SAND... ...o
decade... ...g
indus...es in Australia a... ...y writes
a column for Australia's ... ...aper, *The Sunday Telegraph*, in New South ... ...mer assistant editor, foreign correspondent and columnist for *The Daily Telegraph*, she was recently editor-at-large at *marie claire* magazine. Sandra is the author of two books: *Beyond Bad, The Life and Crimes of Katherine Knight* and *The Promise, An Iraqi Mother's Desperate Flight to Freedom*. Sandra Lee lives in Sydney with her husband.

DO OR DIE

DO OR DIE

THE TRUE STORY OF AN SAS HERO'S BLOODIEST BATTLE AGAINST AL-QAEDA IN AFGHANISTAN

S E Lee

JOHN BLAKE

Published by John Blake Publishing Ltd,
3 Bramber Court, 2 Bramber Road,
London W14 9PB, UK
www.blake.co.uk

First published in Great Britain in 2007
This paperback edition published 2008

First published in 2006 by HarperCollins Publishers Australia Pty Limited

ISBN: 978-1-84454-580-3

British Library Cataloguing-in-Publication Data:
A catalogue record for this book is available from the British Library.

Design by www.envydesign.co.uk

Printed and bound in the UK by CPD Group, Blaina, Abertillery, Wales

3 5 7 9 10 8 6 4 2

Papers used by John Blake Publishing are natural, recyclable products made
from wood grown in sustainable forests. The manufacturing processes
conform to the environmental regulations of the country of origin.

For my brother, Gavin Lee.

*And for the soldiers of the Australian Army,
past, present and future.*

*'We sleep safely in our beds because rough
men stand ready in the night to visit violence
on those who would harm us.'*
GEORGE ORWELL

Swift and Sure
The motto of the Royal Australian Corps of Signals

Who Dares Wins
The motto of the Australian Special Air Service Regiment

GLOSSARY

1-87	1st Battalion, 87th Infantry Regiment, from US Army's 10th Mountain Division
ADF	Australian Defence Force
AF	Afghan Forces
ALICE	all-purpose lightweight individual carrying equipment (pack)
AO	area of operation
AQ	al Qaeda
ASIO	Australian Security Intelligence Organisation
AWACS	airborne warning-and-control system
BP	blocking point
C2	command and control
CAS	close air support
CCP	casualty collection point
CentCom	US Central Command
CFLCC	Coalition Forces Land Component Command
CIA	Central Intelligence Agency
click	slang for kilometre
CO	commanding officer
CSAR	combat search and rescue
Dishka	Russian-made DShk machine-gun
E&E	escape and evasion plan
FAC	forward air controller
FARP	forward air-refuelling point
FLIR	forward-looking infrared camera
FOB	forward operating base
FUP	form-up point
gatt	gun
helo	helicopter
HLZ	helicopter landing zone
HUA	heard, understood, acknowledged; roughly articulated as *hoo-ah*
HVT	high-value target
IDS	infrared detection set
intel	intelligence information
JDAM	joint direct attack munition bomb
K2	Karshi-Khanabad air base

KIA	killed in action
locstat	location status
LRPV	long-range patrol vehicle
LZ	landing zone
medevac	medical evacuation
MEU	Marine Expeditionary Unit (US)
MREs	Meals Ready to Eat
NOD	night-observation device
non-com/NCO	non-commissioned officer
NVG	night-vision gear (or goggles)
OP	observation post
OpOrd	operations order
OpsO	operations officer
QRF	quick-reaction force
Rakkasans	troops of the 187th Infantry Regiment, from US Army's 101st Airborne Division
ROE	rules of engagement
RPG	rocket-propelled grenade
RPK	Russian-made light machine gun
Rupert	senior officer
SAM	surface-to-air missile
SASR	Special Air Service Regiment (Australia)
SAW	squad automatic weapon
SF	Special Forces
sitrep	situation report
SKEDCOs	sled on which ammunition is loaded
SLR	self-loading rifle
Spooky	slang for AC-130 Spectre gunship
SR	surveillance and reconnaissance
SRV	surveillance-and-reconnaisance vehicle
Stinger	*see* SAM
TOC	Tactical Operations Center
UAV	unmanned aerial vehicle, e.g. Predator drone
UBA	unauthorised boat arrival
USAF	United States Air Force
WO2	Warrant Officer Class Two
Zulu time	Greenwich Mean Time

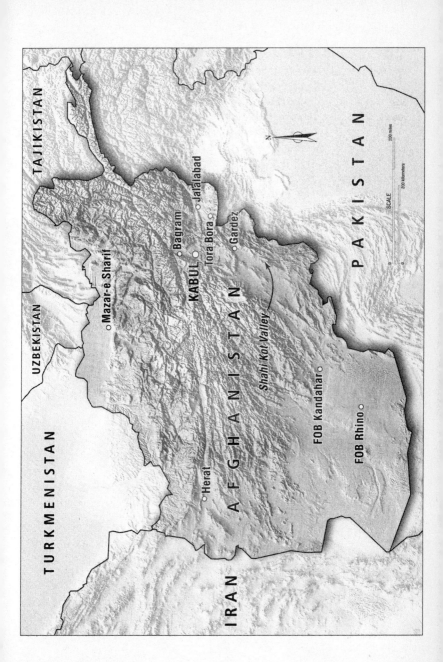

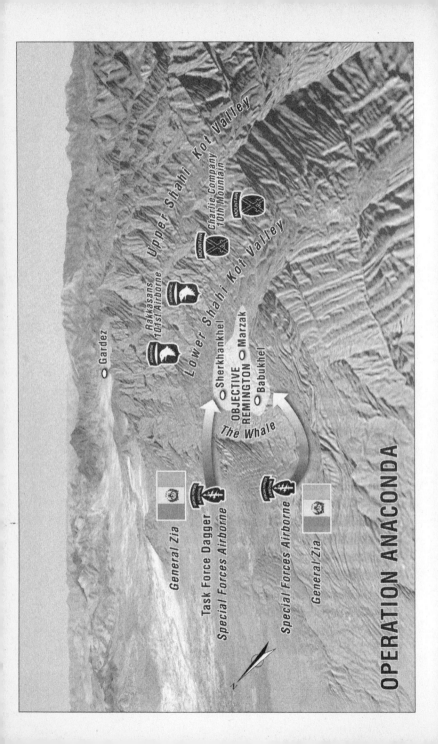

OPERATION ANACONDA

PROLOGUE

*They represented the elite, and today they were going to
face the public, which had devoured tales of their heroics in
the nation's newspapers but had yet to put a face or name to
the stories of incredible survival and battlefield triumphs.*

Army Signalman Martin Wallace didn't feel much like a
modern-day war hero. If anything, he felt slightly awkward
as he stood on the perfectly manicured deep-green grass outside
Government House in Canberra; conspicuous for all the wrong
reasons. Wallace, a member of the Australian Army's elite Special
Air Service Regiment, had been called to the nation's capital
where, in a few minutes, he would receive the prestigious Medal
for Gallantry, one of the nation's highest decorations for bravery
in perilous circumstances. Wallace had earned it one hellish day
nearly nine months earlier while serving his country in the War on
Terror in Afghanistan. He had been fighting the remnants of the
religious fundamentalist Taliban regime and their terrorist
partners, al Qaeda, after the murderous September 11 attacks in
the United States.

Their Excellencies, the Governor-General, Peter Hollingworth,
and his wife, Mrs Ann Hollingworth, had issued official white
invitations, stamped with King Edward's golden crown atop a
sprig of wattle, to the investiture. Proceedings would commence
at 10.50am and conclude exactly 70 minutes later at noon, sharp,
on 27 November 2002. The dress code on that sultry Wednesday
morning was appropriate to the occasion – service dress

ceremonial and accoutrements. Signalman Wallace was proud to wear the Australian Army's uniform, and proud of being a soldier in 152 Signal Squadron at the SAS base in Swanbourne, Perth, but the dress code had presented a slight and oddly amusing problem for him.

Despite being the star of the morning's pageant of pomp and ceremony, and despite his impressively chiselled good looks and ramrod-straight posture born of years of military service and parade ground marches, he felt like an impostor. While his lean, athletic physique gave it a definite and dignified authority, most of the all-khaki ceremonial uniform he was wearing had been borrowed, hastily. It came from his fellow soldiers in the Special Forces crew that lives by the credo 'Who Dares Wins'. Wallace appreciated the irony, and had a laugh at his own expense: he was a member of the most elite and highly organised regiment, renowned for its adaptability in any environment, and here he was decked out in an improvised uniform. *Bloody perfect*, he thought.

The uniform he wore belonged to his troop commander at 152 Signal Squadron, a top bloke called Marty whom Wallace respected and admired. The shoulders had had to be widened slightly to accommodate Wallace's build, and the badges changed to recognise his rank. Wallace had borrowed the gold buttons for the jacket from a corporal within the SAS Regiment's 1st Squadron, an old mate named Mick. They had served together on their first overseas mission twelve years earlier, and like Wallace, Mick had also served in Afghanistan. The wide black leather belt and brass had come from a fellow signaller at 152, another chook, as signallers are known, who had also completed a rugged tour of duty in Afghanistan in the early days of the War on Terror.

It was all a bit of a laugh, but what did irk Wallace later after the ceremony was that he was asked to remove his royal-blue beret for the official photographs thereby robbing his Royal Australian Corps of Signals of the honour he felt they deserved at this proud occasion. 'I felt like an op-shop dude going up to get an award in a borrowed suit and tie,' Wallace remarked later, humour mixed with a small measure of embarrassment. At least he wore his own corps' blue-coloured lanyard over his right arm, clearly identifying himself as a member of 152, something he would toast privately with his best mate and fellow SAS trooper, Mooka, over a beer after the ceremony.

But Wallace's awkwardness went beyond the borrowed uniform, and if truth be told, he focused on the uniform to conceal the real cause of his discomfort. His awkwardness was deeply entrenched in that rare characteristic possessed by brave men and women who would prefer not to be singled out for simply doing their job, no matter how extraordinary and courageous their actions have been. His reticence was rooted firmly in something that could only be described as the humility of heroes; he felt uncomfortable that the ceremony about to unfold would spotlight him and celebrate his gallantry and courage under fire. Soldiering is about mateship and teamwork.

There was something else, too. Martin Wallace – or Jock, as he automatically became known, thanks to his Scottish ancestry, when he signed up as a seventeen-year-old in 1987 – also felt sorely the absence of another brave Australian who was with him the day all hell broke loose in the largest combat operation in the War on Terror, and the biggest to involve Australians since the Vietnam War.

It was 2 March 2002, in a freezing place called the Shahi Kot Valley high in the Afghanistan mountains, where the air is so thin it's hard to breathe. Of historical significance and breathtakingly beautiful, the area was the last stronghold of the multi-national terrorist group al Qaeda, and American intelligence had placed its Saudi leader, Osama bin Laden, in the region. Warrant Officer Class Two Clint was right beside Jock for most of the eighteen hours they were in the valley, pinned down after being ambushed by an estimated thousand al Qaeda terrorists and Taliban fighters. Clint and Jock fought for their lives and those of 80 soldiers from the US Army's 10th

Mountain Division who had been deposited there that morning by three fully loaded CH-47 Chinook helicopters. If Wallace had his druthers, his brother in arms Clint would be standing right beside him again now, being similarly honoured. Instead, Clint was hard at work, having been overlooked for any award, something Wallace thought was wrong.

Wallace couldn't pinpoint the exact emotion he felt but the ceremony seemed somehow superficial, a bit hollow. A bit of a show, put on more for others than for him. The dangerous work had already been done, and yet more was needed back in Afghanistan. As a soldier, Jock wanted nothing more than to get back to the business, but he also knew the medal ceremony was bigger than him, bigger than one man who had done his duty. *It's about the nation and about being Australian*, he thought to himself as he surveyed the smartly dressed politicians and dignitaries who had come to salute Jock and the other soldiers who were being honoured.

Wallace was in good company. With him were the tough-as-nails commander of the regiment's 1st Squadron, Major Daniel McDaniel, and his squadron sergeant, Warrant Officer Class Two Mark Keily. Both were superior officers in the SAS who, with Wallace, took part in what the Australian Defence Force called Operation Slipper as part of the American-led coalition's Operation Enduring Freedom. The three soldiers had notched up several decades of military service between them and had seen action in various countries on several continents. They represented the elite, and today they were going to face the public, which had devoured tales of their heroics in the nation's newspapers but had yet to put a face or a name to the stories of incredible survival and battlefield triumphs.

Three other SAS soldiers – a corporal, a sergeant and a captain – would receive awards anonymously due to their current operational status. And the SAS Regiment's absent commanding officer, Lieutenant Colonel Peter 'Gus' Gilmore, would receive the Distinguished Service Cross for his command and leadership.

4

Wallace had been Gilmore's signaller, keeping him connected to the outside world and to his troops on patrol in Afghanistan throughout the early days of Operation Slipper. The boss had recently returned to Afghanistan where he was once again running the show for the Australian contingent.

Wallace might have been a reluctant hero but he knew what to expect. That morning, after a good night's sleep in a serviced apartment in the Canberra suburb of Dickson, he and McDaniel and Keily were given a thorough media briefing by those higher up the chain of command. There was the small matter of journalists descending on the wartime heroes to record their moment of glory and sing hosannas in their honour. They had to know what they could say, but more importantly, what they couldn't say. Operational, tactical and security matters are highly sensitive issues for active SAS soldiers. Top secret, in fact. Wallace knew the drill and respected it. Men and women's lives, including his own, depended on it. The pre-ceremony briefing was essential. Some things would be off limits.

As befitted the occasion, the Australian Defence Minister, Senator Robert Hill, was at the investiture and so too was the Chief of the Australian Defence Force, General Peter Cosgrove (*no doubt in a perfectly tailored uniform*, Wallace thought to himself with a chuckle, self-consciously tugging at his borrowed jacket).

The ceremony began precisely at 10.50am, in a splendidly decorated room in Government House. Wallace, McDaniel and Keily stood perfectly still, their chins thrust forward, their hands clasped in front of them. They didn't flinch. They didn't smile. They listened with a practised solemnity, in true military style. Wallace was first cab off the rank. The order of service recognised the fact that he was to receive the highest decoration that day – the Medal for Gallantry, no mean feat for a digger who was outranked by all those around him.

With a practised regal bearing that would, months later in the dying days of his governorship, be described as arrogance, Dr Hollingworth called on Wallace to step forward. 'For gallantry in action in hazardous circumstances while undertaking communications responsibilities in Afghanistan during Operation Slipper,' the citation read.

Jock's mother, Margaret, sat a few rows behind her son with his elder brother, James, and best mate, Travis Standen, aka Mooka, and Travis's fiancée, Frances. Jock was permitted to invite four people to share his moment of glory and he'd chosen them carefully. James and Margaret had taken the Hume Highway from Sydney to Canberra and had been so excited that they couldn't eat breakfast. Mooka and Fran had flown across from the west, where they then lived, courtesy of the Australian Army. Jock would be Mooka's best man a few months later, performing the honour over the phone all the way from Iraq, when Mooka, a second-generation SAS man, and Frances tied the knot in a surprise wedding. They wouldn't have missed seeing their best man get the distinguished medal for quids, and the fact that they made the trek meant more to Jock than he could say.

Despite the significance of the moment, Margaret Wallace was not easily impressed by the pomp and ceremony. She had always been extremely proud of her second son, as she was of James, and while she knew little of what Jock had done six months earlier in an isolated and nearly unpronounceably named place in eastern Afghanistan, she knew instinctively that it wouldn't surprise her. Jock had grown up with a dogged determination and strength of character that was unwavering. He had a way of excelling at everything he attempted, even when he was testing the boundaries with typical teenage exuberance, which he had done regularly and often spectacularly.

What Margaret Wallace secretly wished for was that her late husband, Reg, was alive to see their son being honoured by his country, but Reg had died ten years earlier, a victim of mesothelioma, a virulent form of cancer associated with asbestos. Margaret looked over at James and spotted a splash of tears on his cheeks. 'It was a lovely ceremony and James was a little bit moved,' she recalled later. 'And I suppose he felt it with his dad not there and him being the eldest male in the family. But it wasn't spoken of.'

In the ornate room, Dr Hollingworth continued reading the citation. 'Signalman Wallace displayed gallantry and courage under fire when performing communications responsibilities during Operation Anaconda, as part of Operation Slipper in Afghanistan. He maintained composure under sustained heavy attack from enemy forces while performing his duties as a signalman, attending to the wounded and providing leadership to those around him ...'

As the words echoed through the hallways, Jock's thoughts slipped back to the battle. Jock could see it all in his mind's eye in vivid technicolour, as clear as when it happened. A young soldier lay beside him, his camouflage uniform stained, sticky and wet with blood from a sucking chest wound. He was only a kid, eighteen, maybe nineteen if he was lucky, a pimply faced American terrified of dying on foreign soil. As the drugs flowed through his body, anaesthetising his pain, Jock told the kid not to worry.

'You'll make it, mate,' he said. 'You'll make it.'

Jock lit the kid a cigarette and rugged him up, checking on him every few minutes to make sure he was still alive and hadn't slipped away. Jock smoked half a pack of cigarettes that day, something he remembered thinking his mum would not be happy about. *Stuff it*, he thought, as bullets cracked overhead and mortars exploded metres away, ripping apart his fellow soldiers and sending shockwaves through his body. There was a good chance he could be killed – *what's a few durries?*

As the battle raged on, Jock had no way of knowing that those opening eighteen hours of Operation Anaconda would later be regarded as one of the most intense battles against al Qaeda.

That day was just nine months ago and the memories were still so bloody raw and real, but it could have been another lifetime. Jock's attention snapped back to the present as he heard his name called out.

'Signalman Wallace's gallantry has brought great credit to

himself, the Special Air Service Regiment and the Australian Defence Force,' Dr Hollingworth said.

Jock Wallace stood perfectly still. He looked at Dr Hollingworth as the Governor General leant forward to pin, above Wallace's left breast, a shining, round gold medal, hung from an orange ribbon lined with chevrons – or inverted Vs – a deeper shade of orange. The medal featured a Federation Star surrounded by flames representing action under fire. It was surmounted by a St Edward crown affixed to a bar inscribed 'FOR GALLANTRY'.

The hero soldier and the Governor-General shook hands and the audience applauded politely. And that was that. Wallace was directed to the back of the room where he stood at ease watching McDaniel and Keily receive commendations for their conduct in the war.

With the official business out of the way, Senator Hill directed the human traffic out onto the lush lawn of Government House where plastic chairs were set up for a true-blue celebration with beer and biscuits.

'These soldiers epitomise the professionalism, dedication and courage of the Australian Defence Force. Their efforts in difficult and dangerous situations have been outstanding and have received international praise,' Senator Hill said later. 'They have done their nation proud. The awards are just recognition for a job well done. That the awards cover such a wide range of ranks, from signalman through to lieutenant colonel, reflects the quality and depth of leadership throughout the entire Special Forces Task Group.'

The politician had not overstated the impact of the Aussie SAS on the international community. The US Army had already sung the regiment's praises. Indeed, soon after the battle, the commander of Operation Anaconda, Major General Franklin 'Buster' Hagenbeck had said, 'You won't find a more professional group than the Australians that have served here with us.'

After the festivities and good-natured backslapping, Jock

Wallace took a moment to read the citation that outlined, in broad strokes, the reasons for the medal pinned above his heart, a medal that had elevated him to an elite rank of brave and gallant soldiers and enabled him to sign his name as Martin Wallace, MG. As he read the citation, he shook his head in wonderment. It all sounded so easy on paper, so clean and straightforward. Out there in a place dubbed Hell's Halfpipe by some young American soldier who thought the unforgiving terrain looked like a skateboard pipe back home, it was anything but.

CHAPTER 1

*'Oh shit! Is this going to be the last photo
of me, the last image of me taken – at least by
Western photographers?'*

SAS SIGNALLER JOCK WALLACE

Jock Wallace was freezing his arse off. For the past hour the SAS soldier had been cooling his heels at the form-up point on a muddy patch of earth used as a carpark beside the main runway at bombed-out Bagram Air Base. As he waited to go into battle, he could feel the mercury sink deeper and deeper into the sub-zero zone. It was just shy of 2400 zulu time (Greenwich Mean Time) – 4.30am on the local clock in eastern Afghanistan – and the sun wasn't due up for a good two hours and 22 minutes, well after the time he'd have landed at a destination nestled in the Shahi Kot Valley, a couple of hundred clicks south in Paktia Province, Afghanistan. Known as 'bandit country', this was one of the 34 provinces that made up the war-torn and lawless country.

The moon was bright, at least 80 per cent illumination according to the strategic note-takers who purposefully record such things when sending men into harm's way. Cutting through clouds and fog, it cast an eerie light over 200 or so soldiers steeling themselves for a gunfight with al Qaeda terrorists hiding in the nose-bleed-high mountains that surround the Shahi Kot Valley. The mission had been called off the previous two nights due to sleet and snow blanketing the base and preventing the Chinook helicopters from delivering the warrior cargo.

Fierce enough to freeze the balls off a brass monkey, Jock reckoned, feeling the bone-chilling cold through the GORE-TEX pants he wore over his camouflage gear.

Every few seconds a flashbulb exploded, assaulting the senses, as a photographer from the US Army official newspaper, *Stars and Stripes*, took for posterity pre-battle pictures of the soldiers waiting for Operation Anaconda to start rolling.

He's coming around like one of those dicks in a restaurant, Jock thought, watching the bloke work his way through the gathered men from Charlie Company of the 1st Battalion, 87th Infantry Regiment at the US Army's 10th Mountain Division.

'Can I take your photograph?' he asked.

'Yeah, mate,' Jock nodded, cool as a cucumber.

Jock now says: 'I remember thinking of that SAS book *Phantoms of the Jungle*; there's a photo of one of the guys taken before a patrol in Vietnam. It was the last photo ever taken of him and I'm thinking that's a good idea, having a photo taken before the patrol. That way you've got the most current photo.'

Jock didn't need to be told, but the most current photograph was just in case anything went wrong. This was war; things went wrong.

The snapper fired off a few frames, temporarily blinding Jock with the flash.

'I've gone, "Oh shit! Is this going to be the last photo of me, the last image of me taken – at least by Western photographers?" Then I told him to piss off, he was taking rolls and rolls and rolls. "Go and talk to my agent,"' I said.

'When you think about it, you think it could be the last photograph, and you go, "Oh shit, that's big." And then you go, "Stiff shit." There's nothing you can do anyway. I'm on this vehicle whether I like it or not at this point. I've given my word that I'm going to do this, and whether or not I'm starting to have an inclination that I'm not going to come out of this ... I've given my word and I'm not changing anything.'

Wallace, at 32, was one of just two Australians attached to the

1-87, as it was known. He'd spent the past few days bunking in with the troops from the 10th Mountain and had got to know a handful of them pretty well, particularly Frank Grippe, the sergeant major of the infantry regiment.

Grippe could have come straight from central casting. He was a soldiers' soldier and everything about him was big, including the GI Joe haircut that stood defiantly on end on top. His barrel chest threatened to burst open with each muscle-rippling move; his biceps and triceps were the size of well-worked quadriceps that in turn could take their own special punishment, and would later that day. And he had a pockmarked face made even more interesting by the gruelling climates it had weathered while serving Uncle Sam. He was a finely tuned warrior whose voice, when he spoke to his men and women at times just like this, before heading into battle, echoed the staccato delivery of a machine gun fully loaded. *Rat a tat tat. Rat a tat tat. Rat a tat tat.* Only a fool argued with the sar-major and there were no fools at the form-up point (FUP) that early morning; scores of naive, young men on their first combat mission, but no fools.

Jock felt like he'd won the lottery when he was assigned to the 10th Mountain. The regiment had been given a key role in Operation Anaconda, a mission that had one objective: to capture or kill al Qaeda and Taliban elements that had been regrouping in the Shahi Kot Valley in the four months since the rapid fall of Kabul the previous November, and Tora Bora soon after. Intelligence estimates in the weeks before the operation variably put the enemy numbers at between 100 and 250. The valley was in the foothills of the magnificent Hindu Kush, a range in which some mountains soar to 7000 metres, and had always been a redoubt for Afghan guerrillas hiding from and fighting foreign invaders. Poetically known as the Valley of the King, it had been where thousands of occupying Soviet soldiers were annihilated by the mujahideen in the 1980s while fighting the ten-year Soviet occupation. It had a history, and it was an ominous one that did not augur well for intruders.

Anaconda was a three-pronged operation. Combined allied and Afghan forces would launch an assault at two points from the west in the Shahi Kot, crushing the enemy into submission the way an Anaconda envelops and crushes its prey. Seven blocking points would be established by American soldiers on the eastern side of the valley to stop any surviving enemy from fleeing through treacherous donkey trails and goat paths, dubbed rat lines, which snaked over the eastern Takur Ghar mountain range into Pakistan. Troops from the Australian SAS would act as another blocking force and set up observation posts at the southernmost end of the valley.

The SAS had gone to Afghanistan as part of the multi-national coalition force fighting the war on terrorism and were engaged in vital long-range reconnaissance and surveillance missions. The patrols comprised some of the most highly skilled and rigorously trained soldiers in military history; men, only men, who had developed a reputation for fearlessness, independence, resourcefulness and self-sufficiency in the most adverse of conditions. They also came with their own long-range patrol vehicles, known as 'devil vehicles' by the enemy. The six-wheeled, open-air Land Rovers were armed to the teeth and had the motorised agility of a mountain goat, giving them a superior advantage over other nations' Special Operations forces. The Americans loved the Aussies' audacity and respected their courage. They wanted them on board. It was a done deal.

H-Hour, the precise moment when Anaconda would all begin, was scheduled for 6am local time, when two flights, each consisting of three Chinook helicopters, would touch down, first in the north – infiltrating 100-plus troops of the 187th Infantry Regiment from the renowned 101st Airborne Division (Air Assault), otherwise known as the Rakkasans or Screaming Eagles. Five minutes later, Chinooks would land in the south, depositing Jock and his fellow SAS trooper, Warrant Officer Clint, with troops from the 1-87. It was the first time since World War II that the Rakkasans and 10th Mountain battalions had worked together.

Anaconda was given added importance because of the high-value targets (HVTs) thought to be hiding in the valley. The greatest HVT, according to the vast but not infallible US intelligence network, was Osama bin Laden, possibly hiding in the extensive cave systems that lined the precipitous mountain ridges. There wasn't a single soldier braving the conditions in Bagram that winter who hadn't dreamt of nailing the hate-filled monster who gloated in a videotape that he had orchestrated the murders of nearly 3000 people in four separate terrorist attacks in the United States on September 11, 2001.

For many of the men from the 10th Mountain, based in the verdant and rolling hills of upstate New York, it was even more personal. Some were native New Yorkers, like Sergeant Major Grippe, who grew up about 90 minutes from the 10th Mountain's home, Fort Drum, 530 kilometres away from the World Trade Center. There were dozens of soldiers who had lost family or friends in the attacks on New York and on the Pentagon in Washington DC. They were in awe of the bravery of the passengers on board the hijacked United Airlines Flight 93 that had crashed into a field in Pennsylvania. Thousands of US bullets that night had one name indelibly etched on them – Osama bin Laden.

Wallace was attached to the 1-87 as a signaller from the Australian Army's Special Air Service Regiment. He ran communications for Clint, whose job as SAS liaison officer was to coordinate movements between 1-87 and the 1 SAS Squadron which was operating in the area.

The SAS soldiers, members of the Sabre, or fighting, squadrons, had been let loose in Afghanistan the preceding December, and by January had operated in an area in the Shahi Kot Valley that the American generals had dubbed Area of Operation Down Under, often abbreviated to AO Down Under. The men were renowned for their knowledge of the region.

Jock and Clint's mission with the 1-87 was vital. They had to ensure that the 10th Mountain Division did not stray into AO Down Under and that any enemy forces could be engaged without

15

endangering the lives of Australian and American soldiers. It was Clint's job to ensure the Americans didn't accidentally open up on their allies with misplaced and ironically named friendly fire, or 'blue-on-blue' action. In military terms, the job to prevent friendly fire incidents is known as deconfliction. Jock provided the lifeline, a high-tech communications network that kept the Aussies in touch with each other and their chain of command, and Clint liaised with the commanding officer of the 10th Mountain's battalion. Together, they would keep the SAS men away from friendly fire. The rest, staying alive, was up to the hard-hitters from the SAS Sabre squadrons.

'The Americans supplied their own nets, they had their own sigs,' Jock explains, abbreviating networks and signallers. 'I was there as an Australian communicator to work on the Australian net. I was not working on an American net. My signal went to Australians and their signals went out to their blokes in the field. We did the same thing, but we had different missions. Clint and I were with them to deconflict with the Aussie SAS patrols that were deployed ahead of the American arrival into the Shahi Kot Valley.

'They [the SAS patrols] were up there for SR – surveillance and recon – which is a pretty standard operation,' says Jock. 'So we talked directly or indirectly to the Australians from exactly where the Americans were firing from, and if they were getting fire from the Americans, we were there to stop it.'

Now in the freezing cold Jock was champing at the bit to get out there and close with the enemy, to get on with the job. The wickedly biting cold wind howling across the FUP offered extra motivation.

The engines of three tandem-rotored CH-47 Chinooks started to turn and burn about 250 metres down the apron, ready to take the soldiers to their landing zones: 82 to the southern end of the Shahi Kot Valley and another 40-odd slightly further north.

Most of the young 1-87 Americans were Generation Y soldiers who looked like they had stepped from an end-of-year school photograph, as they sat on their packs in a place they called 'the

'Stan', shooting the breeze, making small talk to distract themselves from the dangerous mission ahead. Bagging Osama and the al Qaeda murderers. Debating the relative merits of their iPod playlists back in their footlockers in tent city: Britney v White Stripes v Busta Rhymes, pop versus rock versus rap. Bumming cigarettes, having a laugh, talking about wives, girlfriends and the piss-poor substitute of internet porn. Jive talk, shit talk, small talk to pass the time.

'Everyone is tired, sleepy and has just woken up and it's two in the fuckin' morning and you're sitting in a muddy paddock for another two hours, beside the runway, waiting to go to a place where people are going to try to blow your head off,' Jock recalls. 'It's just half-awake soldiers; men, all milling around with a delay in front of them before they are going into a really, really serious event.'

As the departure drew closer, the soldiers went about their business, mentally ticking off the drills they had memorised, and checking their webbing, weapons and ammo.

'Making sure your gatt was good to go, wouldn't seize up under fire in the cold hills 10,000 feet above sea level,' Jock says, using the soldier slang for 'weapon'.

Days earlier, a three-metre-square mud map had been scratched into a patch of snow-covered dirt to chart the AO known as Remington, which included three villages in the Shahi Kot Valley – Sherkhankhel, Marzak and Babukhel. The sar-major had pointed out the 1-87's landing zones on the map: LZ 13 and L2 13a.

Bloody beautiful, thought Jock, *thirteen, lucky for some.*

Their objective was in the south, to establish security at a place known as Blocking Point Ginger.

Jock could hear one of the senior non-commissioned officers barking out final instructions over the increasing *thwack* and *thwomp* of the Chinook's blades, repeating the most basic rule of engagement.

'Stay fuckin' alive,' the NCO hollered.

The troops didn't respond with the usual *hoo-ah* chorus they frequently used as a mass psych-up, and one they had used outside tent city at Bagram the day before when US Colonel Frank Wiercinski jumped on the back of a Humvee for a rallying war speech. *Hoo-ah* came from the acronym HUA, for 'heard, understood, acknowledged'.

Dispensing with the *hoo-ah* war cry, Jock instinctively knew the blokes were conserving their energy, steeling themselves for the job ahead.

'It's like they've got a marathon to run; they're just sitting there waiting, not doing laps around the bloody airport,' he reflects now. 'Everyone is trying to stay as reserved and focused and calm as possible.'

The 10th Mountain's only mortar platoon going into the southern landing zone checked their equipment, pleased they were taking the awesome firepower of the 120mm mortar into the field. Based on the intel he had received, Platoon Sergeant Michael Peterson thought the 120mm – with its 7200-metre reach – was the right system for Operation Anaconda because he could range all the blocking positions, including that of the 101st Airborne which would land further north in the valley. The generals decided against importing field artillery, known as the king of battles, so the 120mm provided the best indirect support. The platoon would also take 56 mortar rounds, each of which weighed in at 15 kilograms, as well as their own 50–60 kilogram rucksacks loaded with survival equipment, cold-weather gear, ammo and rations.

Peterson, a lanky twenty-year army veteran and father of two, had no doubts about the capability or commitment of his men, even though the youngest was just seventeen, slightly under the age at which soldiers are legally permitted to go into combat. The kid was just four years older than Peterson's son, but he didn't know that then.

'I had no idea. I'm a platoon sergeant. You send me somebody – unfortunately, it's like a piece of equipment. Although I do love my men.' Peterson adds: 'But you know, "Hey, you are going to

the fight, kid. I don't care how old you are, everyone fights."
Daniel Menard: great kid.'

Peterson's troops were fired up. Two days before Anaconda
kicked off, one of the privates in his close-knit outfit had received
a CD from his girlfriend back home, along with a few other odds
and sods to remind him of the comforts he was missing while at
Bagram. It couldn't have been more perfect. Kenny Loggins'
'Danger Zone'.

'I made him play that song like twenty times right before we
went in,' Peterson says. 'And we're all sitting there, everyone is
fired up and everyone is listening to "Danger Zone".'

Peterson and Jock had already met on the tarmac at Bagram
at the end of the mission rehearsal for Anaconda the day
before, when the entire complement of soldiers ran through
their objectives in preparation for the real thing. Sergeant Pete
and his seven men had just disembarked from the Chinooks
with their loaded SKEDCOs when another aircraft began
taxiing towards them.

'Each sled weighed about 600 pounds and we've got six of
those and there are eight of us,' Peterson says now. 'We got those
things off the bird and everyone takes off and we are trying to
drag these things. And there's a plane taxiing, getting ready to hit
us, and the only guy that came back was your buddy [Jock]. He
actually came back and helped us pull them, and I was, like,
"Thanks man, thanks a lot."'

As Peterson recalls, the two soldiers exchanged pleasantries
and then 'went about our merry way'. As meetings go, it was
brief, but it meant that Peterson knew exactly who the Aussie was
who was willing to help them out of a tight spot when they met
again the next morning in the Shahi Kot Valley, up on the high
ground as the mortar platoon set up its perimeter.

Jock looked over at Clint and noted that he looked concerned.

'You got your chook shit?' Clint said, meaning Jock's comms gear.

'Yep. Everything's ready, mate,' Jock said to reassure the
seasoned SAS man who had a decade of experience on him.

Jock was methodical to the point of being anal, but methods and processes were what kept men alive on battlefields. Jock was a strategic thinker, a man who had quit the Army once to do a bachelor's degree in science, only to re-enlist after graduating a few years later. Naturally, he headed straight back to the SAS Regiment and 152 Signal Squadron in Swanbourne. Apart from having the hubris of youth on his side (*well, compared to Clint who clocked in at 45*, he thought), and the fervent belief that wars were what soldiers did, Jock had checked, in triplicate, his equipment and codes.

He was diligent about adhering to and maintaining information security principles and his were as right as rain, but the American network had been compromised the day before by some goose who left his radio in a place where the enemy could have found it. As a result, Jock took extra measures to protect the integrity of the Australians' communications networks. Nothing was left to chance in this man's war. Then there was a similar incident involving yet another one of Uncle Sam's finest, requiring more safety measures from Jock.

Just one of those things, he thought, *always factor in Murphy's Law.*

The night before, Ando, another real hard man of the SAS who had climbed through the ranks to be in charge of the regiment's water operations, had been in the Australian radio ops tent throwing questions nineteen to the dozen at Jock, who was going through his checks.

'Is ya gear ready?'

'Yeah, mate.'

'Got the batteries for your NOD yet?'

'Yeah, mate.'

'Need a hand with anything else?'

'All good, Ando, but thanks, mate. Much appreciate it.'

Jock packed his night-vision goggles in his pack along with roughly 60 kilograms of other equipment, including his Kevlar-lined armour-plated vest to stop ballistics weapons ripping his guts apart. As soon as he'd confirmed he was going into the Shahi Kot Valley he had marched down to see Sergeant Simon, a decent bloke who ran the Aussies' Quartermaster Store at Bagram. Jock needed to borrow a vest, having previously lent his own to an SAS trooper heading out on patrol.

Simon gave his own vest to Jock. 'No worries, mate,' he said, handing it over and wishing Jock the best on his way into battle.

'Simon – always a pleasure to work with him,' Jock says. 'He gave me his personal vest because he understood that I needed it. And I really appreciated it. He's in the right job, he wants to give, he wants to help you, he knows the true value of teamwork. I spent five minutes with him. There was no piss-farting around. Everyone knows where I'm going.'

Jock also stuffed in his pack half a packet of cigarettes, ten litres of water, some pre-packed rations with unique and challenging flavours which could be classified as dangerous to the taste buds, plus cold-weather gear and a sleeping bag. He also packed ammo for his personal weapons, an M4 automatic rifle and a 9mm Browning pistol. He didn't bother to pack any reading material, figuring someone else always did that and there might not be any time for a trip to the library, anyway. His radio and comms gear was all set, too. Jock had even stocked up on new batteries from the Q the day before and was now squared away and ready to deploy.

'How's ya gear?' Ando asked, sussing Jock out again.

'Good, mate.'

'Got ya thermals?'

'Yes, Mum.'

Ando laughed.

'Jock, mate, you look after that silly old bastard, Clint, out there,' Ando said, an edge of seriousness creeping into his voice.

'Yeah, no worries, Ando.'

Jock knew that Clint and Ando were close mates, having trodden similar paths through the regiment. Hell, they'd probably even kicked a lot of the same arses on the way up the

ranks. It took a special breed to get into the SAS and an even
tougher one to survive and thrive. Jock knew Clint could be a
hard taskmaster, but Clint was a man Jock wanted standing
beside him on the battlefield. He thought Clint was rock solid.
Jock knew instinctively that he could trust Clint and rely on him
if things went wrong. They'd be looking out for each other out
there in the valley.

Other blokes had come and gone, wishing Jock well, patting
him on the back. Not really saying too much and not needing to.
Their presence said it all.

'Not everyone realised it was going to be a shit fight – but there
was going to be a gun battle at least,' Jock says now. 'What size,
it wasn't clear. So everyone was mentally stepping up into a higher
gear and making sure that all the guys around them were alright.'

At 9pm Jock had been on his way to get some shut-eye outside
the green canvas tent that was home for the time being. En route,
he ran into the recently arrived commander of the Aussie
contingent, Lieutenant Colonel Rowan Tink.

A tall, taut fellow with a balding pate, Tink had arrived in
Afghanistan on 31 January and taken command of the Australian
contingent from Lieutenant Colonel Peter 'Gus' Gilmore, who had
orchestrated the close working relationship between the Australian
and US Special Operations forces. Gilmore had recently returned
to Australia, having completed his two-month rotation. Jock had
been Gilmore's signaller but, with Anaconda about to get under
way, the CO's sig was available for use in the field.

Tink had been intimately involved in the planning for
Anaconda. He had spent the past two weeks engaged in the daily
briefings and strategy sessions with the US brass from the 10th
Mountain, the US Army's 5th Special Forces Group and the US
Army's top dog, a three-star general named Paul Mikolashek, who
had overall command of the Coalition Forces Land Component
Command (CFLCC – or C-flick, as it was pronounced).

'How're you going, Jock?' Tink asked.

'Not bad, sir.'

'You all ready?'

'Yep. Sure am.'

'Hope you're ready for it. It looks like you're going to meet a bit more resistance than expected.'

'Oh, yeah?'

Jock kept walking, thinking about the briefing that the troops from the 1-87 Infantry Regiment had received earlier that day. They'd been told that US Air Force jets would launch a devastating bombing raid in the valley in the 60 minutes preceding H-Hour, obliterating more than a dozen enemy targets that had been identified as established fortified positions. Pilots flying B-1B and B-52 bombers, and two F-15E Strike Eagle fighter jets had thirteen targets in their sights along the valley. Teams of AH-64 Apache helicopters would hover overhead, watching the bombs wreak havoc before swooping down to check the strike zone and determine if the incoming Chinooks would be flying into hot or cold LZs. Cold was good. Hot was not; it meant they would be under enemy fire.

Once infiltrated, the conventional infantry troops should be prepared for a gunfight with any surviving pockets of enemy fighters. The briefing anticipated that the HVTs, the high-value targets, would – if they were there and if they survived the bombing raid – flee through the rat lines leaving small groups of well-armed and well-trained foreign al Qaeda to do the fighting. The message from the briefing was clear: expect the enemy to fight to the death.

Jock figured it was all the same, regardless of the numbers mentioned at the briefing or Tink's late-night words, which sounded like a warning. One hundred, two hundred, two-fifty, or even a hundred more, it didn't matter. There was no going back. Whatever came would come, and Jock Wallace had done everything possible to prepare for it.

Bring it on, he shrugged.

CHAPTER 2

'Everyone of our generation has been called to do
something for his country. We are no different. We have
been called on to fight the war on terrorism.'

COLONEL FRANK WIERCINSKI, COMMANDER OF THE 3RD BRIGADE,
101ST AIRBORNE DIVISION (AIR ASSAULT)

The mission on which Jock and his fellow soldiers were about to embark, and the list of dangers it entailed, could not have been clearer. Seven days earlier, on 23 February, Major General Franklin 'Buster' Hagenbeck, the commander of Coalition Joint Task Force Mountain, who was running the show, published the Operations Order (OpOrd) for Anaconda, which was originally planned to take 72 hours.

Major General Hagenbeck's OpOrd contained four key goals. The first was to capture or kill key al Qaeda leaders. The second: destroy AQ's foreign fighters. Third: prevent the escape of enemy AQ. And finally, fourth: defeat Taliban forces that continue to resist the Afghan military and their coalition partners.

'I will use a combination of conventional and special operation forces working in conjunction with Afghan Forces to complete the destruction of identified al Qaeda leadership, organisation and infrastructure and prevent their escape to Pakistan,' Hagenbeck stated in his OpOrd.

The battle plan for Operation Anaconda was a classic Hammer and Anvil strategy. Hagenbeck's plan involved a series of simultaneous 'non-linear operations in the non-contiguous areas of operations'. The convoluted military jargon aside, the plan included about 400 Afghan soldiers under the command of the fiercely anti-al Qaeda and anti-Taliban Afghan, General Zia Lodin, who hailed from Logar Province. The Americans wanted the main thrust of the fight to be led by the Afghan Forces (AF), mainly for political reasons: it was their country and the US did not want to be seen as an occupying force. The heroes and liberators of Afghanistan had to be Afghans.

The AF would work with about 30 advisers from the US 5th Special Forces Group who had trained them in warfare tactics. Alternatively known as the Green Berets, the 5th Group's area of operation was in central and southwest Asia and fell under the command of Colonel John Mulholland. The Green Berets, whose motto is 'To Liberate the Oppressed', had been sent to war in the immediate aftermath of the 9/11 terrorist attacks and had set up a base at the Karshi-Khanabad Air Base, dubbed K2 for obvious reasons, in Uzbekistan. Their skills were unconventional warfare. Their goal was to oust the Taliban and capture or kill al Qaeda. In Afghanistan the US Special Forces were known as Task Force Dagger and included various teams such as Cobra Seven Two and Texas One Four.

Agents from the Central Intelligence Agency were also to be embedded with the SF and Afghan troops, marking the first time in history that CIA and Special Forces operators worked together in war. A patrol of Aussie SAS troopers would also be attached to the US 5th Special Forces Group and General Zia Lodin's Afghans as liaison officers. Their job was to coordinate movements between US, Afghan and Australian forces and prevent accidental friendly fire on small SAS patrols on surveillance and reconnaissance missions in the valley.

The 5th Special Forces men and Zia's Afghan Force were dubbed the Hammer. They would approach the Shahi Kot Valley from the west via the Zermat road in a heavily armed convoy. It was a treacherous track across rugged terrain in difficult countryside which left troops vulnerable to ambush. The road was muddy and frequently impassable, and at that time of year was still at risk of being snowed in. Live landmines and other ordnance left over from the mujahideen's war against the Soviets were yet another danger.

Zia's men would set out at midnight with their US and Australian Special Forces soldiers charged with the primary role of entering the Shahi Kot, passing potentially ambush-rich positions around a smaller mountain that rose up from the valley floor dubbed the Whale, so called because it looked like the back of a humpback whale. As the Hammer and main thrust, Zia's forces would move across the face of 1 SAS Squadron in the field and flush out AQ and Taliban enemy in the three villages within Objective Remington. Intelligence estimated the enemy numbers in the villages at between 100 and 250.

Two other units of Afghan soldiers, together with their own Special Forces operators, would be tasked with controlling the perimeter to the east and southeast. The complete thousand-strong Afghan component comprised many soldiers from Afghanistan's Northern Alliance (a loose coalition of men under the control of various Afghan warlords who had been, at one time or another, at war with each other), members of the local mujahideen, and even, ironically, some former Taliban. Loyalties frequently shifted in the country, partly the result of pragmatism and partly due to the Afghan tradition in which the conquered would side with the victors without any loss of face. In all, the AF was integral to the success of the mission.

Four companies of incoming air-mobile infantry troops from the 10th Mountain and the 101st Airborne would land on the eastern side of the Whale in the south and northeast of the valley, setting up blocking points lyrically named Ginger, Heather, Eve, Diane, Cindy, Amy and Betty. They would cover any escape routes – rat lines – over the eastern Takur Ghar into Pakistan. Together, these four components formed the Anvil.

A second wave of air assault troops would be inserted later on D-Day to reinforce secured positions.

The Australian SAS soldiers were so respected that they had

been assigned the difficult role of establishing a blocking force and observation posts across the southern end of the valley – several kilometres wide – and had been in place for days.

The plan did not involve the use of heavy artillery or protective armoured vehicles. It was extremely difficult to airlift these to the oxygen-starved heights of the Shahi Kot but the decision not to take artillery would be the subject of debate later. The troops would rely on their own light infantry weapons including rifles, machine guns, mortars and explosives. It wasn't ideal because it gave the soldiers a smaller 'kill circle', meaning that their fire range was not as far as they would have liked. But Hagenbeck's plan allowed for the lethal firepower of close air support from the US Air Force, Navy and Marine fighter jets which, when called in by the SF or infantry units in the valley, would bomb enemy targets.

The general's OpOrd had another thing going for it. Immediately before H-Hour – the time the flights of Chinooks touched down and disgorged their combat troops – fast-moving jets and bombers would swoop in and unleash holy hell on known enemy locations spotted by the covert SF patrols in the Shahi Kot in the preceding weeks. If everything went to plan, the bombing raid would be a crippling 55-minute reign of terror.

Hagenbeck had spent weeks planning the mission, but the 10th Mountain almost missed the show.

On 25 January, Hagenbeck had flown to Kuwait for a meeting with the overall CFLCC boss, General Paul T. Mikolashek, who commanded America's conventional ground forces in 25 countries in the Middle East, Central Asia and Horn of Africa. The massive area was known as US Central Command, or CentCom, and was one of the Pentagon's five regional commands around the globe. Mikolashek answered directly to General Tommy Franks, a towering Texan with a southern drawl who commanded CentCom out of Florida and had a direct pipeline to US Defense Secretary Donald Rumsfeld and the 43rd President of the United States, George W. Bush. Hagenbeck wanted to talk to Mikolashek about redeploying the 10th Mountain, which was based at K2 and had been operating as a quick-reaction force for Task Force Dagger (the 5th SF Group). It was a perfect fit for the infantry unit, particularly since its commander, Lieutenant Colonel Paul LaCamera, his command sergeant major, Frank Grippe, and Grippe's operations officer in 1-87, Sergeant First Class Robert Healy, had all been Special Forces operators, members of the 75th Ranger Regiment.

But the battalion-size regiment of 500-odd soldiers from the 10th Mountain had seen little action since the stunningly rapid collapse of the Taliban just 62 days after the 9/11 terrorist attacks, and the subsequent installation of Hamid Karzai as president of the interim Afghanistan Government. As the political landscape changed, so too did the requirements of war, and Hagenbeck's infantry would not be needed for the new phase of security and the reconstruction of Afghanistan.

A week later, though, the top dog of the 5th Special Forces Group, Colonel Mulholland, called on Hagenbeck with information that would change the course of the 10th Mountain's redeployment.

'Colonel Mulholland was the commander of Task Force Dagger, a special operations outfit, and he told me that there were what we called compartmentalised intelligence of foreign al Qaeda that were coalescing in Shahi Kot Valley,' Hagenbeck recalls, explaining that intelligence was coming in from various sources.

'And he was assuming that he was going to be given the mission to go destroy them, defeat them. And he said, "Sir, if this is as many as I think there's going to be, I don't have the means or the command and control to do that. And I'm going to talk to General Franks about it. Would you mind if I suggested that you take on and be the commander of the larger fight because we are going to need more than just our assets to do this?" So, absolutely, I jumped at the chance. It really began from that small conversation.'

A few days later, once the politics and strategic command-and-control elements had been established, Mikolashek, via a video-teleconference from Kuwait, told Hagenbeck: 'I want you to learn how to spell Bagram.'

Even though the conference was conducted over secure lines, Mikolashek was using a form of veiled speech. Technology was not limited to the coalition forces. Who knew who might be listening?

'I knew immediately what he was talking about and so I picked up the phone afterwards, on a secure and confidential line, and spoke to him about it,' Hagenbeck says.

By the second week of February, the 10th Mountain had moved from K2 into the boggy air base at Bagram and the planning for Anaconda began in earnest.

Jock Wallace arrived at Bagram Air Base in mid-February as part of an advance party for the SAS squadron, who would be known as Task Force 64, in preparation for the Aussies' role in Operation Anaconda. Anaconda would be the first real action Jock had seen since leaving the SAS Regiment's headquarters at the Campbell Barracks at Swanbourne, not far from Perth, the previous November. For the past four months he'd been putting in time as the regiment commanding officer's signaller – or CO's chook – chilling his balls through a glacial winter at forward operating bases in Doha in Kuwait, then Rhino in southern Afghanistan, followed by Kandahar. Finally, he made it to Bagram.

The Australians had been secured for Anaconda earlier in the month after Lieutenant Colonel Rowan Tink had a series of meetings with the US brass about what the diggers could bring to the table. A lot, as it turned out.

Jock and his superiors in the advance party were given a table in the 10th Mountain Division's headquarters which was under the command of Major General Hagenbeck, and were initially hosted by the 5th Special Forces Group, who gave them quad bikes to get around the boggy air base.

Bagram was a mess. It was the tail end of winter and the ground was covered with snow and huge puddles that resembled muddy lakes. The duckboards that served as pathways were surrounded by bogs as deep as the soldiers' ankles and there was no way to keep clean, no matter how hard the blokes tried. Jock just gave up. Bird baths would have to do, and anyway, he wasn't out to impress anyone.

The 10th Mountain's HQ tent was attached to the massive hangar located off the side of the runway near a place called the Cross Roads. It was dominated by the air-traffic control tower that was flanked by the Spanish hospital on one corner and the form-up point on the other. The main gate at the front of the base was about a kilometre away. Outside, the muj, as Jock dubbed the friendly locals, had set up a small market selling a range of local arts and crafts, including the traditional Afghan dress and woollen *pakhul* hats. Captured Soviet military belts, local hashish, and rations and supplies that made their way into the ramshackle stalls from the base supermarket (the PX) or from the Bagram rubbish dump were also given a price.

US engineers had built a line of offices with demountable walls lengthways down both sides of the hangar, and the yawning belly of the edifice was given over to sleeping accommodation for some of the US soldiers. Parts of the hangar looked like an old-fashioned dormitory with bunk after bunk lined up in neat rows, and footlockers and rucksacks tucked at the end of the beds.

A chow line was set up across the narrow end at the back of the hangar. Later, the base was lined with rows of tents to accommodate the growing number of soldiers who arrived in the country, and while some blokes had stretched modesty screens around their personal patch, they were useless when it came to blocking out the noise and stench of grown men snoring, belching and farting.

The Americans' Task Force Dagger had hooked their own tent at one end of the hangar about a dozen metres away from the Aussie SAS Regiment, who had in the meantime arrived, and their Regimental Aid Post, which would eventually house the regiment's doctors and medical equipment. A US intelligence tent was tacked on to the 10th Mountain's HQ, and all were interconnected with a series of flapping canvas doors. The Australian tent paled in comparison to the air-conditioned tents employed by the Americans, who eventually took pity on their antipodean compatriots and lent some supplies. To Jock the US tents were flash, but there were some things he was not willing to compromise over, not even in a war and not even when it was bloody freezing outside.

'They were swish until you realise that none of the smell comes out,' Jock says now, laughing at the memory. 'I refused to sleep in them – I'd sleep outside and have fresh air. I found the cold weather clothing was sufficient to keep me warm; even still I'd rather be a couple of degrees colder than live in that stench. It reeked.'

Towards the end of February, Lieutenant Colonel Tink dispatched Jock and Clint to the 10th Mountain Division's headquarters. They were tasked as the SAS's liaison officers with Lieutenant Colonel LaCamera's 1-87 in Operation Anaconda, and would be bunking in with them, getting to know the way they did business.

'We were introduced to everyone there,' Jock recalls. 'They made us welcome. [They were] running around doing their battle plans and battle preps and we were going to all their briefings et cetera, between theirs and [Colonel] Wiercinski's HQ. The next couple of days involved a lot of briefings and liaison with them – just keeping abreast of the situation and getting my equipment ready and making the necessary changes as they came up.'

Jock Wallace has an innate bullshit detector. He knows how to read people and, while not one to condemn a man or woman on first impressions, for Jock they do count. The 10th Mountain's Command Sergeant Major Frank Grippe took Clint and Jock under his charge and the chook instantly sized him up. *He's a no-nonsense straight talker*, Jock thought. Jock never found Grippe wanting. Not that Grippe would have cared. He was there to do a job – capture or kill al Qaeda and Osama bin Laden the knucklehead, as Grippe called him – he wasn't interested in winning popularity contests.

'He's a big bastard, got the normal [GI] haircut and he's starting to be a silverback – it's grey and short and cropped,' Jock says, recalling the first time he met Grippe at Bagram. 'Pitted complexion, but also weatherbeaten. He had done some hard yards, you could see it in his eyes, you could see it in his body and the way he carried himself. He's a big, loud man, when he speaks he's got this booming voice.'

Grippe instantly dubbed Jock 'Digger' and in doing so acknowledged both the Australian tradition of handing out nicknames and the nation's proud military history. And he clicked with Clint, who held the same rank in the Australian Army.

'Just the fact that Grippe, the senior sergeant major, was showing us around and giving us the intros meant that we were made men,' Jock recalls.

Jock felt confident with Grippe, and his instincts were confirmed by the way the men from Charlie Company treated their command sergeant major with genuine respect and admiration. They jumped up and gave a strong and good-natured greeting of 'Sar-Major' when Grippe went by on his introductory tour, chest out, head high, arms swinging purposefully.

They're not just pissing in his pocket, Jock thought, as Grippe cut a swathe through the 10th Mountain's HQ.

The men looked to Grippe for guidance, courage and leadership, and he never let them down when it came to that holy triumvirate.

'I was a digger, but I was an Aussie; the American diggers had to have the compulsory respect for officers. I'd call Frank Grippe "Sir", but I was saying that out of respect, not out of obligation. He's the RSM [regimental sergeant major, the Australian equivalent to Grippe's rank of command sergeant major]. He's a real one, not a wanker one; not one who had done the courses but hadn't really understood the ideology or the concept of the position.

'The RSM position is all about being a soldier's soldier. In the soldiering skills department, he is the benchmark. And if you have an RSM who is not displaying the skills or applying them in his own bearing and demeanour and approach, then it's obvious. And it's also obvious when you've got one who does, and Grippe is that one, the one who does have the skills.'

For his part, Grippe was equally pleased to have Clint and Jock working with his unit. Not only did the American have a British mother, he also had relatives living in Australia, which gave him a natural affinity for the Commonwealth and Aussies. And being a former Special Forces man himself, he appreciated the incredible skills of the Australian Special Air Service Regiment. It was, after all, among the best in the SF global community.

'It was great having them on board, they lent a different view, and Clint's a hoot. And young Digger? I had a good time talking to him. They are both extraordinary gentlemen,' Grippe says now. 'And because of my background in SOF [Special Operations Forces] I knew what they had been through, training-wise and indoctrination-wise, and so we thought alike quite a bit. And we all wanted to get in the fight and hunt down al Qaeda. They just lent another capability to my battalion to – bottom line – fight and kill al Qaeda.

'And, of course, because of their background I just had an immediate respect and an immediate calm because I just knew that ... when the chips were down, those two guys would fight.'

Jock Wallace was happy to be working with the 10th Mountain for another reason. The Americans prided themselves on their generosity and hospitality, and the American population was well behind their troops fighting terrorism in far-off lands, sending succour and support with care packages loaded with sweet offerings. Jock was bemused but at the same time pleased to be sharing in the Americans' booty. He got to a point where he didn't think it would be too outrageous to expect a chocolate on the pillow each night. Hell, the hard hitters from the 5th Special Forces Group had even dubbed their accommodation Motel 6.

'They'd try and give you anything they had. The Americans were very hospitable,' says Jock. 'We [Jock and Clint] had our own bedroom. The Americans had heaps of lollies sent over by the American population. It wasn't like "Homer Simpson land of chocolates", but they had lollies. There were also walls full of care letters.

'It was significant. And it kept your focus and kept your mind on the job. You also knew the Australian population would be backing you – with the exception of people with an ideological disagreement with it. But by and large, even those people would wish success for the Australian team, I imagine.'

No soldier who had ever been deployed on a mission – whether to a war zone or for peacekeeping purposes – could help but feel the sting of public opprobrium when, and if, it came. Soldiers don't play politics. They follow orders and fight wars. Jock, like thousands of volunteers who had enlisted in the Australian Defence Force, remembered through gritted teeth the hell the Vietnam veterans endured when they returned home to Australia, decried and vilified in the most vicious way imaginable. The memory of that appalling treatment was like a festering sore for all the men and women willing to put their lives on the line for their country.

'The reason we are there is the politicians,' Jock says. 'Like when the Vietnam vets came home – why did people throw eggs at *them*? Throw them at the politicians, throw them at Parliament House, throw them at yourself because you voted them in.'

★   ★   ★

Ever since bunking in with the 10th Mountain, Jock and Clint had been working on their mission, getting to know the men they would be going into battle with. As D-Day approached, the US soldiers began focusing explicitly on the job ahead, going over their individual and collective objectives in the Shahi Kot Valley, staging the rehearsal, and checking their equipment. Jock visited his mates Ando and Simon, prepped his sig's equipment and sorted all his high-tech gear. He was as good to go as he had been at any other time in his life.

On the eve of Operation Anaconda, outside tent city not far from the huge rusting aircraft hangar in the middle of Bagram Air Base, a solid hulk of a man in battle fatigues climbed on top of a Humvee military jeep to the approving roar of several hundred soldiers. The troops formed the international operation charged with eliminating al Qaeda and the remnants of the oppressive Taliban regime hiding in the Shahi Kot Valley.

The man on the Humvee was Colonel Frank Wiercinski, the commander of the 3rd Brigade, 101st Airborne Division (Air Assault) and chief of US ground forces for Operation Anaconda. The only airborne infantry division in the US Army, they were known as the Rakkasans, a term that came from World War II when the 3rd Battalion, 187th Infantry Regiment – now part of the 101st Airborne Division – parachuted into Japan. The Japanese dubbed the brave parachutists the Rakkasans which translates, literally, as 'falling umbrellas'.

Standing taller than 180 centimetres and with a booming voice, the career officer was the type of man who instantly commanded attention. As soon as he opened his mouth, the troops fell silent.

'It's Friday night and everybody here has been invited to the party. *Hoo-ah!*' Wiercinski roared, grinning from ear to ear as his rallying cry was met with cheers from the troops.

'I'm gonna get serious with you for a minute. Everyone of our generation has been called to do something for his country. We are no different. We have been called on to fight the war on terrorism. You are part of that fight,' boomed Wiercinski, his pistol strapped to his thigh over his camouflage pants, a pumped-up picture of raging testosterone and manliness.

'Every man, every woman has some defining moments in their lives. Today is one of your defining moments. You will never forget this ... You are representing your country.

'A lot of us have two questions always going through our minds: Why? How will I do?

'As for why, each and every one of you has to answer that for yourself. For me it's 9/11, for those families that watched as their loved ones never came home. For those firefighters, emergency workers and policemen who charged up rather than came down. It's for them. We do this for them.'

Jock Wallace stood to the side of the action, his fists shoved deep in his pockets, his army-issue GORE-TEX cold-weather gear protecting him against the freezing conditions, listening intently to Wiercinski. Winter should have been thawing out, at least according to the calendar, but the temperatures at Bagram still plunged way below zero. Nothing could prevent the bone-chilling cold that came with the location: Bagram was 1770 metres above sea level in the middle of the breathtaking Panjir Valley on the Shomali Plains in north central Afghanistan. Winters were brutal; summers, too.

Jock cast a look around at his fellow soldiers, their rapt attention lasered onto the commander. He'd never experienced anything quite like Wiercinski's rallying cry or the impact it had on the soldiers who had gathered to hear it. The anticipation and excitement were palpable. The adrenaline was pumping; the atmosphere was supercharged.

Jock laughed to himself. *Fuckin' Americans, what a show.*

It was not the way the Australian Defence Force did business.

'It's a mass psych-up. It's a method of building your energy and getting the fervour going, but I didn't need the fervour, I was there for a reason,' Jock says now. 'I didn't need to wind myself up, I'm there cold and hot, you know what I mean? They are trying to incite passion and instil strength and resolve. You shouldn't be there if it ain't there. That's just my perspective. And, in essence, if other people need that gee up, I'm glad they got it.'

Jock thought the most significant part of Wiercinski's rallying cry was that the big boss had taken the time to address the workers. Though he found the colonel's speech entertaining and distracting at the same time, he appreciated the symbolism.

Wiercinski, totemic on the Humvee, was on a roll, his voice rising to a crescendo as he came to the second question.

'How will you do in combat?' he thundered. 'You are thinking you've never been in combat – "I don't know how I will do." You will be good in combat because of a lot of reasons. The first one is because of who you are. You volunteered. It started in here,' Wiercinski said, tapping a closed fist to his chest over his heart.

'That's what makes you good in combat. You are the best in the world – you will do it for each other. And you will watch each other. We have two missions tonight. One is to defeat an enemy and [the other] is to never leave a fallen comrade.'

'*Hoo-ah!*' the soldiers chanted in agreement.

Never leave a fallen comrade was part of their code. They lived by it, swore by it and upholding it was the difference between honouring the Army and dishonouring the uniform and yourself.

'There are two kinds of people out there,' Wiercinski said. 'There's innocents who don't want any part of this fight. And there are those out there who want nothing better than to kill an American or kill a coalition fighter. Do not be afraid to squeeze that trigger. You will know when and you will know why. Take care of one another. Take care of all of us. I wouldn't want to be anywhere else in the world today but right here with you.

'Today is your climb to glory. Today is another chapter in Rakkasan history. Today is our rendezvous with destiny. You all be proud of yourselves. God bless each and every one of us. See you when you come back.'

Wiercinski paused and panned the expectant faces before him – so young and vital. A career officer and veteran of the first Gulf War, Wiercinski knew what was ahead – he had all the intelligence reports and he was going in with his men in just a few hours' time. Jock knew the colonel's message had to matter to them.

The troops were waiting. Wiercinski rose to the occasion.

'Remember our motto,' he thundered. 'Let Valor Not Fail.'

'*Hoo-ah!*' came the chorus from the troops.

'Rakkasan!' Wiercinski roared back.

Their credo was no-nonsense.

They were ready to move and ready to fight.

CHAPTER 3

*Jock caught sight of the two Apache AH-64s that
had taken off five minutes before the Chinooks
and were escorting them in.*

The men from the 1-87's Charlie Company were all bombed
up, gunned up and ready to roar. They'd been sitting in the
dark in their chalk positions for more than an hour, and were
waiting for the three Chinook pilots to finish their ear-splitting
tests on the new 714 engines that lifted the massive airframes.
The flight was scheduled to take off around 5am local time.
Three more Chinooks would fly in the 100-plus soldiers from the
101st Airborne.

An NCO held the flight manifest for the six choppers and the
roll call of volunteer soldiers began in flight order. As each
soldier's name was bellowed over the increasing din of the rotor-
blades, he grabbed his pack and weapons and walked silently
through the darkness to the back of the waiting helos. Jock, Clint
and another 40 troops from the 1-87 were on Chalk One, as the
helicopter was called, for the flight in. Jock was happy to see
Sergeant Major Frank Grippe and the sar-major's boss,
Lieutenant Colonel Paul LaCamera, on their helo.

The bellies of Chalks Two and Three would also each have
about 35 troops crammed in, sitting shoulder to shoulder, some
with their backs to the wall and their legs around their loaded
weapons, properly positioned with barrel pointing down, as per the

safety drills that had been drummed into the soldiers in the unlikely event of accidental discharge. A handful of unlucky bastards, including some of the men from Sergeant Peterson's mortar platoon, sat on the floor in the middle, tucked around the 120mm mortar and SKEDCOs on which the ordnance was packed in wooden boxes. No seat offered a first-class ride, but in the middle with nothing to rest your back against, it was particularly rough.

Jock was one of the first up. His in-flight position landed him a few metres behind the pilots. He would have preferred to be at the rear of the helo for one good reason – last on, first off. Helicopters with a full load of combat-ready troops heading to a war zone instantly become HVTs – and the longer a soldier is on one, the longer he's a target.

The only advantage of being up the front was that some soldiers had a view of the FLIR screen. The nose of the chopper is fitted with a forward-looking infrared camera, a piece of high-tech equipment that senses heat emissions and sends the data to a video screen between the two pilots where it is converted into a moving map. Heat-emitting objects such as engines, recently fired weapons, small homes with heating, villagers and enemy combatants are easily detected by the highly effective and powerful infrared camera. Nothing escapes.

The FLIR was a crucial piece of technology and more so this morning, given the extensive cloud coverage and low visibility. Other than possibly watching a few of the younger and more nervous battle-green troops hurling last night's dinner into their helmets with each pitch and roll as the Chinook tore through the darkness like a roller coaster, there was no in-flight entertainment. *A bit like flying in a Third World country's ancient plane*, Jock thought with a chuckle. No entertainment, no food, cramped conditions.

The joker to Jock's left, a man wearing civvies whom he suspected was an American special operator, had no problems with the vertiginous tacks and turns of the flight or the cold and cramped conditions in which they travelled. In fact, as soon as the chopper was in the air and *thwack-thwack-thwacking* its way south over the Afghanistan countryside, he rested his head on Jock's shoulder and fell asleep. *Like a fuckin' baby*, Jock thought.

It gave Jock a fair fit of the shits and, as the flight screamed along, he got more and more pissed off as the bloke got more and more comfortable. After a while, Jock delivered a solid wake-up call to the sleeping stranger's ribs. *Oomph.*

'Sit up straight. Stop leaning on me,' Jock growled.

'Awww, come on bud.'

'You're not my fuckin' girlfriend.'

'The guy looked like a little puppy that had his nose rubbed in a puddle of piss,' Jock says now.

Screw him, he thought, *I'm going to war, I don't want one leg not working because it's got pins and needles.*

Everyone was uncomfortable and this wanker was making it more uncomfortable.

Jock had nothing to confirm that the bloke was a special operator other than that the sleeping stranger, who was travelling with another man, was not wearing the US Army's full field uniform, which included a flak jacket plus high-tech GORE-TEX and polypro gear for warmth. Clint had been talking to the strangers earlier at the FUP and had told Jock that they had discussed their E&E (escape and evasion) plan with him.

'If it all goes to shit at LZ 13, they bloody well intend using it,' Clint had said.

'That's a good idea, Clint,' Jock had replied, 'but you want to know where you're going in these parts.'

'An E&E plan is a double-edged weapon,' Jock explains now. 'You can walk five metres in exactly the right direction towards the nearest friendly forces and still hit a mine, because although it's the right bearing, it might not be the right route. Or you may just wander into a dodgy warlord's land and get picked up and compromised.

'Having an escape plan was a good option but trying to get out of that joint by yourselves was pretty risky.'

The Chinooks made good speed, travelling south from Bagram at about 110 knots – 200 kilometres per hour – as the first halo of light started to break through the pitch black of night. Gunners wearing night-vision goggles manned the right and left doors of the helos as well as the rear ramp. Some blokes tried to steal a few minutes of sleep here and there, but whenever their necks slackened and their heads nodded, they jerked awake. Sergeant Peterson nearly jumped out of his skin when the Chinook gunner test-fired his weapon out the tail end of the chopper. His young soldiers cracked up.

A few more sanguine troopers treated the flight as a sightseeing trip and had their faces glued to the windows, taking in the scenery as the chopper tacked sharply and pitched down closer to the rugged terrain of the mountains. As they flew the stomach-churning route banking fiercely every few seconds, Jock noted the fragmented beauty of the country.

One second he could see rocky mountain faces so close he could almost touch them. The next second he saw snow-covered peaks towering above the helo as it banked fiercely in the other direction. The scene changed from sky to cliff to valley floor like a slide show. When the Chinook lurched in a sharp turn, he could spot an occasional village nestled into the valley at the foot of a huge mountain. Here and there he snatched a glance at Chalks Two or Three as they peeled off and plummeted down, contouring the mountains to metres above the valley floor, conducting evasive zigzag manoeuvres as they went. Jock also caught sight of the two Apache AH-64s that had taken off five minutes before the Chinooks and were escorting them in.

The helo was blacked out for security purposes and the only light came from dull red globes mounted on the walls and emitted a red-hued spectral fog. Jock was wearing army-issue earplugs to block out the deafening roar of the 714 engines and it was impossible to talk with, let alone hear, Clint or his American colleagues. Not that he needed an in-flight chat to work out what most of the young blokes around him were thinking. He only needed to look at their faces to recognise fear of the unknown ahead. Jock was more experienced than the young blokes and had been in a few dangerous places before this one. He knew those looks. He'd had those looks himself.

'You can see it in their face, they're scared and they don't want to be there. But they're not acting scared or that they don't want to be there,' says Jock now.

'But by and large, it wasn't the overwhelming thing you noticed. Everyone was confident and everyone was really willing and everyone knew what was coming – as in, we were going into battle.'

The two flights of three Chinooks ferrying Charlie Company's 120-odd men and the 100-plus from the 101st Airborne had left Bagram, altitude 1770 metres, and were flying into potentially hot LZs at no less than 2600 metres. It was the highest altitude battle ever fought by American soldiers. They had been drilled that altitude is your enemy almost as much as al Qaeda is. One American officer had been advised to expect, realistically, an altitude attrition rate of up to 40 per cent. It was one of the last things the troops heard at the form-up point – that and their NCO yelling at them to stay alive.

The SAS soldiers weren't worried; they were well prepared, having undertaken extreme training in the mountain ranges of Australia, New Zealand, Europe and even the Rocky Mountains in Colorado. As Jock peered out the window, he had one overriding thought: *Let's get into it.*

It was around 5am on D-Day – 2 March 2002 – and Major General Franklin Hagenbeck had been in the Tactical Operations Center for hours, getting ready for the bombing raid before H-Hour. This was going to be a baptism by fire for his infantrymen; the first time conventional forces had been used in Afghanistan. The Special Forces had invited them to the party and Hagenbeck had command. He wanted to be there for every minute of what he had sent his troops to do, and in the era of high-tech modern warfare he could watch it play out in real time.

Two unmanned Predator drones were in place over the valley, being flown by remote control by US Air Force pilots sitting in a top-secret compound at the Prince Sultan Air Base in Saudi Arabia. Armed with state-of-the-art satellite technology, the drones beamed live video footage of the action back to two screens at the front of the Tactical Operations Center.

The TOC was attached to an austere bombed-out hangar that the Soviets had used during their ten-year invasion of Afghanistan two decades earlier. That military effort was an abject failure during which the Soviets lost 15 000 troops. One of the worst days saw the mujahideen kill 250 soldiers – 200 of whom were rumoured to have been stoned to death after being captured. The Soviets also sustained 55 000 casualties. After the Soviet Union's ignominious defeat, it retreated from Afghanistan, leaving Bagram littered with disused and unexploded mines and ordnance.

Hundreds of destroyed Russian aircraft shot down by the mujahideen's CIA-donated weapons, including the lethal American-made surface-to-air Stinger missiles, lay wrecked alongside the useless shells of Afghan MIG fighter jets that had met a similar fate. The roof of the main hangar had been blown off, and walls were almost non-existent.

After the Special Forces soldiers removed the Taliban from Bagram in December, Army engineers began transforming the aircraft graveyard-cum-minefield into a tent city to house several thousand troops from dozens of countries that formed the coalition in the War on Terror. They built paths known as duckboards for soldiers to safely circumnavigate the base without stepping on the explosives. Huge wooden signs stuck in the mud warned the troops of the dire and potentially fatal consequences of any diversion. Dire is an understatement.

When Major General Hagenbeck moved in, he found an unexploded bomb protruding from the hangar wall. Stunned, he called in the ordnance and explosives unit who detonated it without a hitch.

'Everywhere around the place, if you stepped off the concrete you risked getting hit. In fact, in the first 30 days we were there, eleven people either were killed or lost a limb stepping off the concrete, that's how many bombs there were,' Hagenbeck says now, reflecting on the conditions into which he had moved his control-and-command element. Some of the 'streets' on the base were subsequently named after the dead troops.

'The Soviets had just saturated the countryside in their ten years with mines and bombs, and so there was a lot of unexploded ordnance, not just mines.'

The TOC had been set up to accommodate the various forces that were involved in Operation Enduring Freedom. A curved wooden table was built on a raised platform in the centre of the tent. It was long enough to seat at least a couple of dozen officers. The TOC was crowded with officers, intelligence operatives, communications experts and soldiers. As the overall commander of Operation Anaconda, Hagenbeck was allocated prime position bang at the centre of the table, with top-ranking officers from other units and coalition forces fanning out to his left and right. Sunken boxes were attached to the desk to hold telephones with lines to the field, other unit commands and back to General Tommy Franks, who was running the entire show from US Central Command in Tampa, Florida – 11 000 kilometres and ten time zones away.

Information was coming in from all over the valley and other areas of operations in that part of Afghanistan. Directly in front of Hagenbeck at the front of the tent stood a one-and-a-half-metre-wide video screen displaying an image of the battle map. To the left were screens for the live Predator feed and a log of action coming in live from the field via the communications networks. A whiteboard with maps was elsewhere with the words: 'Who else needs to know?'

It was well before dawn on the blistering cold Saturday morning and the atmosphere in the TOC was tense, the anticipation palpable. There was a real sense of expectation and a quiet acknowledgement that this day was to be historic in one sense or another. A US Army chaplain was on hand to lead the officers in prayer when Anaconda began. Hagenbeck knew what every general going into battle knows: the plan is only good until the first shot is fired.

'Let me tell you who these terrorists were, because I think it's important,' Hagenbeck says now, sitting in his office in the east wing of the Pentagon which was rebuilt after the hijacked American Airlines Flight 77 crashed into it on September 11.

'You've seen all the little film clips on TV about the terrorist camps that Osama bin Laden ran,' Hagenbeck says, his voice sinking an octave. 'These were the guys that ran the camps. These were the Chechens, the Uzbeks, the Mongol-Chinese, some Pakistanis.

'These were, by and large, veterans that would, in our Army, be captains or majors or sergeant majors that run our training bases back in Australia, back in the United States. And so the purpose was not just to kill them because they are al Qaeda, but to kill them because they're the ones that were producing all of these terrorists in those years in Afghanistan.'

Major General Hagenbeck meant business.

His predecessor by two, Lieutenant General Timothy Maude, was at his desk inside the famous Department of Defense headquarters when the Boeing 757 exploded through the walls, killing him instantly. It was less than twenty metres down the hall from where Hagenbeck and I are talking. A memorial to those killed at the Pentagon adorns the wall in the corridor leading to Hagenbeck's office. Maude, a three-star general, was the Army's deputy chief of staff for personnel and had been Hagenbeck's golfing buddy and close personal friend. General Maude was 53 when he was killed, and his death made this war very personal for Major General Hagenbeck.

Lieutenant Colonel Rowan Tink, the commander of the Australian forces in Afghanistan, arrived in the TOC before 5.30am and took a seat to the right of Hagenbeck. Tink had been dragged out of bed a couple of hours earlier by a liaison officer to discuss the positions of Australian SAS patrols doing long-range surveillance and reconnaissance in the Shahi Kot Valley. Tink was concerned about the potential for conflict on the ground with other US Special Forces operators and wanted to ensure that his SAS troopers, who had been in the valley for a while, were in no danger of being accidentally fired upon by members of the US Special Forces teams as they were resupplied or withdrew through the Australian lines.

The SAS and the US SF would not know the whereabouts of their counterparts for security reasons. The last thing Tink wanted was a friendly-fire fatality (or fratricide) before the real fight began and he'd already discussed his safety measures, via phone, with Brigadier Duncan Lewis, the commander of Special Operations who was in Australia, and the national component commander in Kuwait.

The staff in the TOC had their attention drawn to the Predator screen and electronic C2 – command-and-control – display. They had already seen surreal images of an attack by a US Navy SEAL patrol, call sign Mako Three One. (The number 31 is pronounced Three One in accordance with standard radio protocol, as are all numbers in call signs.)

The only men over whom Hagenbeck did not have direct command were the Special Forces soldiers from the US Tier One Delta Forces, and SEAL Team 6. The US had various known Special Forces operating in Afghanistan but it also had 'black operations' Special Forces outfits – those whom the Pentagon does not formally acknowledge – including one known as Task Force 11. Task Force 11 was a Tier One group and worked closely with strategic assets. Its main operation – to hunt down and capture or kill Osama bin Laden and the al Qaeda command – had top priority. Named in memory of September 11, the burly and usually bearded blokes in the task force worked in utmost secrecy and were commanded from Florida. They had their own mission. As Robin Moore says in his book, *The Hunt for bin Laden*, Task Force 11 'would concentrate on POW snatches, grabbing suspected and known terrorists and taking them into custody, kidnapping AQ leaders and killing individual terrorist threats'.

Around 4am the five-man American SEAL team had snuck up on an al Qaeda crew and its Soviet DShK anti-aircraft gun that had been strategically placed on a rocky slope overlooking one of the landing zones designated for the incoming infantrymen of the 10th Mountain. The enemy position on a small mountain feature could have wiped out the entire battalion, including Jock and Clint.

Mako Three One's snipers approached and opened fire, killing two AQ fighters and wounding another. Two others escaped, but the patrol radioed the coordinates of their kill to an AC-130 Spectre gunship flying above, as per Hagenbeck's OpOrd.

The Spectre's call sign was portentous – Grim Three One. It responded ferociously, unleashing a barrage of lethal fire into the position while tracking the two escaping AQ and opening fire. It was a good kill.

Shortly after, Grim Three One received the co-ords from a second SF patrol in the valley for another confirmed enemy observation point on the Whale. It circled over the valley and flew into action again, blasting the target and enemy combatants into oblivion. Strike two successful.

CHAPTER 4

'We weren't expecting to make a major contact although we were ready to make a major contact if need be. We are all fighters.'

SERGEANT MAJOR FRANK GRIPPE, THE TOP NON-COMMISSIONED OFFICER OF 1ST BATTALION, 87TH INFANTRY REGIMENT, 10TH MOUNTAIN DIVISION

At 0100 zulu time – 5.30am in the valley – General Zia's Hammer stopped west of the Whale. It hadn't been easy going, and the formation was spread out over several kilometres. The Zermat road was a joke; parts had been turned into impassable muddy bogs by rain and melting snow. The *jinga* trucks loaded with the Afghan Force broke down, or couldn't traverse the terrain. Some tipped over, injuring soldiers. The AF, knowing the countryside and the enemy as they did, believed it would get worse.

A mini-convoy of about 50 US soldiers and 40 Afghan fighters, whom the Americans dubbed 'jundees', had already broken off from the main column to secure another position a couple of kilometres north of the Whale. About 30 were on foot as they closed on their location. The SF guys, riding in Toyota pickup trucks, were decked out with all the high-tech equipment needed to see at night. All of a sudden, *boom*. A hail of mortars and machine-gun fire rained down on them.

They were under attack, but from where? They suspected AQ had seen them coming from positions hidden along the ridgeline of the mountains overlooking the valley floors. Shrapnel exploded all around, hitting coalition targets and inflicting a string of casualties among Zia's men and the hard men from Task Force Dagger. It was chaos; pure destruction.

Back in the TOC at Bagram, the fight was being monitored over the radio and screens for the Predator vision, as well as being fed back to US Central Command in Florida.

'Attention in the TOC,' a voice boomed, silencing the continuous hum of talk.

The stern announcement indicated a call for fire was about to be declared. Grid coordinates for the target were yelled out to ensure that the coalition forces in the valley were not in the kill zone. It was standard operating procedure.

This time the coordinates were for a target locked on by the crew of Grim Three One, the same AC-130 gunship that had laid waste to the two al Qaeda positions earlier that morning.

A Special Forces patrol had radioed the crew of the AC-130 and asked it to fly over one site of potential ambush around the Whale – to check for enemy positions. The Spectre's crew replied that they saw several trucks and personnel on foot and relayed the information to Special Forces on the ground, asking them to check their locations. All reported no friendlies at the location co-ords cited by Grim Three One. Somehow, though, Grim Three One's coordinates did not match its location, but the crew were unaware of the error. The gunship was actually over the mini-convoy that included the Cobra Seven Two team and General Zia's AF, not over the location of the coordinates it read out.

Grim Three One opened up the 105mm howitzer, relentlessly strafing the target with deadly ammunition. Cobra Seven Two soon suspected that the precise targeting of the ammo could only be friendlies, not mortars or machine-gun fire from enemy al Qaeda.

As shells began blasting the earth around the mini-convoy, a male voice came over the radio yelling they were taking incoming.

The voice belonged to Warrant Officer Class Two Stanley Harriman, a 34-year-old Green Beret and second-in-command of Cobra Seven Two.

They were being pasted bad. The convoy raced to evade the shells spewing razor-sharp shrapnel in every direction upon impact. A piece of torn metal cut through the door of Harriman's truck and ripped through his back. Two other SF soldiers were seriously wounded. Harriman and the wounded were medevaced out minutes later after an incoming Chinook had delivered the Rakkasans from the 101st Airborne in the northern end of the valley on the eastern side of the Whale. Despite the best efforts of the American medics and the chopper pilots who got the wounded SF man back to Bagram, Harriman died. According to Robin Moore in *The Hunt for bin Laden*, the father of two was the first Green Beret warrant officer ever to be killed in action, and the first fatality of Operation Anaconda.

General Zia lost three of his men, and twenty more sustained injuries.

Anaconda had begun. Badly.

Back in the Tactical Operations Center, the Australian SAS's commander, Lieutenant Colonel Rowan Tink, listened as it was reported that Dagger had taken fourteen casualties.

'Confirming Texas or Cobra,' Tink wrote in his war diary, referring to two of the US Special Forces patrols in the valley.

It was Cobra Seven Two.

Out in the valley, Zia's main column heard the attack and deployed a quick-reaction force to their stricken comrades. Meanwhile, they halted progress, as planned, to wait out the scheduled bombing raid before troops were inserted into the remaining LZs in the valley.

While stopped, parts of the convoy came under heavy attack from al Qaeda terrorists on the Whale. Eventually, with the growing chaos, casualties and destroyed trucks, the Afghan Forces would make the decision to withdraw.

Zia's decision to withdraw would ultimately result in a crossfire of accusations between US and Afghan forces about who had let whom down. The arguments would also consume some Special Forces soldiers who had spent time training the Afghan soldiers – each of whom was paid US$200 per month – and who defended Zia's men, and the US conventional soldiers who believed that relying on the Afghan Forces was a serious mistake.

'We got our arses mortared off,' the SAS liaison officer recalled after the battle. Before Zia's force pulled back, SAS observers with the convoy discovered more AQ positions on the Whale, something Brigadier Lewis later confirmed at a press conference in Australia.

'Just prior to that [air assault going in], literally just before the sun came up – these guys [the Afghan militia] got fired upon,' Hagenbeck says now. 'Two things happened. They were fired upon by the al Qaeda with mortars and D30 howitzers, but unfortunately – and we suspected shortly after it happened and we later confirmed it – there was a fratricide [in] which an AC-130 inadvertently opened up and killed some Afghan militia and killed one Special Forces guy.

'We had to shift our main attack to the air assault elements because they [Hammer] had to withdraw and they did not get back into the fight for three days or so. And it was understandable. It would have happened to any military force.

'While this was going on, some special operators in the hills killed some al Qaeda that were in the hills; they had heavy machine guns lined up and also some mortar positions,' Hagenbeck said, referring to the Mako Three One incident. 'So they were instrumental in making sure the air assault got in ... So that's the opening salvo. That is the way it all began.'

It was now around 6.15am.

The first air strikes of the pre-H-Hour bombing raid screamed through the darkened skies in the east and west of the valley. A fast-moving F-15E dropped a massive thermobaric bomb on an intricate cave system used by al Qaeda. The so-called fuel-air munition hadn't been used before in Afghanistan. The massive explosion should be efficient and deadly, sucking the oxygen out of the cave system and incinerating anyone in its way. The thermobaric was chased by a barrage of joint direct attack munition bombs – or JDAMs – which exploded along the back of the Whale, supposedly destroying enemy positions with withering accuracy.

Some of the pre-planned targets were perilously close to the US Special Operations forces that had infiltrated the mountain. Months after Anaconda had ended, an Air Force report revealed part of what happened next. 'As bombs started to fall, teams on the ground were uninformed of the pre-planned fires and believed they were being fired on by friendlies, which resulted in them broadcasting a "knock it off" request part way through the strike.'

Friendly aircrews heeded the call and did indeed knock it off.

In a much discussed and controversial interview about six months after the operation, Major General Hagenbeck told *Field Artillery* magazine why the pre-H-Hour bombing raid was so limited.

'We knew the enemy's "centre of gravity" was inside the caves where his soldiers and logistics were. But we did not know how much C2 he had inside that valley. I did not want to attack dozens and dozens of cave complexes arbitrarily without having some sense of what was in them.'

So that was it. The anticipated 55-minute bombing raid that would have obliterated thirteen enemy targets hardly eventuated.

Jock Wallace and most of his fellow baby-faced fighters on the incoming airlifts were oblivious to the catastrophe unfolding on the ground below them. For all Jock knew, everything would be in place when the chalks landed. They'd had their briefings and everyone had a job to do and knew how to do it.

Lieutenant Colonel Paul LaCamera had been wearing cans – earphones – and was getting some sense of the chaos on the ground below. He informed his number two, the indefatigable Sergeant Major Frank Grippe, the big bloke whom Jock had got to know over the previous five days down at the 10th Mountain headquarters at Bagram.

'We weren't expecting to make a major contact although we were ready to make a major contact if need be. We are all fighters,' Grippe says, sitting in his office at Fort Campbell, Kentucky.

'There was definitely a sense of urgency, definitely a sense of adventure. About 45 minutes out from landing we got the word. I was sitting next to LaCamera and he had the headphones on and we were getting the word that the Special Forces and the Afghan Forces were taking heavy mortar and heavy machine-gun fire and I thought, "Well this ought to be interesting. We will definitely be making some contact."

'But again, we didn't know if it was just an anomaly – a small strongpoint or just a cell of al Qaeda and Taliban forces. I knew the Special Forces had lost a soldier, there was a report on that, but I can't recall if it was killed in action or wounded. We said there was some contact made, as simple as that. Bottom line, up front, you are going to go flying into this valley and land, either way.'

Charlie Company was minutes out from landing and everyone was switched on, even the previously sleeping bloke beside Jock. Jock was getting revved up. This was the adventure he'd been waiting for since November. One of his best mates in the SAS, Johnny, was already out in the Shahi Kot. Jock was a signalman, a comms expert, and he knew the Aussie blokes had been taking numbers in the mountains. The SAS patrols had done sterling work and located enemy positions. Jock wanted to join the fight, just like Johnny.

The Chinooks were flying low and fast. The doors were open, the back cargo ramp was down, and an icy wind ripped through the helo. A US soldier standing at the back of the aircraft held up two hands with his fingers splayed and shouted: 'Ten minutes, wheels down.' The hand signals were SOP, standard operating procedure, in the US and Australian military.

Ten minutes to showtime, Jock thought.

He was pumped; his heart was pounding. He did a mental checklist and reassured himself that he was good to go. And he was. No pins and needles in his legs; gear ready and in working order; radio and satellite equipment well juiced; weapon in action condition, locked and loaded. Jock looked at Clint and gave him a smile and a wink that would have been equally at home on a fifteen-year-old boy about to pop his cherry.

The bombing raid should have ripped the guts out of the al Qaeda and Taliban positions by now, Jock was thinking.

In the Tactical Operations Center at Bagram, Jock's boss, Lieutenant Colonel Rowan Tink, had his eyes on the Predator footage on the big screen.

Tink turned to his diary and noted the time as 0158 zulu time. 'Commander realised the bomber did not hit the AQ caves,' he wrote. The intention was to wipe out all the known al Qaeda caves in the valley with the aerial bombing. But the aerial bombing had not gone entirely to plan.

Two minutes later, at 6.30am, the helos in the first flight carrying the men from the 2–187 from the 101st Airborne touched down in the north of the valley. Then came Jock's Chinook at BP Ginger further south.

'Wheels down,' Tink noted.

It was 6.38am in the valley.

Chalks One and Two touched down 400 metres apart and about one click south of Marzak, heading for blocking points Ginger and Heather, the two southernmost points on the eastern side of the valley. Chalk Three landed two clicks north. The Rakkasans were further north again. The twin rotors of the massive beasts sent a blinding blast of dirt, dust and gravel into the air.

'Go,' Charlie Company's sergeants bellowed as their men deplaned and took their first steps in the Place of the King, trying to suck what little oxygen there was in the high-altitude air into their pounding chests.

Peterson's mortar platoon were running as fast as they could, considering they were hauling their mortar tube and dragging their SKEDCOs, each stacked with fifteen to twenty rounds of ammo and weighing what felt like a tonne – roughly 275 kilograms each – trying to get out of the way of the following troops.

Jock bolted off, holding his M4 fully automatic carbine diagonally across his chest with his right hand while automatically tapping his belt to triple-check that his Browning 9mm pistol had not been dislodged on the flight and was still on his belt. He felt the weight of the 60-kilogram backpack and, as soon as he was out from under the tail of the Chinook, he looked up and saw the snowcapped mountains around him – the eastern ridges of Takur Ghar and the deep crevices of the rat lines that ran to Pakistan. To the northwest was that monstrosity known as the Whale, a huge piece of rock rising hundreds of metres high, cutting the valley in half, north to south, and home to a hidden enemy. Closer west was a smaller mountain feature dubbed the Finger, where Mako Three One had earlier wiped out an al Qaeda terrorist position and set up its own observation point overlooking the valley.

Fuckin' awesome, Jock thought. *Could've been a ski field if the Russians and Taliban hadn't screwed with the country and riddled it with landmines.*

Clint was right behind him, breathing down his neck. Next came the thunderous footsteps of Sergeant Major Grippe, followed by Lieutenant Colonel LaCamera. Clint and Grippe would stay close. They had to – Clint was the liaison officer for his fellow SAS troopers on patrol in the surrounding rugged terrain.

Within two minutes, the empty Chinooks lifted off and were hurtling down the valley, growing smaller in the distance. Jock now noticed something wrong. He had been expecting an overwhelming odour of cordite to be hanging in the air from the ballyhooed bombing raid. But there was nothing.

Jesus Christ, he thought.

'There was absolutely no evidence that there were any bombs dropped in our vicinity as we had been led to believe in the briefings – that they were going to smash that place, both ridges, before we came in,' Jock says now. 'And if they were talking about the eastern ridge, then it had surely settled down pretty quickly and had blown all the cordite to the other side of the valley. Which is crap. It seemed like there were no B-52s that bombed anything. If a B-52 drops its guts, you know about it for a long time later.

'Basically we were told there was going to be a helluva lot of ordnance dropped before we got there, that they were going to lay it on thick on the ridgelines – the Americans were going to intensively bomb this area prior to us alighting from the helicopters and prior to the helicopters even arriving, so it'd end just before our arrival. And we'd get out and into position with the enemy still having his ears ringing et cetera.

'When I got off, that's the first thing that I noticed: there was no smoke, no indication of battle damage or recent bombing. We are in this pristine, beautiful, snowcapped and ringed valley with patches of snow on the ground. The air was just mountain winter air – cold, crisp. You could hear a chicken crowing from miles away.

'That sort of put me a little bit on guard in my mind, in that I knew basically once again no matter who is calling the shots it comes down to you. You just switch into another mode – "Okay, you blokes are unreliable, I can't rely on what you're saying and I have to do it myself."'

An eerie silence settled on the LZ. Jock started to hump his gear north, creating a formation with Clint, Grippe and Grippe's right-hand man and operations officer, Robert Healy, aka 'Ops'. Standard drill. Heading for the blocking point called Ginger, under the majestic Takur Ghar.

Jock thanked the early morning light that had cast long shadows on the valley floor, helping him get his bearings – vital for him setting up his communications network and radio antennae. The sun had been up for sixteen minutes but had done nothing to alleviate the sting of the sub-zero temperatures. He breathed the thin air and exhaled, instantly creating white clouds as his hot breath condensed on contact with the cold.

The formation moved forward, crunching the snow-patched rocks and dirt underfoot. Jock scanned the ridgelines looking for enemy. The men from the 1st and 2nd Platoons of 1-87 had fallen in and were on the move.

Where's the fuckin' cordite, Jock thought to himself, badly wanting to smell the acrid aftermath of the bombing raid, a telltale sign that Anaconda was on track.

He didn't have long to think about it.

Within minutes, Jock's world exploded. Cordite was the last thing on his mind.

CHAPTER 5

The RPG hit the ground about five metres
away from Jock and he could hear it sizzling
through the snow as it closed in on him.
Closer, closer, sizzle, hiss.

Major General Franklin Hagenbeck's battle-plan aphorism did not disappoint. No plan survives the first round, and the first round in the Shahi Kot Valley was about to be fired at the adamantine men from the Special Forces Mako Three One patrol. The five-man team had earlier obliterated the al Qaeda position on the Finger and now occupied the destroyed enemies' vantage point with its uninterrupted line of sight down the valley. It was a perfect sniper hide and the men watched as the CH-47 Chinooks emptied the soldiers of the 10th Mountain at LZ 13 and LZ 13a.

As soon as the formation began to move on the valley floor, the special operators emerged from the cover of the rocks and displayed a bright orange VS–17 fluorescent marker panel to signify their presence and identify themselves as coalition soldiers. It was standard operating procedure. If they were hoping for a friendly reaction, they were wrong.

A handful of men in the lead section from the 10th on the valley floor instantly went to the ground, took up positions and opened fire on them with their M4s and squad automatic weapons.

Clint and Jock followed the tracer fire and found the target: a small team of men wearing what looked like traditional Afghan gear. They were about 500 metres away, up the hill, and could have been al Qaeda or Taliban fighters.

Human intelligence from local warlords and militiamen as well as from the surveillance and reconnaissance patrols in the mountains estimated the enemy numbers in the valley at up to 250, concentrated mostly around the small northernmost village of Sherkhankhel and around Marzak, which was further south. AQ terrorists and Taliban loyalists had been on the run since the systematic fall of the country's major cities, beginning with Mazar-e Sharif in early November, followed in quick succession by Herat, Kabul, Jalalabad and, by early December, Kandahar, the spiritual home of the Taliban.

Many sought sanctuary in the villages in the valley or took up residence in the intricate cave system tunnelled deep into the mountains, which had been used for thousands of years. In preparation for a fight to the death, al Qaeda and Taliban loyalists gave food or small amounts of cash to 700 or so locals, particularly women and children, to get them to leave the villages. They also gave them sheep as an inducement to depart so they could take over their modest homes.

'They told us that we should go and they would stay,' one villager told a reporter from *The New York Times* in early March. 'They told us that Shahi Kot will be bombed by the Americans and if we stayed, we would probably be killed and they would not be responsible for our deaths.'

Terrorists later distributed to the villagers pamphlets known as *shabnama*, or night letters, promising them a reward of US$50 000 if they captured or killed a Western soldier, aid worker or journalist.

Conspicuous strangers get shot in these parts and covert operators did what they could to melt unobtrusively into the local scenery.

When Jock and Clint looked to where the American troops were pounding the ridgeline, something didn't add up. The two quick-thinking Aussies instantly recognised the VS–17 marker for what it was and realised that the heavily bearded and scruffy blokes wearing the brown wool *pakhul* hats, *lungee* (turbans) and local woollen coats weren't the enemy at all. They were US Special Forces men.

After weeks out in the field with no access to the modern comforts of hot running water, a bar of soap and a razor blade, they easily passed as mountain tribesmen. Jock didn't think you'd have to be a rocket scientist to work it out, nor should it take more than a second to do so, but the soldiers in Frank Grippe's company had been drilled that men on a battlefield were either shooters or targets.

The signature sound of machine-gun fire burst through the air and tracers streaked across the morning sky, bouncing around the men on the ridge, as bullets splintered rocks, kicking up dirt and debris. The men dropped their marker and began diving for cover. Clint and Jock's instincts kicked in and they charged towards the fire team lying in the prone position, flat on their guts, 50 metres away. The team were squeezing the triggers on their Minimis and M240G 7.62mm machine guns. To some of the young soldiers, the M240 was reminiscent of the M60 used by Sylvester Stallone playing Rambo, jumping out of the river with a big bandolier crossed over his chest and a menacing look on his face.

'Cease fire!' Jock roared as he ran, his pack slamming into his back with each step, his breathing hindered by the altitude. 'Cease fuckin' fire.'

Clint was with him, standing over the soldiers on the ground, knocking their elbows out with his foot.

'Disengage,' Clint yelled. 'Disengage.'

Jock recalls: 'Our assessment of the situation – individually – was that they [the men on the ridge] were friendly. We arrived at that on our own and went straight into action. Obviously we have got packs on so aren't sprinting, and Grippe's boys got some good bursts off, but we stopped the firing. So that was exactly the sort of incident we were there to prevent. The Americans didn't even deconflict their own fire, but that's because their Special Force is so compartmentalised and secretive.

'And that was a big stuff-up, because we were there as liaison officers to deconflict with any *Australian* SF patrols; but it didn't appear that the Americans knew they had a patrol in that area. Their attempts for secrecy failed to allow the same mechanisms that we had in place for deconfliction. Those blokes nearly died as a result of it.'

Jock got his radio up. His job was to ensure that no Australian SAS troops had been compromised or hit by fire. He tuned into the Australian frequencies. No one answered. *Good, not our blokes* he thought, knowing that they would only reply if they were in trouble.

Jock dropped into another frequency, hoping to reach the US Special Forces patrols. Nothing. No reply. He wasn't surprised – the Yanks and the Aussies used discrete nets and wouldn't be sharing frequencies, and US Special Forces soldiers were notoriously secretive, for good reason. It was later confirmed the men being brassed up by the troops from the 10th Mountain were indeed from Mako Three One.

'I was convinced they were friendly but I didn't have any idea whose friendlies they were,' Jock says now. 'Anyway, the decision to kick the boys in the guts and make them stop shooting was the correct one. So we were on the money by stopping them – it just wasn't Australian troops we were stopping them shooting.

'Grippe came up and assisted us in getting them to disengage and was very much doing his best to command his troops and keep order in the situation. I don't remember any of the other Americans attempting to stop it at all, even after we had started to stop it. Grippe came up and said, obviously, "What's happened?" [In the end] he sorted his boys, who were all fired up. They just wanted to bust some caps off and that's what they did.'

The incident was over in two minutes and the Mako Three One patrol disappeared into the hills. Fortunately, no one was hurt

Fuck me, Jock thought wryly, *that didn't take long. We've only just ex-planed and we've already had a blue-on-blue. The boys are toey for a gunfight. Bring it on! Osama, I've got a present for you.*

Command Sergeant Major Frank Grippe had his men from the 10th Mountain rolling within minutes of the blue-on-blue contact, heading north through the valley.

'For a New Yorker like myself, with a Ranger background, I was ready to go and get into another gunfight. That's the way we do business,' Grippe said.

Jock was incredulous at the first contact. He knew instinctively it was blue-on-blue and it offended the professional soldier in him, but he figured that these young blokes were conventional forces, many of them on their first operation. He himself wouldn't have done it, and there was no way on earth that Clint would have either. They were from an elite regiment, had a lifetime of experience over most of their fellow soldiers in the Shahi Kot that morning, and bloody well should be able to read the landscape. That's what years of the toughest Special Forces training in the world had prepared them for.

Jock was pumped. Clint and he had already potentially saved lives and the sun wasn't even fully up yet.

'It felt a bit like Christmas. It was just very exciting. I remember feeling fired up, like we were part of something significant, that we were doing something good and, obviously, very high risk,' Jock recalls. 'There was a lot of unknown.'

He fell into formation with the huge NCO Frank Grippe at the front, flanked by Grippe's Aussie SAS counterpart, Clint. Completing the formation was Sergeant Robert Healy, a former US Ranger instructor who hailed from Michigan and had joined Uncle Sam's Army as a scrawny seventeen-year-old in 1985. Healy had three little kids at home in upstate New York, two boys aged nine and seven, and the apple of his eye, a little girl aged four.

The rest of the company were spreading out across the LZ in

a standard drill: some forward, with the Ruperts – a nickname for officers – in the guts, and more troops bringing up the rear. The valley had returned to silence, broken only by the sound of footsteps on the frosty ground.

Grippe marched fearlessly forward, inspiring the same fearless attitude in his men.

It was no wonder. By February of 2002, Grippe had notched up two decades in the US Army and loved every minute of it. He was Army through and through; lived it, breathed it. There was nothing he would rather do. Grippe had enlisted in the infantry as a nineteen-year-old in his home state of New York in 1981 and over the following twenty years had been a rifleman, a machine gunner, a reconnaissance squad leader, a Ranger, a paratrooper and an instructor. He had led teams, squadrons, units, platoons and battalions in training and into fights.

In 1989, he had been involved in the daring operation that led to the ousting of Panamanian dictator General Manuel Noriega. Grippe, then a Ranger, made a night combat parachute assault onto the Rio Hato airfield and military complex in Panama in Operation Just Cause. He was then a staff sergeant, working one grade up as a platoon sergeant, and assigned to Charlie Company, 2nd Ranger Battalion. He and his men jumped out of a C-130 Hercules at 150 metres after a seven-hour ride from the US. Every one of the thirteen C-130s used in the operation received ground fire damage and sustained bullet holes from Noriega's loyal troops.

The mission in Just Cause had taken Grippe's Ranger platoon just 55 hours to execute. The men had been paged at 7pm on Sunday and went into immediate lockdown on their base in Washington state on the northwest coast of the US, to prevent information leaks. They left home base the next day and arrived at Fort Benning in Georgia where they prepared for and rehearsed the mission, drawing ammo and rigging parachutes. At 1am on Wednesday, they parachuted into Panama and took the Rio Hato airfield which was being defended by Noriega's Panamanian Defence Force. Noriega eventually surrendered and is now doing time in an American prison for drug trafficking. Mission accomplished.

Grippe had also served with the Rangers in the United Nations-led Operation Uphold Democracy to restore democracy to Haiti in 1994.

'We were called in to do a manhunt for a group of renegade Haitian military and police members who thought they were going to start their own insurgency,' Grippe says now. 'They started with threatening the US Special Forces operating in the area and then actually shooting and wounding a Special Forces soldier. We flew a Ranger force in and conducted direct-action operations to police up the renegades. We did just that and brought stability to the southern city of Les Cayes.'

Grippe sure as hell had earned his stripes, working his way through the ranks and garnering respect as he climbed the ladder. He had completed every course possible for a non-commissioned officer.

When decked out in full dress uniform, Grippe's puffed-up chest was a riot of colour. He had been awarded the Bronze Star for Valor a few times over, the Purple Heart, the Army Good Conduct Medal, the Humanitarian Services Medal and the Army Achievement Medal, to mention just a few. His duty to country had taken him abroad and he was one of a few US troops to be able to wear – with pride – the French Armed Forces Commando Badge and the British and Royal Thai Armies' Parachutists Badges.

By any standards, Grippe was an accomplished soldier and, to Jock, a bloody top bloke.

Right now Grippe had his eyes on the scene in front of him. Looking up he saw the rugged brown cliff faces and small crevices and hollows that time and weather had carved into the steep mountain. On the valley floor was a line of shallow hollows known as a wadi. Few things were robust enough to grow and survive at this altitude except a scattering of juniper shrubs and grass tussocks that could endure the brutal winter conditions and the vicious summers when the sun sucked the moisture out of the scorched soil. The towering snowcapped eastern ridgeline was in shadows with the sun coming up behind it and the details of the landscape merged together.

Before leaving Bagram, Grippe had told his men that Operation Anaconda would be a 'sergeant's fight'. The terrain, he explained, would fragment the battalion into sections, and thus each sergeant would be forced to fight a different fight to his compatriot just metres away in a wadi or beside a rock outcrop offering protection from the enemy. No man's war would be the same.

The troops had moved about 100 metres from the LZ, pushing north, when *bang*, off in the east, all hell broke loose.

Jock caught sight of a brilliant flash off the eastern ridge. *Oh, that's pretty*, he thought. Then *whoooomph!* A black dot in the middle of a bright light was *wwssshhhhing* across the valley floor on a direct collision course with Jock in formation. Realisation struck him like a bolt of lightning – *Jesus Christ, it's a fuckin' RPG corkscrewing straight towards me* – and he bolted, running as fast as he could away from it toward what looked like a dry creek bed with a dirt wall rising up a couple of metres high at its closest point to Jock. Others charged after him.

Stuck out in the open with no cover, a rocket-propelled grenade spelt danger. Al Qaeda terrorists had long used the Russian-made shoulder-fired RPG-7, a lethal and versatile weapon that fires a high explosive charge through the air rotating like a football at speeds of up to 294 metres per second. When it impacts, *boom*, it's all over, red rover.

Jock didn't want his morning in the high mountain country to be over so soon, nor in such a nasty way, courtesy of al Qaeda. *Bugger that*, he thought. He sprinted, looking back over his shoulder to check if the RPG was on his tail. It was like something out of a Bugs Bunny cartoon.

'Once I realised it was time to run, there was no slowing me down. It's coming straight at me, leg it, look back. Nah, leg it, and look back a couple more times and it's gaining on me, it's gaining on me, it's coming in,' Jock says.

Back at the TOC Major General Hagenbeck was watching the troop insertion via the Predator vision and keeping an eye on the eastern ridgeline.

He had been holding his breath that there wouldn't be Stinger missiles or RPGs that would knock the helicopters out when they landed or took off again. 'I thought we were going to land – and it turned out to be accurate – by surprise. But they knew we were coming, we couldn't keep a secret; nobody can keep a secret in a coalition outfit. We knew they knew,' Hagenbeck says now.

'The only thing that we could do was effect surprise by the time we came in, the direction we came in and where we went in, and that all worked. And that was some smart guys figuring out how to do that. I felt pretty comfortable that we were going to get the infantry soldiers on the ground. What I was concerned about early enough [was] were the helicopters going to get hit while they were dislodging the troops, when they were getting off, or when they took off?

'Afghanistan, we knew, had gotten thousands of Stinger missiles and it turned out some were shot. We didn't know it at the time, but they were ineffective. I guess they had been stored in these high levels in the cold. I was told after the fact that they were ineffective. But [there were also] rocket-propelled grenades.'

The RPG hit the ground about five metres away from Jock and he could hear it sizzling through the snow as it closed in on him. Closer, closer, sizzle, *hiss*. And then, almost miraculously, it stopped.

'The only thing I could do was witness it arriving. It was coming straight at us. We physically couldn't get out of its way quick enough. I could hear the *sssssssss* behind me because all the snow and dirt was just baking off with this hot round hitting the ground. It just kept sliding up until about a metre from my heels when it finally came to rest.'

Jock wasn't hanging around to see if it would detonate. He took a couple more steps before diving head first into the top of the lip of the creek. But he hadn't accounted for the weight of his pack and didn't make it over the top. The RPG was still there, sizzling menacingly. His arms, legs and rifle flailed as he righted himself and launched at the summit of the creek bed again, finally dragging himself over and into cover. He was in.

'Had it detonated, there would have been ten of us down straight away, and that would have included Grippe and Clint. It would have taken out Grippe – the thing slid up a metre behind me but it probably nearly landed on Grippe.

'I don't know if any of the Ruperts were around then, but if they were, "Tally ho, Rupert". If that initial round went off, shit, it would have just been carnage, mayhem, because that would have taken out half the command group.

'That's how arsey it is.'

Jock was safe, but he was powerless to do anything to help his mate Clint. Suddenly, the air opened up with small-arms fire and lethal rounds from a DShK anti-aircraft heavy machine gun, a weapon the troops called the Dishka.

Jock had been about to stick his head up and sing out for Clint but thought better of it as the DShK opened up and began thumping rounds overhead into the bank. Instead, he reached over and began pulling people to cover.

'The AQ who fired the RPG had jumped on to the Dishka, or one of his mates has come along shortly thereafter and jumped on to their machine gun,' Jock says. 'It just seemed to me he's fired the rocket, the rocket hasn't gone off, he's pissed off because it's been a really good shot, and he's jumped on his gun to finish the job, so to speak. He's very unlucky on all accounts not to get any casualties.'

Frank Grippe hadn't moved. Neither had Clint. It had happened so fast, they didn't have time. The hulking non-com just stared down at the RPG sizzling on the ground beside him and looked over at Clint. This was Taliban country, and their al Qaeda guests – the reason the coalition troops were there in the first place – meant business.

'It's going to be a long freakin' day now,' Grippe said to Clint. Softly, with a touch of irony, Grippe now says: 'I'm like, "Okay, this is going to be interesting" – and this is the first five minutes of the fight. The interesting part at the beginning of the day was the RPG landing between two Americans and two Australians. What an unlikely combination of four soldiers on a combat mission! There is a whole battle going on around you, but there was the four of us. I mean, you talk about the unity of the Australians and the Americans, you know. Australia didn't have to jump on board in this fight. I mean, we were less than six months into 9/11 and who would ever think that you would have this group of four soldiers – two American and two Australian – moving together in a valley floor in Afghanistan and have an RGP land, *bam*, right in the middle of you and not explode?'

Any fatalities could have been reported in the press. 'That would have probably blown the SAS cover right there, having a couple of casualties like that. And of course the fact that it was two sergeants major – it would have been an IO [information operations] campaign victory for the enemy because they would have gone, "Fuck, yeah." You know, I am humble about this, but at my rank if I go and get whacked ...'

The coalition troops were out in the open in an al Qaeda kill zone. As if on cue, the enemy began launching mortars and hammering their heavy machine guns. They had pre-registered their fire positions and knew the precise range of the ammo's trajectory. *It's like shooting fish in a barrel*, Jock thought. *The sneaky bastards have done their homework.* Every position in the valley floor had been covered with tactical planning. The guerrillas had observers, front and rear. It was a fully fledged battle. The enemy had the high ground and good fields of fire, which meant a lethal advantage.

'Holy shit, you alright, man?' soldiers yelled at each other.

'Fuckin' A,' came the positive replies as the earth burst to life beneath them when bullets struck.

Jock noticed some of the troops under heavy fire drop their packs as they bolted for cover. A US captain later said he was worried that the size of the packs would slow his troops down and get them killed. Jock couldn't believe what he was seeing. A soldier's pack is a soldier's best chance of survival – you just don't leave it in the line of fire like a sitting duck on opening day of the hunting season. The men had left priceless equipment on the ground, not to mention machine-gun ammunition that had been divided between the soldiers because of its weight.

For Grippe, also, there were circumstances in which dropping the packs was SOP – standard operating procedure. His men had to do something to get out of the line of fire.

Grippe began moving his troops into position, executing what the Americans call battle drill two. They were reacting to contact. Platoon lines began manoeuvring over the terrain and Sergeant Peterson's mortar platoon humped the fully loaded SKEDCOs into position to set up the 120mm mortar with its powerful range of 7200 metres.

'An infantry company practises offensive operations. That's their craft, closing with and destroying the enemy – that's what we do,' Peterson says now.

Private Jason Ashline's job in Sergeant Pete's eight-man mortar platoon was to fire the rounds. The twenty-year-old soldier was on his first posting at the 10th Mountain Division at Fort Drum in New York and Anaconda was his first combat mission. Another native New Yorker, he'd been a soldier for a mere eighteen months and had a wife and two children, including a six-month-old baby boy, back at Drum. He had every reason to want to come home alive. The baby had been three days old and Ashline was at the local Sears department store collecting the first set of photographs taken of his new son in hospital when al Qaeda attacked America on September 11, 2001. The terrorist strikes had robbed him of the pleasure of being around to enjoy his baby's first few months of life. That pissed him off.

To compensate, Ashline packed pictures of his two little tykes and a Bible in his ruck when he deployed.

'It didn't really feel like we were going into combat at first,' Ashline says now. 'I wasn't nervous or scared. I was really anxious to get there and hit the ground and start doing some stuff. Just really more anxious to get down there and start shooting rounds.

'We expected the enemy there: they [Command] told us during the briefs that there would be enemy forces; that there were suspected enemy in there. But it was a little shock, the amount of enemy forces that were there. We expected it, but I don't think we expected as much as we got.'

In fact, the day before Anaconda kicked off, Major General Hagenbeck had received a call from a special operator who said there were about 400 AQ and Taliban in the valley, many in fortified positions. That was nearly twice as many as previously estimated. The SF operators had also discovered al Qaeda positions on the eastern ridgeline right above the LZs.

Not one single American soldier out there now doubted for a moment that they had been dropped into one of the last strongholds of al Qaeda and Taliban in Afghanistan.

Signalman Jock Wallace was in the dry rock-strewn creek bed where he had taken cover from the RPG. The mortar platoon were about 300 metres from his position and each move brought them a bit closer, worrying Jock. 'I'm not a master military tactician, but it didn't seem smart to me to have your indirect fire support right in amongst your troops,' he says.

Within seconds of Jock taking cover, WO2 Clint had charged into the creek bed, quickly joined by Sergeant Major Grippe and his boss, Lieutenant Colonel Paul LaCamera. More troops – including those Jock and Clint had just kicked in the guts to stop the blue-on-blue fire – found their way into the rocky formation sprinkled with snow. The creek bed was a natural fortification equidistant from the valley floor below the eastern ridgelines of Takur Ghar and the Finger and the Whale on the west. It wasn't a huge area – maybe fifteen metres across and about 45 metres long.

Some of the young GIs nicknamed the creek Hell's Halfpipe

because it reminded them of skateboard ramps back home. Grippe called it 'the bowl', and yet another soldier with him said it resembled a football arena with three sides closed in by slopes that ranged from two to fifteen metres high. The higher wall on one side had a sharp drop into the valley, making it nearly impossible to scale from the outside. The southern end was open and had a gentle slope running down into the valley. It was, Jock says, a fully exposed fire lane.

'The enemy were on the eastern side halfway up the hill – shooting down on us – the bullets going into the earth around us,' Jock says. 'Mortars going off. You couldn't get up off all fours. You couldn't stand up and not be in the line of fire; you couldn't comfortably piss or you'd get shot at.'

Jock took up a position on the southeast end of Hell's Halfpipe near a small boulder. He dropped his pack and began to get set up. 'If I'm looking east, it sort of curves down. I'm right down on the end and there's not too much in front of me,' he says.

Clint helped Jock pull soldiers into the bowl before establishing his own position a few metres further north of Jock.

Clint was an experienced soldier, smart, tough and straight-to-the-point. He'd seen and done enough in the Army to know that things weren't up to speed right from the word go. He was phlegmatic and raised issues and rationalised them with Jock without making the younger signaller feel nervous. Clint's equable presence and soldiering skills masked any angst he might have been feeling.

'Clint was definitely not 100 per cent happy with the way things were going,' Jock says. 'But Clint's a soldier and there's no way he was going to back out.'

The AQ held the ridgelines with pre-registered mortars and the DShk anti-aircraft machine guns. The crew-served weapon fired 12.7mm rounds. The soldiers did everything they could to dodge the 15cm-long rounds spewing out of the DShK. 'The calibre is what gets you, and those rounds are big enough that they don't even have to hit you to hurt you,' Jock says. 'They can go past you and hurt you. They can pull things off you just going past you.

'The rounds were landing down in the pipe on the other bank, which left maybe a metre or so in the bottom of the pipe that was clear. You could do what they call a monkey run, when you're hunched right over and trying to go fast but not expose yourself, just to get anywhere north or south.

'As soon as you went south, that's when the ground to the east folded down and left everything exposed, and then another slope sort of picked up just to the south of that and you had a little bit more cover.

'But there was a good 20 to 30 metres in the open where you were anyone's. There was no cover. Just a free field of fire.'

Grippe and LaCamera established their command post and radio operator at the northern end of Hell's Halfpipe, while troops from the 10th Mountain took up initial fire positions along the east slope, squeezing off rounds directly on enemy locations or in the direction of the machine gun and small-arms and RPG fire. Grippe was building a 360-degree perimeter for his men.

Al Qaeda were in well-fortified positions and were camouflaged in the snow and set back in their positions in the rock crevices. The soldiers on the low ground could barely see muzzle flashes, but every so often, they caught a visual of the enemy moving on the ridge.

'They thought they were pretty *hoo-ah*,' Grippe says now. 'And so a lot of them ran out of the hills to meet us on the HLZ [helicopter landing zone] and we immediately just freakin' killed them because of our superior training and marksmanship. So they ran back up into the hills. They were stupid. They were used to fighting and getting down close and we just killed them, which was to our benefit.

'I wished that however many hundreds were up there all came running down at one time, because we [could have] just killed them all right there on the spot. It would have been more beneficial to us. Would have saved some hours, would have saved some money and munitions. And the all-day fight started.'

Minutes had passed but so much had already happened in the chaos after landing. Jock and Clint struggled to hear each other over the rain of fire ripping the guts out of the valley. Miraculously it had failed to find any warm bodies. *Phhht, phhht, phhht. Bang, bang, bang.*

'Shit, Clint, that bloody RPG was close,' Jock said to his boss.

'Yeah.'

'How come it didn't go off?'

'Might have been the way it was stored, or how old the ammo was – hard to say.'

'Clint, we would have been fucked if that round went off!'

'No shit, dickhead.'

Jock figured the RPG had been stored incorrectly, as Clint had said and Hagenbeck later suggested, or didn't explode because it landed too flat and not on its nose. Or it simply could have been defective and not gone the distance. Whatever the reason, he wasn't bothered; he was alive.

'I was laughing about it, sort of like, "That's fucking close, that would have hurt us, mate, it would have knocked us all out, ten of us",' Jock says. 'And he was sort of, "Yeah you dickhead, you've only just realised?"'

Jock powered up his radio again and hooked up the coaxial cable. Before leaving Bagram he had done a mental calculation of the directions for the antenna, and he was spot on. It was standard operating procedure for Jock, who took enormous pride in his work and left nothing to chance, especially when lives were at risk.

Less than a minute later he had established comms back to the Australian Regimental HQ at a secret location in Afghanistan, which was passing reports to Lieutenant Colonel Rowan Tink in the TOC.

'One Oscar, this is Niner Charlie,' Jock said over his push-to-talk radio, adding the locstat (location status) and exact grid references of his and Clint's position.

'We're in a bit of a shit fight here. Over.'

Back at the HQ, an experienced SAS officer who was walking past the comms desk asked the young radio operator what Jock meant by 'shit fight'.

'By the sound of the gunfire in the background, I'd say they're in a fuckin' shit fight, sir,' the chook said drily.

The penny dropped for the Rupert. Men were in harm's way and he, although safe, was a witness via the radio.

'Ask them for a sitrep,' he ordered.

'This is One Oscar, send sitrep. Over.'

'Niner Charlie, roger. Wait out.'

Out in the field, Jock turned to Clint.

'Give us a grid ref, mate.'

Clint gave the map reference and Jock passed the sitrep to the Australian higher command.

Tink was in the TOC with the US command and a couple of Aussies. 'HLZ 12 and 13 taking mortar fire. HLZ 12 and 13 taking an RPG hit from behind,' Tink wrote in his war diary, noting the time.

It was 0230 zulu, 7am on the battlefield.

The sun had been up for 38 minutes.

And Jock and Clint were under fire in Hell's Halfpipe.

That's some welcoming committee, Jock thought ruefully.

CHAPTER 6

*'The Apaches got pasted up, got the shit shot
out of them. Two of them, one after the other.
You could hear them getting whacked. They
were definitely getting impacted.'*

JOCK WALLACE

Jock Wallace had done his homework. He knew that he and
Clint and the boys from the 10th Mountain had landed in a
place the Russians had named the 'bowl of death' more than a
decade before. Now he knew why it had earned that charming
appellation. Bullets rained down on them relentlessly, RPGs tore
through the air, and mortar shells exploded, sending deadly
shards of shrapnel into Hell's Halfpipe where he'd taken cover.

So this is where the muj smashed the Russkis, Jock thought,
trying to adjust his hearing to the deafening roar of war as he got
his chook gear set up. He'd heard about a book called
Afghanistan, the Bear Trap, which opened with the chilling line:
'Death by a thousand cuts – this is the time-honoured tactic of
the guerrilla army against a large conventional force.'

The man who wrote it, Mohammad Yousaf, had commanded
part of the mujahideen's successful fight against the Russians. He
knew of what he spoke. 'Ambushes, assassinations, attacks on
supply convoys, bridges, pipelines and airfields, with the
avoidance of setpiece battles; these are history's proven techniques
for the guerrilla.'

Jock wondered if any of the US Army's chiefs had got hold of
a copy of Yousaf's battle book. *Fuck, it's for sale on Amazon*, he

thought, *they bloody well should have read it*. It was a strategic template for the Afghan guerrillas' ambush and assassination tactics, detailing with great pride in one section how 250 Russian soldiers had been killed in one day in that very place in the Shahi Kot Valley. The Soviets had even lost the eight helicopters used to deliver the troops. Jock and the 10th Mountain had just been ambushed; small mercy that the three Chinooks which infilled them into the valley got out okay.

'The enemy was on a wide front – a very big front that was initially directly opposite where we were,' Jock says. 'They were just smart. They've been fighting in those hills for thousands of years and the people are well versed in tactics – they knew when you're going to be in the poo and when to inflict things on the enemy. And they pasted the Russians in the bowl of death.'

Jock powered up his radio again and contacted the Regimental HQ, giving a situation report to a fellow chook named Dicko. Despite the noise and gunfire, Jock spoke calmly, detailing as much information as possible while keeping an eye on the battle from his place in Hell's Halfpipe.

'We were probably in the only bit of cover that was worth anything in that entire valley for about 800 metres north or south,' he says now.

The 1st and 2nd Platoons from the 1-87 had spread out and were moving to their BPs, Heather and Ginger, in a similar manner to the way the Australian infantry operates – some forward, the bosses in the guts, and more people bringing up the rear.

Bang. The al Qaeda and Taliban fighters upped the ante, and the soldiers started taking a withering barrage of direct fire and mortar rounds.

'What is that? What is that?' yelled Staff Sergeant Thomas Oldham, one of the 1-87 Battalion mortar crew.

'It's AK-47 fire,' screamed his non-com officer, Sergeant Michael Peterson, who had brought the massive 120mm mortar into battle.

Jock looked up and saw al Qaeda soldiers dressed in black, shooting down on them from the eastern ridgeline.

'That's Smufti and Snegat up there, on the eastern ridge,' Jock said, using a couple of the names the troops applied to the enemy, in the way soldiers have done throughout history.

Small-section sergeants instantly began manoeuvring their troops and locking on the enemy target. Frank Grippe had told his men that this would be a sergeant's fight. Now his 'big four' of training were paying off. Not only had Grippe's peacetime Army focused on peak physical fitness and combat life-saving training for all troops so they could supplement the medics, they had been indoctrinated with battle drill training and shooting skills, paying particular attention to night shooting with lasers. Watching his soldiers pick off the enemy, Grippe knew he'd pulled the right rein.

'We have a saying, "known, likely and suspected enemy positions". So you put down effective fire and well-aimed shots into those positions,' Grippe explains. 'A known target is a knucklehead that you can see or a muzzle flash that you can see. A suspected target is a muzzle flash or some type of movement, or just an area that if I was an enemy, well, that's where I would have a position.' And the same with likely – what looks like a rock outcropping or a bunker.

The Yanks were pouring 7.62mm medium machine-gun fire into the hill, as well as a vicious torrent of rounds from the M240G 5.56mm light machine gun. Jock saw a couple of black-clad figures go down on the ridge and thought, *You bloody beauty.* More AQ had joined the party. The level of enemy fire was rapidly increasing, as was the noise. RPGs landed outside Hell's Halfpipe, some of which failed to go off, like the one that chased Jock into the creek bed. Mortars exploded way too close for comfort.

'The enemy started coming out doing some assaults, lining up across the valley and heading down and trying to dislodge us,' Jock says. 'A couple of times, twenty or so of them went around, trying to come around the rocky cliff face to our northwest, but they were repulsed and shot off the cliff.'

Repulsed is the military's anodyne term for shot dead.

Sergeant Pete's eight-man mortar platoon got the 120mm tube set up within minutes and began providing indirect fire support for the 10th Mountain Division, aiming the weapon in the direction of the AQ mortars in the mountains. *Booooom.*

'I put my guys down, all my soldiers, I put them down as a security perimeter and we just started firing,' Sergeant Pete says.

Peterson fired explosive 120mm mortars onto the AQ positions as fast as the battalion fire control officer could get them into the tube, but it wasn't fast enough. He hadn't counted on the enemy pre-registering their war machinery. Each 120mm mortar he delivered to al Qaeda was greeted with a return 82mm mortar, as the enemy walked their own rounds right into Sergeant Pete's location. This was only the beginning. The mortar section started taking direct fire from enemy sniper and machine-gun positions.

'I can't believe the bastards are firing at us,' Sergeant Pete yelled to his soldiers. 'Let's see what we can do about that.'

'At first we were firing kind of blind, you know, we saw the mountain and we knew where the fire was coming from but we just couldn't pinpoint any of the enemy locations. But we were going to fight,' Peterson says now. 'So we started firing at the mountain. As soon as that 120 took off it seemed like they focused a lot of their direct fire on us. They definitely turned the Dishka machine gun and their mortars on us.'

As the fire intensified, Sergeant Pete and his men ran for cover in a wadi and returned small-arms fire at any target they could see. In between dodging bullets and directing his young troops to take cover, Peterson ran back through the fusillade and armed the mortar tube by himself. It is a job normally done by four or five soldiers. Twenty-nine-year-old Captain James Taylor Jr, who would be injured during the day, later commented: 'When the fire became too intense, Peterson sent his soldiers to a covered location while he remained behind, without regard to his own safety, to man the mortar by himself.'

No wonder Sergeant Pete's men worshipped him.

'I guess the big surprise for me was the amount of people we were fighting,' Peterson says now, adding that they were briefed by their S2 intelligence guy they would be up against 150 to 200 al Qaeda and Taliban fighter remnants in the valley.

'And so I wanted to go in with the 120 [mm mortar] and get as many of those guys as we possibly could, but there was probably twice that number right where we were at when we landed. And it just got bad.

'The 120 is awesome. It's just not good when you are going against about eight other mortars and an artillery piece and there's just one of you.'

'When we got into that fight when it first started, I thought to myself, "This is as scary as hell." No one is born as some brave kick-arse warrior,' Peterson says now. 'You have to make decisions and when we got initially pushed away from my tube – we were driven back a little bit from my mortar tube – I thought to myself, "I'm sitting in a ditch and getting shot at." I didn't care about God and country, didn't care about anything else. I just didn't want to disgrace the Army. And whatever anyone read about this fight – and if we all died – I just wanted them to think that the mortars fought their butts off, that we got up and went back to the tube and started hammering again.'

And they did.

Jock watched out of the corner of his eye as AQ tracked the mortarmen's every step, lobbing 82mm mortars on them one after the other with stunning precision.

It was bedlam, and extraordinary that no one had been killed. Jock was running on pure adrenaline. He was charged. 'We have had about three pisses in the first hour and half a packet of durries,' he says.

He looked over at Clint five metres away and yelled at him. 'Hey, Clint, let's get a bloody photo, get your camera out,' Jock said.

Jock wanted a photograph to capture the moment but Clint was having none of it.

'I was getting a bit cheeky. I shuffled over to him and said, "It's in your bum pack." And he didn't get it. So I went and got it and he's literally trying to get his thoughts together and probably trying to work out the best way to utilise the men on the ground. Taking a photo wasn't his priority,' Jock says.

'So I took a photo of him and he took a photo of me.'

In the photos, Jock looks all gung ho. Clint doesn't look happy. He understood fully the gravity of the situation; Jock, obviously, did not.

Sergeant Pete's mortar was getting belted big time, as were other infantrymen in the kill zone.

About 100 metres away, Jock saw a couple of the packs that the US soldiers had dropped when they ran for cover getting mortared and blown to pieces. The enemy on the hill had started to use the packs as target practice and would continue to do so all day.

What the fuck? Jock thought.

It was then that he realised the valley had previously been DF'd – direct fired – and the reality of the situation became crystal clear. The enemy had already ranged the valley floor and knew exactly where their weapons would land their fire. But as Jock explains, they still needed to know where the US soldiers would be.

'You can have as many of these as you want, but unless you know where the enemy is, it's no good to you,' Jock says. 'Someone must have been on the western ridge to report our locations, and, as it was, we soon learned how many were on the western ridge.'

The soldiers in the halfpipe had all been trained in the best ways to limit the enemy's ability to put effective fire on them, and they fought back with intensity.

Jock Wallace made about five calls back to the Aussie Regimental HQ in the first hour, relaying, via the chooks at One Oscar, details of the firefight and the ambush to Lieutenant Colonel Rowan Tink, and the commander of 1 SAS Squadron, Major Dan McDaniel. Each radio contact updated the sitrep, and Jock called for close air support (CAS) from the Apache gunships and fast movers overhead.

The staff in the TOC were no longer able to watch the action in the lower Shahi Kot Valley on the video screens. At 7.30am the unmanned Predator drone flying above had locked its cameras onto a compound at Sherkhankhel, further north, in the belief that a 'high-value target – UBL' was in the region. UBL was the shorthand the Americans used for Osama bin Laden, the leader of al Qaeda, spelling his first name with a U.

Calls for CAS were answered as the enemy fire intensified, and the Apaches – known as the Killer Spades – from the 3–101's A Company hit targets called in by Grippe's battalion fire-support officer, Captain Taylor, who was in Hell's Halfpipe with Grippe.

Just before 8am, AH-64 Apaches roared overhead again and opened fire on an al Qaeda position north of Ginger, Jock's initial objective before the ambush. The choppers were under fire, but refused to genuflect to the barrage coming from AQ terrorists just a hundred metres below them.

A cheer went up from the men pinned down in Hell's Halfpipe when they saw the fearsome attack helicopters sweep over the valley on rocket runs. The Apaches had been engaged since well before dawn, laying down suppressive fire on known enemy positions, and were now flying in a racetrack circuit over the northern and southern end of the Shahi Kot. With an AQ location captured in its high-tech target acquisition system, the gunner co-pilot sent a fusillade of 30mm chain-gun and rocket fire into the ridgeline, wiping the enemy combatants out in a triumphant puff of smoke.

'It was great. We'd just been jumped, got to ground, got our composure. Vick and Achey [two of the forward air controllers from the US Air Force attached to the 10th Mountain] have put out the calls for fire and have been able to contact some Apaches who were willing to come in,' Jock says now.

The Apache is a terrifying bird of prey. Armed with Hellfire air-to-surface missiles, air-to-air missiles, and a 30mm automatic M230 chain gun tucked under the fuselage, it is capable of flying at a maximum of 197 knots – or 365 kilometres an hour. Able to manoeuvre at enormous speeds, it is an exquisite example of electronic warfare technology and perfect for a close support role like this – where the pilots are almost close enough to the enemy to see the whites of their eyes.

According to Major General Hagenbeck, enemy detainees considered the Apaches the most feared weapons on the battlefield. 'The helicopters were on top of them before they knew what was happening. The Apaches came as close to "one shot, one kill" as you can get,' Hagenbeck told *Field Artillery* magazine.

Even though its metal frame has been engineered to withstand an enormous amount of firepower in combat situations, the Apache is still vulnerable to certain weapons.

'When the helicopters came over, at first they were kicking arse. They were ripping rockets off and hosing the hill with the gun and then they turned, right in front of the rock face they had just been brassing up, and it seemed like the whole hillside came alive with small-arms and automatic gunfire,' Jock says.

Al Qaeda and Taliban fighters opened up on the Apaches, shooting at them with everything they had including Kalashnikov rifles, RPGs and machine-gun fire. One helo took a direct hit, and a bullet ricocheted through the cockpit and hit the pilot.

'The Apaches became stationary to the enemy when they banked right in front of their position,' Jock says, explaining the rocket runs and tactics used by the gunship pilots.

'So the Apaches were coming straight at them, *brrr, brrr*, firing rockets, and then they turned. That's when they're vulnerable because they are now pretty much pulled up in front of them [al Qaeda's machine-gun nests] and they've got to slowly take off. You can belt in there and they have to try and get you, but as soon as you turn broadside and you're closer and slow moving, the choppers are vulnerable. The enemy did it perfectly – they held up, held up, held up, and obviously you duck when the Apache is shooting at you, but then they all just propped up and hooked in.

'And all of a sudden [the Apaches'] guns ceased. You could hear the rotors slap as they were turning and then the mountain came alive and opened up on them. There was just hundreds of small arms belting into these Apaches,' Jock says. 'I might be exaggerating when I say hundreds, but to me that's what it seemed like.

'The Apaches got pasted up, got the shit shot out of them. Two of them, one after the other. You could hear them getting whacked. They were definitely getting impacted.'

Jock had no doubt, especially when the Apaches limped off the battlefield.

An hour after the first Apache blasted the snow-covered ridgeline with cannons, Captain Taylor called for another rocket run.

The gunship roared in but the co-pilot gunner couldn't fire.

'Summit Four Zero. This is Killer Spade Six,' the pilot radioed to Taylor, who had called in the grid coordinates of the targets. 'We've taken small-arms fire and have to return to the FARP to deal with it.'

The forward air-refuelling point, or FARP, codenamed Texaco, was halfway between Bagram and the Shahi Kot Valley. In all, four Apaches were damaged that morning and, with fuel running low, the wounded fleet limped out of the valley.

'That was the last we saw of any choppers until way late in the day,' Jock says now.

Watching the birds disappear was soul-destroying for the men left behind, including Jock, for it meant one thing. The men of the 10th Mountain were on their own and facing shocking odds. *About the same as the Aussies in Long Tan, decades earlier in the Vietnam War*, Jock thought.

'A bit disenchanting, it's not meant to happen like that, they're meant to be able to kick the shit out of things, that's meant to save my arse,' Jock says on reflection.

Any inkling he'd had that they might not make it out of the Shahi Kot Valley alive was magnified when the Apaches got smashed. 'We were stunned. We all looked at each other and thought "What the..." as they limped off the battlefield,' Jock says. 'That's when it first dawned on me that we were in some serious shit.'

CHAPTER 7

It was a three-month crash course in soldiering, the basic training of all new recruits. He was seventeen and a digger. And within days Martin would be known as Jock, in keeping with the Australian military's unofficial tradition of handing out nicknames to its members.

Jock Wallace is a Gen X soldier, having been born at the tail end of 1969. With his parents, Margaret and Reginald, and older brother, James, he spent the first four years of his life living in North Epping, a typical middle-class neighbourhood twenty kilometres northwest of Sydney's CBD. The suburb's greatest claim to fame came in 1972 when a fifteen-year-old schoolgirl named Shane Gould won three gold medals for swimming at the Olympic Games in Munich. The quiet blonde with huge lungs had gone to the local primary school, a geographical coincidence the locals boast of even today.

North Epping was, and is, a tranquil suburb but Margaret Wallace wanted a country childhood for her children, so when her youngest son was four she packed up the family and headed to Tamworth, 440 kilometres north of Sydney on the New England Highway. Tamworth is the country music capital of Australia and in 1973, the year the Wallaces arrived, the city's burghers hosted the first of what would become an internationally renowned annual country music festival. Each January ever since, the festival has welcomed about 50 000 tourists with affection for all things country and western. They are diehard fans, and must be to endure what is unarguably the hottest time of the unforgiving southern summer, when the sun turns the countryside into a sunburnt parchment as fragile as crepe paper and as combustible as rocket fuel.

The Wallaces moved onto a small farm at Winton, west of Tamworth, and the young Martin and James were given free rein to run wild. The family raised cows, chooks and, for a short time, pigs. They had four blue heeler dogs to work the property and a pet beagle named Queenie.

The boys' childhood was typically Australian and typical of the times. It was the 1970s, a period of transition both politically and culturally. Martin, or Jock as he would become known in the Army, was born the year that a man first walked on the moon and he grew up in a decade that marked the start of a new computer and consumer age. Polaroid launched an instant colour camera, a huge leap from the old Box Brownie, VCRs began appearing in homes around the nation, and Nike reinvented the running shoe. Two unknown Americans named Steve Jobs and Stephen Wozniak founded Apple Computers and unveiled the first mass-produced personal computer, and kids began entertaining themselves with Walkmans and arcade video games such as Space Invaders.

The political landscape similarly was undergoing a seismic shift. At home in Australia, the Labor Party came to power in a sudden burst of energy only to lose it just as quickly and explosively with the dismissal of Prime Minister Gough Whitlam. A political scandal dubbed Watergate ended the troubled presidency of Richard Nixon and launched the careers of two journalists, Woodward and Bernstein, and in the United Kingdom a greengrocer's daughter named Margaret Thatcher became the first British woman to lead a major political party.

At the very end of the decade, on Christmas Eve in 1979, the Soviet Union invaded the landlocked country of Afghanistan, an historic act of aggression that at the time meant nothing to a ten-year-old Martin Wallace, but would be of enormous importance to him more than two decades down the track.

For all its change, the 1970s was still an era of innocence for children, a time when they were unafraid and open to the possibilities before them. Martin's mother encouraged him and his brother James to express their personalities and opinions, and they did, particularly in their bedrooms which they painted themselves; red for James and burnt orange, the signature colour of the seventies, for Martin. Their cousins were jealous of their domestic liberties, but to their mum it seemed perfectly normal for such strong-willed sons.

'They were as wild as March hares,' Margaret Wallace recalls fondly.

James and his younger brother were as thick as thieves and, together with their mates, hooned around the countryside and local State forest, first on their pushbikes and then, when they were a little bit older, on powerful trail bikes. Being country boys, they were brought up surrounded by guns, which their dad, Reg, taught them to handle safely. It's a weapon, he told them repeatedly, and you have to respect your weapons. A shooting range in the back yard gave them ample opportunity to hone their marksmanship, which they did with enthusiasm.

In 1980, when he was eleven, Martin asked for a bow and arrow and began a short-lived obsession with archery that was curbed after he fired one too many arrows straight up in the air; it came down, pointed end first, through the bonnet of his uncle's car. The boys also had a back-yard trampoline on which Martin experienced another rite of passage – his first broken bone – an accident that resulted in a trip to the local hospital and a plaster cast on his arm which was duly signed by all and sundry at school. He would break his arm again in 1987 while attached to 104 Signal Squadron at Holsworthy.

The Wallace boys revelled in the great outdoors but they were also bookish and devoured novels with what was, for boys, an unexpected and pleasing enthusiasm. Their love for books came from their mother, who enjoyed reading to them, especially Banjo Paterson's epic poem 'The Man from Snowy River'. She read it over and over. Every time Margaret got to the point where the stripling on the small and weedy beast rode down that terrible descent, she cried and her boys laughed, both at their mum's sentimental and predictable reaction and in awe of the man from Snowy River.

The younger Wallace boy became hooked on wild, boisterous adventures and churned through the Scottish writer Robert Louis Stevenson's *Treasure Island* before he turned eight, an accomplishment that amazes his proud mother still. He fell in love with Stevenson's rollicking storytelling and character-driven narrative. As soon as he could, he'd consumed the rest of Stevenson's library including *The Strange Case of Dr Jekyll and Mr Hyde*. Even as a child, Martin was intrigued by the mutable nature of human behaviour depicted in the book.

But while he loved reading and was intelligent and articulate, Martin did not thrive at school, not because academia proved too challenging for him, but because it bored him. He went to the nearby Westdale Public School for his primary education and, at the age of twelve, transferred to Peel High School for his secondary. Garrulous and quick on his feet, he took up debating in his first year and talked his way, quite literally, into the final of the interschool competition. But boys being boys, he was too self-conscious to accept an invitation by the debating master to return to it in Year 8. It didn't help that his mates were outside playing footy and mucking around when he'd have to be practising his oratory skills and sharpening his arguments. It was as appealing as being forced to listen to your best mate's sister's latest ABBA record.

About the only thing that grabbed Martin's interest was sport. A skilful footballer, he played centre and wing in the school's rugby league competition. He was lean and fast and, while not particularly big for his age, could outrun the opposition. Few sports escaped him. Martin played cricket, hockey, tennis and did karate and swimming; and perhaps inspired by that bloke from Snowy River, became a skilled horseman.

Martin was well liked and something of a practical joker with a keen sense of humour that bordered on the mischievous.

Margaret Wallace had no illusions about her son's intellect or his roguish behaviour. She was called to the principal's office on the odd occasion, but instead of seeing the principal's point of view, she always launched a strident defence of her son's independence and voracious appetite for adventure. Her youngest got good grades when he applied himself, but his mother could see that school bored him rigid. She even developed a certain affection for the words 'too disruptive' that never failed to appear on his end-of-term school reports.

Margaret had no doubt that the teachers would never approve of her son's nomination as class prefect when he was in Year 10, but she took comfort in the fact that he had character and a strong set of personal values. Both Margaret and Reg were proud that their sons tended to favour the underdog, and she detected a quiet kindness in both James and Martin. James was rock solid, and Margaret could see Martin's caring nature and sensitivity in the way he treated his dog, Queenie, and the manner in which he conducted himself with his mates.

Mateship is a foundation stone of the Australian psyche and of the Australian Army, and that's especially true in the bush. And Martin believed in it absolutely. He was fiercely loyal and had a wide circle of friends. In fact, his schoolmates had once given him a standing ovation when he came on stage at the end-of-year assembly. The foot-stomping and applause doubtless would have irked the teachers who disapproved of his pranks.

Martin was also a hit with the girls, not least because he had piercing hazel eyes, a proud chin and a thatch of wavy brown hair that he wore at a length fashionable for the times. If someone said Martin Wallace was a charming young man, they'd be right. Add a good dose of larrikin and you had a lethal combination.

But Peel High wasn't enough to hold him once the footy season was over. Like a lot of teenage boys who grow up in the country, Martin was champing at the bit to get out of Tamworth and see the world beyond the New England Highway. He'd tasted the independence that money can buy with the pay packet from a part-time job at the local Grace Bros department store, and so at the end of the second term in his penultimate year at high school, and for the second time that year, he decided to call it quits. It was 1986; he had just turned seventeen.

By his own reckoning, Martin was a bit of a fiery young man who had the occasional, if requisite, teenager's clash with his father, and he chafed under the family yoke. It could be fairly said that he was a shining example of the testosterone-charged hubris of youth, on the cusp of manhood and wanting to exert his independence and rail against authority. On top of that, he felt hemmed in by the conspicuousness that comes with small-town life. The local police – known in those parts as the wallopers – were also getting to know Martin and his mates. Not that they were ever in any serious trouble or ended up under lock and key, but the boys made their presence known, as popular boys are wont to do. A broken beer bottle here, a misspoken 'get fucked' there, and a drag through the main street in hotted-up cars all earned a stern warning from the local constabulary.

'We used to go shooting all the time up in the State forest, which was illegal – shooting the shit out of everything,' he says now.

Having quit school against his parents' wishes, Martin needed a job. Opportunity had fortuitously presented itself earlier in the year when recruiters from the Australian Army paid a visit to Peel High School. They talked of the career possibilities and adventures offered by Army life. It appealed to Martin particularly because it paralleled his desire to spread his wings and get out of Tamworth. With the words 'adventure' and 'independence' playing a siren's song in his head, Martin agreed to sign up, but as he was only seventeen, he needed his parents' permission to become a soldier.

Reg gave it gladly, thinking the Army would make a man out of his second son, but Margaret was more reluctant. She understood fully the breadth of her son's intellect and saw great promise should he continue his studies, whereas Martin saw only confinement and frustration. But she also accepted Martin's steely will and single-mindedness. Margaret truly didn't want to sign her son over to the Army, but she knew that if she didn't he'd go anyway.

'I saw it as an option to exercise my talents, without curbing them, in a manner that was productive to the community,' the son says now. 'I could be myself and help the nation, as opposed to being myself and being a pain in the arse to my community. Mum didn't really want me to go – they were keen on me going to university. It upset her a lot, but she understood it was a good thing, probably.'

And so in January 1987, Martin Wallace left Tamworth for the Australian Army's training facility at Kapooka in southern New South Wales. It was a three-month crash course in soldiering, the basic training of all new recruits. He was seventeen and a digger. And within days Martin would be known as Jock, in keeping with the Australian military's unofficial tradition of handing out nicknames to its members.

CHAPTER 8

*The regiment has some of the best and brightest
soldiers in the Australian Army. Being a member
of the SAS is as much about the mental side of
soldiering as it is the physical side.*

Jock had been kicking back at his flat in the beachside suburb
of Scarborough, not far from the SAS headquarters at
Swanbourne, on the night of September 11, 2001. It was a mild
Tuesday evening at the beginning of spring, and he was exhausted.
He'd only recently returned to Perth after spending weeks away on
counter-terrorism – CT – exercises, first in chilly Melbourne and
then in steaming Darwin for the annual CT Olympics, an event
where the government of the day gets to appraise the efficacy and
capability of the CT squadron that's on line at the time.

The Special Air Service Regiment at the Campbell Barracks in
Swanbourne has three Sabre – or war-fighting – squadrons. Each
squadron, known as 1 Squadron, 2 Squadron or 3 Squadron,
rotates through three specific functions including counter-
terrorism (also known as special recovery), surveillance and
reconnaissance missions, and offensive and assault operations.
The squadrons are subsequently supported by a troop from Jock's
152 Signal Squadron. Jock was in J Troop, which was then
attached to 3 SAS Squadron, but for the better part of the year he
had been assigned to the Regimental Headquarters as the
commanding officer's signaller.

Jock was glad to be back on home turf after the trips away. He knocked the top off a bottle of beer and settled in for some late-night television while fighting the urge to doze off. A newsflash interrupted normal programming. He called to his flatmate who was in the shower, a fellow soldier named Neil.

'Mate, get out here, you better come and watch this,' Jock said, a sense of urgency in his voice.

Halfway around the world, at the start of the business day, the North Tower of the iconic World Trade Center in lower Manhattan was on fire. Bright orange flames burst through the broken glass and steel structure and thick black smoke billowed out of the shattered building. The newsreader on TV reported that a plane had crashed into the tower at 8.46am. Authorities were unable to say if the crash was an accident. The talking head on the TV didn't know what type of aircraft had ploughed into one of Wall Street's most famous skyscrapers but suggested it might possibly have been a light aircraft, maybe a Cessna.

As Jock and Neil watched the television in disbelief, a second plane came into view, stark white on cerulean, banking over New York harbour and flying towards the burning North Tower and its twin tower to the right. The crew and passengers on the plane knew what the television news presenter broadcasting into Jock's lounge room did not. The plane, like the one before, had been hijacked.

A few minutes earlier, at 8.52am in the state of Connecticut on the northeast coast of America, Lee Hanson answered the phone. On the other end of the line was his son, Peter, who was on the Boeing 767 that would fly across Jock's television screen directly towards the World Trade Center. The plane was United Airlines Flight 175 and had departed from Boston's Logan Airport at 8.14am, en route to Los Angeles. Peter, surprisingly calm considering the circumstances, had rung his father to tell him the plane had been hijacked and could he please alert the authorities?

'I think they've taken over the cockpit. An attendant has been stabbed and someone else up front may have been killed. The plane is making strange moves,' Peter said.

Eight minutes later, at 9am, he made a second call. Scores of other passengers were ringing family members, telling them they loved them – just in case.

'It's getting bad, Dad,' Peter said. 'A stewardess was stabbed. They seem to have knives and Mace. They said they have a bomb. It's getting very bad on the plane. Passengers are throwing up and getting sick. The plane is making jerky movements. I don't think the pilot is flying the plane. I think we are going down. I think they intend to go to Chicago or someplace and fly into a building. Don't worry, Dad, if it happens, it'll be very fast. My God, my God!'

Just as Peter Hanson spoke what would be his last words to his father, Lee Hanson heard a woman's piercing scream come down the line. Then the phone went dead.

At 9.03am, United 175, with its left wing turning down, crashed into the South Tower of the WTC, instantly killing all on board including Peter Hanson, 50 fellow passengers, nine crew and the five hijackers.

'We just looked at each other and nodded and said, "Shit, it's going to get busy from now on,"' Jock says, recalling the moment terrorism changed the world forever. 'It was almost surreal, like Hollywood's outdone itself with special effects.'

Jock had trained in counter-terrorism. He knew the planes had been hijacked by terrorists. The two planes had crashed into the iconic symbols of capitalism in the heart of the United States' financial centre on Wall Street. It was an obscene yet unspoken declaration of war on America.

Jock remained glued to the television most of the night, his outrage growing as a third plane crashed into the Pentagon in Washington DC, and a fourth into an empty field in Pennsylvania. Nineteen terrorists had turned four aircraft loaded with 11 400 gallons (43 000 litres) of jet fuel into guided missiles that killed thousands of innocent civilians, many of whom had just started work for the day.

'People on base were ringing each other up that night. Everyone was talking about how disgusted and appalled they were by these actions,' Jock says. 'It was palpable, you could feel the atmosphere at Swannie. Everyone came alive, there were people coming to work going, "What are we doing? When are we going?"'

Swanbourne was buzzing with speculation about the coming retaliatory response from the US and Jock was sure some element of the SAS would be involved – given the Australian Government's response and the regiment's international reputation as one of the best Special Forces in the world.

The hijackers were quickly identified as members of Osama bin Laden's terrorist organisation al Qaeda – Arabic for the Base – which had been on the US Government's watch list for years. He reckoned the American Special Forces, always on high alert and ready to roll, would be on the move. Under their charter, the US SF operatives have five missions: special reconnaissance, direct action, conventional warfare, counter-terrorism and foreign internal defence. The Australian SAS were also on call 24/7 and were the experts in long-range surveillance and reconnaissance, essential for fighting terrorism.

'Our job is to prevent that, or react to it, basically. That's the whole reason we're doing the job – because idiots are out there who are going to do things like that,' Jock says, referring to the terrorist attacks on 9/11. 'It's a weird way to look at it and it's not pleasant, but it sort of justifies your own training and your own mindset that you were needed; that your training wasn't all for nothing. The word pretty much from the onset was that we knew something would happen. We knew there would be a reaction to this by the Americans and that the Australians would be pretty high on the priority list if something was going to go down.'

Experience taught the soldiers to keep an ear to the ground. They began mentally preparing themselves for any coming action, stepping up into a higher gear and ensuring they were ready for whatever mission the SAS Regiment would be given.

'You accept that this is your role and responsibility,' Jock says.

At 9.30am on 9/11 in the Emma Booker Elementary School in

Sarasota, Florida, the 43rd President of the United States, George W. Bush, stood in front of the travelling White House media and addressed the nation. He was visiting the school to announce a new federal government education initiative and had been reading a book, *My Pet Goat*, to primary school children when he was interrupted and told the second plane had crashed into the South Tower. He looked stunned. His comments, brief as they were, immediately went around the world.

'Today we've had a national tragedy. Two airplanes have crashed into the World Trade Center in an apparent terrorist attack on our country,' the President said. 'I have spoken to the Vice President, to the Governor of New York, to the Director of the FBI, and have ordered that the full resources of the federal government go to help the victims and their families, and to conduct a full-scale investigation to hunt down and to find those folks who committed this act. Terrorism against our nation will not stand.

'And now if you would join me in a moment of silence. May God bless the victims, their families, and America.'

Seven minutes later, the Pentagon was struck.

At 8.30pm, the President addressed the nation from behind his desk in the Oval Office in the White House.

Today, our fellow citizens, our way of life, our very freedom came under attack in a series of deliberate and deadly terrorist acts.

The victims were in airplanes, or in their offices; secretaries, business men and women, military and federal workers; moms and dads, friends and neighbors. Thousands of lives were suddenly ended by evil, despicable acts of terror.

The pictures of airplanes flying into buildings, fires burning, huge structures collapsing, have filled us with disbelief, terrible sadness, and a quiet, unyielding anger. These acts of mass murder were intended to frighten our nation into chaos and retreat. But they have failed; our country is strong.

A great people has been moved to defend a great nation. Terrorist attacks can shake the foundations of our biggest buildings, but they cannot touch the foundation of America. These acts shattered steel, but they cannot dent the steel of American resolve.

America was targeted for attack because we're the brightest beacon for freedom and opportunity in the world. And no one will keep that light from shining. Today, our nation saw evil, the very worst of human nature. And we responded with the best of America – with the daring of our rescue workers, with the caring for strangers and neighbors who came to give blood and help in any way they could.

The search is underway for those who are behind these evil acts. I've directed the full resources of our intelligence and law enforcement communities to find those responsible and to bring them to justice. We will make no distinction between the terrorists who committed these acts and those who harbor them.

America and our friends and allies join with all those who want peace and security in the world, and we stand together to win the war against terrorism ... America has stood down enemies before, and we will do so this time. None of us will ever forget this day. Yet, we go forward to defend freedom and all that is good and just in our world.

Jock Wallace's hunch that the Australian Army and, in particular, the SAS Regiment would be called to action was spot on.

Prime Minister John Howard was in Washington when the planes struck their target. The day before, he had visited the Pentagon and stood shoulder to shoulder with President Bush to commemorate the 50th anniversary of the Australian–US defence alliance and the ANZUS Treaty. Within hours of the terrorist attacks, a clearly distressed Howard held a press conference at the Australian Embassy on Massachusetts Avenue, not far from the American Capitol building, the political centre of the nation. Using strong and colourful language that was uniquely Australian, Howard expressed his country's solidarity with the United States and pledged Australian support in any retaliatory strike.

'We will stand by them, we will help them, we will support actions they take to properly retaliate in relation to these acts of bastardry against their citizens and what they stand for,' the Prime Minister said.

Howard revealed that he already had sent a message of support to the US President in which he expressed a sense of horror at the 'catastrophic events and the appalling loss of life'. In his note to Bush, he said: 'You can be assured of Australia's resolute solidarity with the American people at this most tragic time.'

At 1.30am in Australia on 12 September – less than three hours after the first plane crashed into the North Tower – Howard spoke with the then acting Prime Minister, John Anderson, and authorised a special meeting between officers of the federal Attorney General's Department, the Department of Defence and the Australian Security Intelligence Organisation (ASIO) in Canberra. The meeting, chaired by the Protective Security Coordinator, resolved to take all appropriate measures to protect American assets and military installations on Australian soil, as well as Israeli and other Jewish assets. It also increased ASIO's intelligence gathering and surveillance in the region and extended the close personal protection of American embassy and consular officials in the major cities.

Australia's commitment to join the war on terrorism was sealed when, on 14 September, the White House press secretary, Ari Fleischer, announced that both the US and Australian governments had concluded that Article IV of their recently celebrated mutual defence pact – the ANZUS Treaty – applied to the terrorist attacks.

'Although our alliance with Australia was crafted under very different circumstances than exist now, the events of September 11, 2001, are a powerful reminder that the alliance and our shared commitments are no less valid today,' Fleischer said in an official statement from the White House. 'Australia shares our assessment of the gravity of the situation and is resolute in its commitment to work with the United States and all freedom-loving people to combat international terrorism. In the days and weeks to come, we will consult closely with our Australian allies regarding an effective response to these attacks.'

As the public grieved, the upper echelons of the diplomatic, political and military worlds were carving out a strategy. Within weeks, Lieutenant Colonel Peter 'Gus' Gilmore, the commanding officer of the SAS Regiment at Swanbourne, was negotiating a role for the Australian Special Forces in the war against terrorism. Top brass from the Army began lobbying General Tommy Franks who was running the US Central Command (CentCom) in Florida, sheeting home the most effective way the Australians could join their coalition partners in the fight.

By mid-October it was decided. President Bush rang John Howard in Canberra to discuss the anti-terrorism campaign and asked that Australia act on its pledge to assist the coalition.

The following day, 17 October, the Prime Minister announced that Australia would deploy two P3 long-range maritime aircraft to assist maritime patrols and reconnaissance; a 150-man Special Forces detachment from the SASR for combined operations with allied SF groups; and two B707 tanker aircraft to support air-refuelling operations. As well, a guided missile frigate, already in the Middle Eastern theatre to support the multi-national interception forces implementing the United Nations Security Council resolutions in the region, would remain.

To Jock and the blokes at the SAS Regiment in Swanbourne, Howard's words were music to their ears. The regiment has some of the best and brightest soldiers in the Australian Army and, while the troops are a tightly bonded band of brothers, they are also highly competitive. They are trained to be able to handle any situation – combat, counter-terrorism, rescue and emergencies – and when the opportunity arises, they want to put their training to the test. Being a member of the SAS is as much about the mental side of soldiering as it is the physical side.

The regimental commanding officer, Gus Gilmore, and the regiment's 1 Squadron, led by Major Daniel McDaniel, got the job. As the CO, Gilmore took his own close personal protection team and Jock, being the CO's signaller, was along for the ride. They shipped out with little fanfare in late November 2001.

'I thought I was kissed. It was good, everyone was very envious and jealous just because I got a guernsey,' Jock says. 'It's highly competitive – people will send their mum to jail to get these jobs.

'My work ethic is, when I work, I work till I drop, and Gilmore knows that.'

The commanding officer had seen Jock and his fellow chooks in action in the centre of Darwin weeks earlier, busting a gut to get the comms system up and running after hitting the ground for the counter-terrorism Olympics exercise.

'We have to set up the link back to Australia for the higher command, and you've got to be ready for anything,' Jock says, explaining the chooks' role.

'We just bust a move, trunks go flying and trucks are all waiting, and you just hook into it and throw in all the equipment that you need, and you whack your system up. When Gus Gilmore hit the building, he came in and said to my squadron commander for 152, "Col, am I ready to go?" And Col had the greatest pleasure in saying, "Yeah, sit down and start," because we had been so proficient at setting up. And that staggered the CO. It was a great surprise to Gus Gilmore to find that it was already actually set up. Although we were lathered in sweat and huffing and puffing, at the time he was asking this we were actually sitting on our arses having a rest because it was already done.'

CHAPTER 9

The SAS troopers were adaptable,
beyond capable, resourceful and innovative,
and their ability to live off the land had earned
them the nickname of 'chicken stranglers',
much to their amusement.

ONE OF THE SAS REGIMENT'S most highly trained sniper-scouts
was sitting in the Shahi Kot Valley south of where Jock was
under ambush. Johnny and his six-man patrol had infilled into the
area after leaving Bagram Air Base the previous Monday. Their
job was to conduct surveillance and reconnaissance in the region.

Johnny had been in the SAS since 1996. He and Jock were
great mates, as tight as could be, and had worked together in
the same squadron at Swanbourne. They had a shared
philosophy when it came to soldiering. Loyalty – watch out for
your mates. Ability – do whatever it takes. And honour – do it
to the best of your capability and do not let your fellow soldiers
down. They also had a shared philosophy when it came to
socialising – party hard.

They were separated in age by three years and, though Jock
was older, they were equals. Both began their careers at Kapooka,
named after an Aboriginal word for 'place of wind', and after
basic training Johnny joined the infantry, ending up in the 1st
Battalion Royal Australian Regiment (1 RAR) in Townsville,
where he excelled in the reconnaissance sniper unit.

In January of 1993, he was dispatched to Somalia in Operation
Solace, under the auspices of the United Nations humanitarian

mission to the war-torn country. Somalia was in the throes of anarchy. Thousands of citizens were starving to death as warlords reigned through a campaign of fear and terror. The 1 RAR was charged with undertaking security operations while aid was delivered to the needy.

In 1996, Johnny was selected to undergo the SAS Regiment's gruelling, almost unbearable cadre course, which he passed with flying colours. It was a major accomplishment. About 300 soldiers start the selection course each year and only a handful of them go on to become a 'beret-qualified' operator, allowing them to wear the sand-coloured beret and 'Who Dares Wins' insignia on their uniform. Johnny was then 24 years old. After surviving the regiment's rigorous eighteen months' training, he was designated as a scout – the man who goes up front to ensure safe passage for the rest of his squad. Danger work.

'More or less, I was the scout tracker, the guy up front I suppose, the eyes and ears,' Johnny says. 'You wouldn't know that now, though; I've lost quite a bit of hearing in my left ear – that was through Iraq.'

By March of 2002, Johnny was a water operator in B Troop – aka the infamous Beagle Boys – in 1 Squadron. He had two tours of duty under his belt in the thick, almost impassable jungles of East Timor, and had seen active service in Bougainville. He had also been involved in other action in other parts of the world. At the age of 30, Trooper Johnny had seen a lot more in his thirteen years of Army life than a man twice his age would anywhere else.

Johnny was in Bravo Two Patrol, which had arrived at Bagram late on a Sunday in February, flying in with the rest of the 1 Squadron soldiers on a blacked-out US aircraft. The Aussie soldiers, known as Task Force 64 in Afghanistan, bedded down for a few hours' sleep, then rose for a hot breakfast before pushing out into the wilds of the Shahi Kot Valley. It would be the last hot meal they'd get for days.

The patrols exited in the Aussies' famous and fearsome looking six-wheel long-range patrol vehicles (LRPVs). Ostensibly, the truck was a Land Rover cut down and gunned up to each patrol's needs, and was the envy of other Special Forces groups in Afghanistan. Johnny's had two machine guns attached to the front and back and the resourceful soldiers had custom-built long-range fuel tanks for extended patrols. Pack racks held vital radio, medical and war-making equipment, as well as ammunition, water and fuel carriers. The LRPV, with the 50-calibre ring-mounted machine-gun, was a deadly mobile fighting and supply unit but it could only go so far. When the terrain became less accommodating for the converted Land Rover, the patrol camouflaged the vehicle and went in by hard foot slog.

The trekking was tough enough, but being a native Queenslander, Johnny had never felt cold like Afghanistan cold. It had even frozen the diesel in their vehicles, providing the men with yet another challenge.

Major General Hagenbeck was at the hangar when the SAS men began to roll out of Bagram in a convoy of LRPVs. Lieutenant Colonel Tink had wanted the two-star general to meet the Australians face to face, to see the men who were putting their lives on the line for the US-led mission in the clearly defined AO Down Under in the valley.

'It was important that he could identify with what their capabilities were and what their vehicles were and how they were armed,' says Tink now. 'But the second thing I wanted was to make sure that he could identify with them as individuals.'

It was an impressive moment. The snow-covered mountains provided a picturesque backdrop for the Aussie SAS Regiment, a wild and woolly looking bunch bundled up in cold-weather gear and sporting two months' growth after recent patrols in other parts of Afghanistan. Weapons bristled off the mud-splattered vehicles. An Australian flag flapped in the breeze on the Aussie accommodation tents attached to the hangar.

Hagenbeck understood Tink's motive for the meet-and-greet. He had run into a few of the SAS troops in the region, maybe in the chow line or while grabbing a cup of joe to keep him going in the long, cold hours in the TOC or the terrain-model tent, which had the battle terrain laid out on the ground. But he had never met them formally as a unit.

'This was the first time I could really look them in the eye and just talk to them, very briefly, about what they were getting into. And they exuded an air of confidence,' Hagenbeck recalls. 'That's what sometimes can make it tough on a commander – you realise when you are making decisions that these are not faceless people and you've already seen this person.'

Hagenbeck walked through the ranks and gave each man a firm soldier's handshake.

'Good luck and good hunting,' he told them.

The Australians' roles were clearly mapped out. The patrols were to provide special reconnaissance of the area in the days ahead of H-Hour, when Operation Anaconda would commence. Tink was worried about getting his surveillance and recon elements into position on the rim of the valley without their cover being blown. Locals, most of whom were either sympathetic to the Taliban and al Qaeda or too frightened to fight them, would see all movement through Gardez and the Shahi Kot Valley.

Several reconnaissance and surveillance patrols inserted themselves by road and foot under the cover of darkness. Tink had clandestine observation posts on high ground and the patrols would be the eyes and ears in the valley, reporting on what they could see in the AO from the rim of the mountain. The SAS troopers had been trained to stay out for as long as needed and could cope with the sub-zero conditions, the rain and sleet, and the jagged mountains.

The SAS troopers were adaptable, beyond capable, resourceful and innovative, and their ability to live off the land had earned them the nickname of 'chicken stranglers', much to their amusement.

'It was a good plan as it worked, but the valley was a hornet's nest, that was the problem,' says Tink now. 'And we didn't have tanks and we didn't have artillery.'

There was also another problem. Weather.

On Monday, bad weather delayed the helo insertion of the SAS and on Tuesday, a patrol in another target area was hampered by rain and sleet, with cloud at ground level and visibility between 800 metres and two clicks. Johnny and his 1 Squadron brethren were now operating in temperatures that plummeted to minus 10 degrees Celsius at an altitude of 2100 metres. Snow was eight centimetres deep on the ground. But the patrols pushed on, edging closer to AO Down Under.

Another problem for the US command was the shifting sands of intelligence.

A CIA report cited a Taliban informer in Gardez who revealed to Task Force Dagger operators that the number of enemy fighters in the valley ranged between 580 and 700 and worked in squads of twelve to fifteen men. They were hidden in well-fortified positions in the mountains, not in the villages on the valley floor. They were well armed, and some of the squads had Stingers, the surface-to-air missiles that the CIA had secretly armed the mujahideen with in its war against the Soviets. But, as Sean Naylor writes in his authoritative book on Anaconda, *Not a Good Day to Die*, the CIA intel from the informer never formally made it to Hagenbeck's or the Rakkasans' intelligence planners.

'There was nothing to tell us they were there [in the high ground],' one of Hagenbeck's intelligence planners, Major Francesca Ziemba, would say later.

According to a report in *The Christian Science Monitor*, intel, including photographs, listening devices and old-fashioned spying, had turned up no sign of AQ in the mountains, and some analysts wrongly believed the hideouts would be too cold for the enemy.

Another factor was bothering Tink. He had been informed that the American Special Forces had put patrols in his area of operation. The secrecy under which the US Special Forces work could have jeopardised the Aussies in their AO. A real potential for blue-on-blue conflict existed. Tink earlier had said that no forces other than Australians could operate in AO Down Under unless he had given the all clear and knew where they were in relation to his own men.

He was a hard-arse on the point. Deconfliction equalled safety; ergo, deconfliction was non-negotiable. He had liaison officers embedded with the American Special Forces command in Gardez who were operating with Afghan commander General Zia Lodin, as the Hammer. Tink had also deployed Jock Wallace and Warrant Officer Clint to the 10th Mountain.

'Deconfliction negotiations continue with the US SF,' Tink noted in his diary in late February – two days after the SAS patrols had set out. 'This centres on the layered control measures we develop and implement to avoid fratricide between forces working in the vicinity of each other. Working on this for a while.'

The deconfliction issue was the cause of some argy-bargy between the top US brass, but Tink was running Task Force 64 – the Aussies – and he would run it his way. 'Confronting and unfortunate as our stance is, I am not negotiating away safety,' he wrote later that same day. 'I believe the US commanders see our measures as largely excessive and perhaps the Australians being difficult.'

Three years later, Tink says wryly: 'I think that was a very astute observation.'

One of Major General Hagenbeck's intelligence planners later told author Sean Naylor that Tink 'was a pain in the butt sometimes'. But he added that Task Force 64 was 'very cooperative and extremely effective'.

'Extremely effective' turned out to be an understatement.

One patrol was inserted and Tink recorded that it had 'eyes on target'. Another unit went in soon after and took the high ground. An ambush patrol was in yet another location, as were a handful more scattered throughout the valley. All were working in horrendous conditions, weather included. The snowline began about 30 metres above the valley floor and the rugged peaks of the mountains were blanketed white. But the Aussies were in play and perfectly located when Anaconda started constricting its prey in the early hours of Saturday, 2 March.

Johnny's SAS patrol reached its designated observation point in good time, and had become acclimatised to the surroundings. The patrol was on top of a steep mountain, and had breathtaking views down into deep valleys. The mountain was cocooned in a silence so haunting that they could hear themselves breathe. The soldiers spoke in low whispers to maintain their covert position. His small team of men were joined by an American soldier and, subsequently, they could hear what the Yanks were up to over their comms nets. Johnny's patrol was lying in wait for the Hammer and Anvil action to push the enemy down to its cut-off position. Then they would do what they had been trained to do: capture or kill any fleeing enemy.

The Aussie blokes were ready for war in one of the most dangerous places on earth at the time, but instead of engaging the enemy, they were watching a herd of goats grazing on the rare scrubby tufts of grass that dotted the rocky mountainside. They pissed themselves laughing. You know you're in Afghanistan when a herd of goats gets in the way of war. They only hoped that the local goatherd wouldn't stumble across the SAS patrol while trying to move his woolly investment to a safer spot. There would be no glory in a herd of goats blowing their covert operation.

The amusing cultural juxtaposition was rudely interrupted by a squall of war bouncing off the mountains across the valley a few kilometres north in the Shahi Kot. Johnny could hear the incoming *thwomp*, *thwomp*, *thwomp* of the Chinooks and knew the 10th Mountain and Rakkasans were inbound.

His ears had already become finely attuned to the sound of combat that began in the dark earlier that morning with the bombing raid.

'You could hear it echoing down the valley and being only that far away [a few kilometres], you could see the aircraft coming in and bombing,' Johnny says now.

It was lighter now and Johnny waited and watched. The choppers took off, then silence filled the crisp morning air. Noises were trapped and voices travelled along the valley floor and up the ravines.

Minutes later, staccato bursts of machine-gun fire delivered the unwelcome message that the landing zone was hot. Johnny waited some more. Maybe five minutes had passed, could've been ten. No one really counts when the fire is raining down.

Suddenly, their radio burst into life.

'One Oscar, this is Niner Charlie,' said a calm and coolly detached voice over the radio. 'We are in a bit of a shit fight here. Over.'

'Holy fuck,' Johnny said as he huddled around the radio with some of his mates, instantly recognising Jock's voice.

Hearing Jock was a shock. His call sign – Niner Charlie – was not one that the SAS patrols would expect to hear on the battlefield because it was the regimental commanding officer's call sign, and the Regimental HQ was not in the area being used by American troops in conventional warfare.

Johnny also recognised how controlled his mate sounded. Professional. Clinical. Calm. Telling it straight.

Yeah, that'd be Jock, he thought.

'We all kind of crowded around the radio, apart from the guys who were out on sentry,' says Johnny. 'We just didn't expect Anaconda to turn the way it did; I suppose no one did. The initial brief we got for Anaconda was that we were mopping up the ragtag of the Taliban. I think the old Taliban gave us a bit of a surprise there.

'You could hear it all, it was amplified over the radio handset. You could hear the battle from where we were, but when Jock pressed the presser switch to [let us] hear his voice, it did bring home how close he was to the bad guys.

'There was a lot of fire, heavy fire; a lot of yelling. The Americans were yelling and you could hear them in the background – it sounded like a lot of confusion over the handset, but old Jock remained calm the whole time.

'You would not have thought that he was in that much trouble.

'I thought to myself, the poor bastard. I didn't know the full story of why he was out there. But I can remember thinking, "I've got to go and get him, I've got to go and get my mate." In a real world he shouldn't have been anywhere near there.

'He said they'd been put into a hot LZ, and they're in the shit and they need some air support.'

Johnny also felt the irony of the moment and experienced a twinge of what he would later describe as 'professional jealousy'. His mate was a signaller in the SAS, whereas he, Johnny, had trained his whole life for combat and close fighting roles. 'I'm thinking, "Why am I watching this herd of goats?"' Johnny says now, laughing at the twist of fate. 'That was my original thought.'

Johnny was frustrated. He wanted to hoist his pack on his back and start marching to Jock's position. He could hear the bullets and machine-gun fire ricocheting in the valley and hissing through the static of the radio. That was what the beret-qualified SAS operators were trained to handle, and yet it was Jock who was under fire in a full-scale ambush. It was one of war's volatile ambiguities.

'It was a feeling of hopelessness really, that our mate was in that kind of situation,' he says now.

Johnny broke all radio protocols and grabbed the handset from the radio operator.

'Niner Charlie, this is Bravo Three-Four, over.'

'This is Niner Charlie.'

'How you going, bro?'

'Yeah, not bad, Johnny,' Jock replied, a smile playing across his lips upon hearing his mate's voice.

'You hang in there, mate. Hang in there, mate, don't give up, you'll be right.'

Johnny says: 'I would have preferred [the battle] come down to us than have it where Jock was because, I'm not saying we are better than anyone else, but we had made a position and, if we did have to fight there, we had the location.' Johnny is referring to their strategic spot on the high ground, always an advantage in war and just plain good common sense.

It was a classic military strategy.

'Where Jock was the opposite – he got thrown into something

where they were waiting for him. I was hoping it would trickle down [south] to us so it would take the heat off him. I jumped on the handset and told him to hang in there and I'm thinking of him. You could hear there was a bit of humour in his voice; he and I are pretty close. He knew exactly who was on the handset.'

Johnny told Jock that he would come and help out, and Jock knew that he was the type of soldier who would – and could – do it. For a minute, Jock wouldn't have minded, but in truth he didn't want Johnny and the boys coming anywhere near him because, at that stage, he didn't think he was getting out of there alive.

'I knew exactly where I was going to go and how long it was going to take me,' Johnny says now. 'But it would have been a stupid thing to do; even at the time I thought it was probably not the smartest thing. But when your mate's in trouble! I didn't know what I was going to walk into, but at the time you put all professionalism aside and think of your mates.'

★ ★ ★

Tink was in the TOC when Major General Hagenbeck's radio operators received confirmation that Stanley Harriman had been killed, possibly by friendly fire. Tink may have been playing hardball when it came to inserting liaison officers with Task Force Dagger operators and insisting on deconfliction protocols in his AO, but he had been right. The lieutenant colonel was not going to negotiate away the safety of his troops, and had done all he could to prevent blue-on-blue fire. Tink felt vindicated for taking such a strong stance, but it was a hollow victory because a good, brave man had been killed.

Calls for close air support were coming in thick and fast from the men under fire at different LZs in the valley, but none were answered.

'Continue to wait for a bomber strike, now overdue by an hour,' Tink wrote in his war diary at the time.

The weather was encroaching. Fog had rolled in and blanketed

Above left: Martin Wallace and his older brother, James, at the family's country home outside Tamworth in rural New South Wales, circa 1974.

Courtesy Margaret Wallace

Above right: Jock Wallace flanked by his father, Reginald, and brother, James, after his march-out parade at Kapooka, 9.5km southwest of Wagga Wagga in country New South Wales.

Courtesy Margaret Wallace

Below left: Martin 'Jock' Wallace and his mother, Margaret, the day before Martin officially completed the basic training for all new recruits at Kapooka Army Base in 1987.

Courtesy Margaret Wallace

Below right: Jock Wallace (second from right) standing at ease on the parade ground at Kapooka, an Aboriginal word for 'place of wind'.

Courtesy Martin Wallace

Above and right:
Jock Wallace threw
himself into the
basic training for
new recruits after
joining the
Australian Army
in 1987.

Courtesy Martin Wallace

The Australian Army appealed to the adventurer in Jock Wallace and gave him a chance to escape the borders of his boyhood hometown.

Courtesy Martin Wallace

Above: Jock Wallace landed in the dead of night on this desert runway outside FOB Rhino in southwestern Afghanistan at the end of 2001.

Courtesy Martin Walla◄

Below: With the Australian flag flying patriotically above their temporary accommodation in Afghanistan, Australian SAS troops take a break from action during Operation Enduring Freedom.

Courtesy Martin Walla◄

Top: US Army Major Bryan Hilferty (left) who delivered the daily press briefings during Operation Anaconda at Bagram Air Base in Afghanistan, stands with colleagues under the Rakkasans' symbol at FOB Kandahar in 2002.   Courtesy Lieutenant Colonel Bryan Hilferty

Above right: Jock wrote frequently to his mother, Margaret, often penning a quick note on whatever he could find, including an MRE package.   Courtesy Martin Wallace

Left: Jock Wallace never went anywhere in Afghanistan without his 5.56mm fully automatic M4 weapon – even the gym. He called the gun his 'American Express card'.

Courtesy Martin Wallace

Top: Despite the freezing temperatures in the high mountains of Afghanistan, the sun could burn through winter cold giving Jock a warm but brief break outside the Australians' sleeping quarters.

Courtesy Martin Wallace

Middle right: After a visit from Major General Franklin 'Buster' Hagenbeck, who wished them 'good luck and good hunting', the Australian SAS patrols leave Bagram Air Base for their patrols in the Shahi Kot Valley.

Courtesy Australian Army

Below right: The long-range patrol vehicle (LRPV) was effective in all weather conditions in Afghanistan and could traverse snow-covered muddy tracks, vast deserts and mountain terrain.

Courtesy Australian Army

Above and below: At dusk on the eve of Operation Anaconda, American troops from the 101st Airborne and 10th Mountain divisions gathered for Colonel Frank Wiercinski's rallying speech outside tent city at Bagram Air Base. Standing on a Humvee, he told the soldiers: 'We have been called on to fight the war on terrorism.'

Photo by John Berry, courtesy The Post-Standard

Above: Major General Hagenbeck (legs crossed) reviews the battle plan for Operations Anaconda around a terrain model in late February 2002. Commanders of all divisions were involved in the planning, including the Australian SAS Chief, Lieutenant Colonel Rowan Tink (third from right).

Photo by John Berry, courtesy The Post-Standard

Below: Illuminated by a nearly full moon, on 2 March 2002 Soldiers from the 101st Airborne Division, C Company, 2nd Battalion 187th Infantry Regiment, prepare to board a CH-47 Chinook helicopter for the flight into Shahi Kot Valley to attack al Qaeda and Taliban forces. Photo by John Berry, courtesy The Post-Standard

the valley, blocking the Predator's vision and thereby limiting visibility of the battle in the TOC. One of the SAS patrols radioed that visibility had dropped from four clicks to 100 metres in the space of ten minutes. Forget the oft-quoted line about the 'fog of war' in Karl von Clausewitz's nineteenth-century magnum opus *On War*. This was literally the fog of war.

With deteriorating weather, Hagenbeck called off a planned second air assault of infantrymen from the 10th Mountain into the valley later that day. Some of the soldiers waiting were the remaining troops in Sergeant Pete's platoon. They were like cats on a hot tin roof, eager to get in and help their brothers in arms. They paced back and forth in their khaki-coloured general-purpose tents at Bagram, kicking chairs over and hating the fact that their buddies were under fire and there was nothing they could do to help them. They had been about to fly in as reinforcement a couple of times but Hagenbeck had made the call: it was too dangerous to attempt a second lift. It was 0353 zulu time, 8.23am in the bowl.

Tink then briefed the officer commanding 1 SAS Squadron on the battle that was not going to plan. He told Major Dan McDaniel to be prepared to set up a blocking effort outside AO Down Under to the west and northwest of Objective Remington. Task Force Dagger and General Zia's failure to move into place around the Whale had left the gate open, and Tink wanted the Aussies to be in position to close it if necessary.

Tink's briefing to the 1 SAS commander was a 'be prepared' only task. Tink was all about preparation based on information. Two weeks before D-Day, Tink had attended a ConOps (concept of operations) meeting at Bagram with Mikolashek, Hagenbeck and other commanders preparing for Anaconda. They were told that there was 'potential for a serious fight'.

Back in the TOC, Tink also noted that twenty-plus personnel had disappeared into a tunnel in one corner of the compound at Sherkhankhel further north. 'Movement was sighted in this compound,' he wrote.

The name Osama bin Laden was still on everyone's mind.

CHAPTER 10

Jock wiped the blood from his hands onto his camos, grabbed his M4, stood up and raced back into the line of fire to help the last of the wounded to safety.

Jock Wallace was thinking about survival. About 30 blokes had managed to get into Hell's Halfpipe but the rest were still scattered out on the valley floor, finding whatever cover they could and engaging the enemy with their small arms. Bullets cracked overhead; men jockeyed for position in the halfpipe.

Jock was set. He had his pack to one side, his radio to the other and his M4 5.56mm rifle switched to semi-automatic, with his rounds ready to rip.

Signallers often felt like a bit of a dick drag, being tied to the radio, but Jock wasn't going down without a fight. He was nose to nose with the enemy.

'Incooommmming.'

'Incoming' was the warning to get down before the round detonated.

Jock looked out of the halfpipe and saw Sergeant Pete's mortar platoon about 200 metres away, setting up then blasting off a 120mm mortar and racing for cover in a wadi to avoid a return AQ mortar.

Check him out, Jock thought as he watched Sergeant Pete, *that bloke inspires confidence. Those kids will do anything for him.*

The enemy onslaught was constant. Frank Grippe's men were

117

shooting at anything that looked like an enemy target, picking off terrorists from 500 metres, *hoo-ah*ing when one went down.

'Any time we could actually visibly see a target, we'd eliminate that al Qaeda element,' the sar-major told reporters at a Department of Defense press briefing five days after the opening round of Anaconda. 'We're here to kill and destroy al Qaeda. It's that simple.'

In times of crisis, people make double-handed deals with their god, promising all types of good behaviour in exchange for a break. Don't smite me, Lord, and I'll give up the fags, quit the grog, never ever say the word 'fuck' in church again, not even in anger, and never in front of the kids. Jesus, I'll even go to Mass on Sundays, I swear.

Jock Wallace was having none of it. Never a by-the-book religious man, he didn't place any store in being touched by the hand of God in the hellhole in which he'd found himself. No amount of believing and praying was going to help him in the Shahi Kot Valley at 9am on a Saturday morning with the enemy on the hillside making the dirt dance viciously around his feet.

If anything, Jock was making a straight-up deal with the gods of self-reliance and close air support. He was a chook, a signaller, and he had the radio – one of the few means of communication back to the Aussie headquarters after the Americans dropped their packs in the kill zone while running for cover.

Well that's reassuring, Jock thought.

He had wanted to go to the gunfight, but hadn't been expecting this.

The Apaches were long gone. At 9.53am local time, Lieutenant Colonel Rowan Tink in the Tactical Operations Center noted in his war diary that a number of Killer Spades were unserviceable, and some had taken direct RPG hits, something the soldiers in the halfpipe already knew. One pilot had been hit in the face. While the pilot and all the helicopters would survive to fight another day, they had been KO'd on Day One of Operation Anaconda.

Out in the valley, Sergeant First Class Michael Peterson was getting jacked off. Al Qaeda mortars had nailed his eight-man mortar platoon for more than an hour. Sergeant Pete had ordered his men to take cover in a wadi and shoot at the enemy on the hill with their small arms, leaving the 120mm tube perched on its tripod out in the open and sitting pretty. Whenever there was a lull in gunfire, he charged across the rock-covered terrain to the mortar, set the target coordinates on the laptop computer, rammed a bomb down the barrel, and let rip.

Sergeant Pete and his young bucks were taking down targets, but their successful strike rate had turned them into al Qaeda's biggest target. If the terrorists wanted to survive, they had to knock out the mortar, which was the most dangerous weapon the Americans had. AQ were punishing.

'I've had enough of this shit,' Sergeant Pete yelled.

He gave his men a rapid-fire pep talk and led them at full gallop into enemy fire to break down their mortar and move it to a better location. Peterson enlisted Sergeant Darren Amick and another fire team leader from 2nd Platoon, Charlie Company, who'd flown in on the Chinook with his crew. He barked out instructions, ordering them to provide security and lay down suppressive fire.

Jock looked over and saw Sergeant Pete and Private First Class David Brown heaving the mortar tube about 50 metres from its original location toward Hell's Halfpipe. The riflemen from 2nd Platoon ran out to help haul the mortars on the their SKEDCOs to the new spot while shooting at the enemy and dodging the steel rain of direct fire.

'I had more help than I could ever ask for, that's how great these kids are,' Peterson says now. 'They were out of control. You know, all you had to do as a leader is be the first one out and they will follow you to hell.'

It was pure bravery, but Jock was concerned.

Don't you bring the enemy to me, he thought, *I've got 30 blokes in here looking for cover so they can fight the terrorists.*

'I didn't understand why a heavy weapon like that was

employed so close to us when we've got radios. Mortars don't need to see where the enemy are, they just need to be told where to shoot,' Jock says.

Jock thought the move closer to the halfpipe would compromise their position, give it away, and he was already privately questioning the overall planning. Had the mortar platoon been infiltrated a couple of clicks up the valley, the enemy attacking the soldiers in the halfpipe would not have known where the US mortars were coming from, giving the coalition troops the critical advantage of surprise.

But Jock knew that the strategies and principles of warfare often gave way to the fluid realities of a battlefield.

'You appreciate if you send a mortar crew off unguarded further away, then they're running a real likelihood of compromise or death,' he says. 'It was bad planning and they should have been supported and put into a position where they could have applied effective fire from a safe distance.'

Jock was applying basic battle strategy. The 120mm mortar has a range of 7200 metres and could have reached targets further north in the valley, which was one of the reasons Sergeant Pete decided to import the weapon. But by bringing the big gun, the big mortar, he had sacrificed mobility, something he was starting to regret.

'We all know the intel was pretty jacked up. In hindsight I would have gone in with two guns of 81 millimetres,' Peterson says now.

'Common sense tells you, don't land on the low ground when the enemy is on the high ground. It's always the first rule of war; seize the high ground. But, whatever; I'm not going to second-guess anyone in my chain of command because I pray to God they know more than me. I think they do.

'I thought for sure the intel was jacked up, somebody dropped the ball in the intel, but again, who cares? That's where the enemy is and, alright, there could be a million of them, let's fight. And I am not trying to sound all bravado now; I think that was our mindset.

'We're there to fight, we're from New York, we want to fight. It was absolutely personal for us, for that battalion. You know, we didn't sit back in the United States and get to mourn these people – everything in our heads was fresh from 9/11.'

Sergeant Pete didn't have time to ponder the possibilities. He had other pressing concerns, including guiding a bunch of young soldiers in their first ever real life battle. They had done plenty of live firing in exercises back at Fort Drum, home of the 10th Mountain Division, but most had never fired a shot at a real enemy in real combat conditions.

Peterson had seen action with the 82nd Airborne Division in the first Gulf War and, while he only fired about six mortars during his entire deployment, he knew what war was like, how the sound of mortars exploding and shrapnel whizzing past could make a man piss his pants or rise to the occasion.

His young guns didn't know first-hand what war was like. Leadership was king.

'One of my fire team leaders [Raul Lopez] crawls up to me and says, "Sergeant Pete, can I fire my two-oh-three?" And I'm like, "Jesus Christ, you're *not* firing your two-oh-three?" And you know, the kid is just so used to the peacetime army and he just went crazy with that two-oh-three and took out quite a lot of people with that thing. You know, he was awesome. He crawled up to me and I'm like, "Fucking fire your two-oh-three."'

Peterson had seven men under his control, and the blokes from 2nd Platoon were also in the vicinity. He felt personally responsible for every single one of them and wanted to get them all home.

'You don't worry about yourself, you know what I mean?' Peterson says. 'It's getting it done, and getting your guys home. You are tense, because you have a lot of responsibilities. One is to do the job that the American taxpayer has been paying you to do. And I think the biggest one is to make sure you get your guys home. You know, you are kind of the mother hen and although there's a blood lust – you want to take these guys [al Qaeda] out

– the number one priority for me is to make sure all of my men survive. And sometimes ... you can be the best leader in the world [but] men die, that's what war is.'

Sergeant Pete set up the 120mm in a wadi across the open valley floor from Hell's Halfpipe and used a weed on the hillside as a reference point. Mortars were scattered between the first and second locations; the SKEDCOs were spread out; and three of his men's rucksacks had been blasted to pieces by al Qaeda RPGs. *Boom, boom, boom.* Food, water, cold-weather gear, ammo, night-vision goggles and a raft of other vital supplies were gone.

What a bloody waste, Jock thought.

Section Sergeant Thomas Oldham manned the computer and registered the target coordinates and fire trajectory.

'Watch this shit, I'm going to kill all these guys,' Sergeant Pete yelled to Oldham, a half-Irish half-Japanese soldier whom Sergeant Pete regarded as a brother.

Riflemen from 2nd Platoon ran into the open field to deliver ammo to Sergeant Pete who began hammering away at al Qaeda positions. Once the gun was going again, the enemy massed all their fire on the mortar, firing shells that bounced all around them.

The battle was a free-for-all – in the valley and in the small washout of Hell's Halfpipe. Al Qaeda mortars and RPGs exploded every minute, and bullets from Kalashnikovs filled the spaces in between, coming from the eastern ridge, effectively trapping the men in the pipe. The soldiers responded with machine-gun and small-arms fire from their M4 carbines and M240s; Peterson did his supreme best with the 120mm.

Sergeant First Class Thomas Abbott sent his men to help Peterson move the remaining mortar equipment. A former Ranger, Abbott had been in the Black Hawk Down hell fight in the hostile Third World country Somalia back in 1993, in which eighteen American soldiers were killed.

Suddenly, *boooom*. Sergeant Pete's crew – now about 100 metres from Hell's Halfpipe – took a hit.

Jock saw the explosion out the corner of his eye while sweeping the terrain for the al Qaeda terrorist who kept lobbing mortars at him.

'I went, "Fuck. Oh fuck." My heart's just dropped out. My heart sank for those guys because I thought they were all dead, Jock says. 'They literally were there one second and there was a puff of smoke and when the dust and smoke cleared there [were guys] screaming and lying around and writhing on the dirt. And more mortar rounds are coming in while these bastards are lying there.

'If you wanted to see a mortar team getting blown up, it would be a good piece of cinema.'

The platoon literally was blown off its feet. Six soldiers were hit. Blood gushed out of wounds and men screamed in pain. They were the first injuries of the day, and Jock hoped they would be the last. Al Qaeda made the most of their direct hit, and began firing artillery along with the rest of their deadly arsenal of 82mm mortars and RPGs. It was an onslaught, coming from every direction.

Shells from a D30 howitzer blasted the ground, but they were off target. They enemy didn't have the smarts to know how to fire indirect artillery, and were launching it with a flat trajectory, sending it straight into the side of the mountain where it exploded without too much damage. There were no greenies in the valley that day to care about a mountain copping a caning.

Thank God these cats don't know how to lob it, Sergeant Pete thought. *Thank God they don't know how to fire high artillery.*

'So now you've got a bunch of 82s and now there's a D30 and things are kind of getting crazy, mortar rounds are still landing around us,' Peterson recalls.

Sergeant Pete was unscathed, but his ears were ringing. He did a quick recce to see the damage and began searching through the smoke and dust for Sergeant Oldham, screaming his name.

He didn't want to lose one of his guys.

It seemed like things were moving in slow motion, but that was the trick of war. Oldham came running out of the smoke, straight at Peterson.

'And his small Japanese eyes had turned this big and I'm like "Tommmmmmmmmmy",' says Peterson. 'And he came running at me and I grabbed him and we both were like, man, holy cow!'

Sergeant Abbott had been struck by a piece of shrapnel in the right shoulder. Just before he flew out, his wife had told him: 'Don't be a hero, come back to us.' A father of four, he had every intention of doing just that. He looked around and saw injured men clutching at their wounds, blood seeping through their camouflage gear which had been shredded by razor-sharp pieces of red-hot shrapnel. They were lying on the ground, half stunned, half shocked and trying to work out whether they were dead or alive.

'If you don't get up you are going to die,' Abbott roared at his fellow soldiers, at the same time thinking that the enemy fighters he was up against were the more skilled trainers, not the callow locals forced to join the jihad.

Lieutenant Brad Maroyka, the commander of Charlie Company's 1st Platoon, looked like a piece of Swiss cheese, having copped a burst of shrapnel. He had holes all over his body, but he knew what he had to do.

'We just needed to get the hell away from where we were,' Maroyka later told *Time* magazine. 'Even those of us with leg injuries had a simple choice: get up and run, or die.'

Maroyka could barely walk. Shrapnel had ripped his calf to pieces.

Private First Class Kyle McGovern was lying on his stomach covered in blood. The tall 21-year-old from New Hampshire had enlisted straight after high school, where he had starred at basketball and soccer. McGovern's sturdy boot was blown half off his foot, exposing his wounds. He lost the two middle toes on his right foot and shrapnel smashed his ankle and tore a hole through his hand. McGovern's eardrums had been blasted, and his vision was blurry.

Command Sergeant Major Frank Grippe was in Hell's

Halfpipe with Lieutenant Colonel Paul LaCamera and Sergeant Robert Healy, watching Peterson's mortar platoon when the mortar struck.

'I figured I had four or five guys dead,' Grippe says now. 'That was quite interesting, just watching this explosion and all the dust flying around and smoke. And before you know it I'm thinking, "Okay, I've got four or five guys dead" – and they all get up. It's amazing. You know, I'll put it this way: it seems like we Westerners quantify a fight by how many were killed in action – and we didn't have anyone killed in that fight.

'Lieutenant Maroyka, he got tuned up by some shrapnel. Sergeant Abbott, he had his arm ripped open by shrapnel. Those people were out of the fight, literally, they were just too weak to go on. No fault of their own.'

Sergeant Pete had a decision to make. The terrorists had scored a direct hit and knew their fire line was accurate. Any second yet another mortar would be hurtling through the sky and exploding exactly where the first had tossed the men off their feet like toy soldiers. He had a bunch of wounded soldiers who needed medical attention fast, including a kid who was barely conscious. A piece of shrapnel had pierced through the side of another soldier's Kevlar vest and lodged near his heart.

Sergeant Pete was also out of mortar ammo – having fired all 56 rounds for the 120mm. All he had left were six illumination rounds.

'Why I brought those I have no idea, maybe I was going to throw them at 'em, I don't know,' he says now, somewhat sardonically.

Major Jay Hall, LaCamera's operations officer who had flown in with Peterson on the Chinook, was, at age 41, a Desert Storm veteran who knew how to issue orders in the heat of battle. Hall wanted his sergeant to consolidate his troops in the bowl near where Jock and Clint were making calls back to the Australian headquarters.

'Roger that, Major,' Sergeant Pete said to Hall over the personal two-way radio each soldier had clipped to his webbing.

Peterson told his men to move and those that could do so

under their own steam did. McGovern, who went by the nickname of Crazy K in school, didn't want to get hit again. Ignoring the searing pain in his leg, he got up and ran like hell on his injured foot, leaving a trail of blood behind him.

'So people started hauling arse,' Peterson says. 'We are trying to get everybody out of our location and get them to the bowl. Everybody's gone and all I've got is some of my guys and a couple of guys from Charlie Company and some wounded folks.'

Peterson had to get his men across the open terrain to the relative safety of the bowl, but he was on the reverse slope of Hell's Halfpipe. He set up a perimeter around his troops and got them moving, but al Qaeda was not going soft on the wounded men. They had a mission to kill the American soldiers who dared enter the bear trap.

Direct and indirect fire rained down on Sergeant Pete's men from another position on the hillside.

Holy cow, we're fuckin' surrounded, Peterson thought.

'And these guys had us dead-to-rights because we were right out in the open now,' he says.

A 30-year-old staff sergeant named Randal Perez took over from the injured Maroyka and showed incredible courage – standing up and exposing himself to al Qaeda fighters, and firing at the enemy as the injured soldiers ran for their lives.

Artillery screamed by and once the smoke had cleared another mortar exploded where they had been.

Boom.

The mortar blew up two medical kits that had been left out in the open with the sea of packs, ditched in the first run for cover.

That's not real helpful, Jock thought.

Jock could see the huddle. Injured soldiers were limping towards the bowl, not really sure where they were going. They were dazed and confused and the anaesthetic of shock was starting to take hold.

'Mate, over here. This way,' Jock bellowed through the cacophony of war, gesturing to the halfpipe.

Peterson, a rangy, athletic man who stands about 193 centimetres in bare feet, was struggling with some huge fella wrapped around his shoulder. The soldier wasn't seriously wounded but he had gone into shock. A dead weight.

Charlie Company's field doctor, Major Thomas Byrne, was patching the kid with a shrapnel wound and raced out to help Peterson. The 32-year-old doctor is a small, stout bloke with Coke-bottle glasses who had never seen combat before, but his actions were those of a seasoned war veteran. Jock Wallace was inspired.

Jock recognised the sounds of artillery and saw mortars and RPGs dogging the fleeing soldiers, exploding right behind them. *Bugger this*, he thought.

Jock dropped his radio and without a second's thought for his own safety, bolted into the line of fire. He didn't monkey run, just straight up sprinted to the wounded, not thinking about the hail of bullets cracking across the valley from al Qaeda hot spots. His lungs screamed from a lack of oxygen and he could see AQ popping out of their hiding spots, taking aim and shooting.

Like ferrets on a fuckin' fence, Jock thought.

A wave of pure hate collided with bloody-minded determination as he ran. Like most soldiers in a war, Jock didn't fear injury or death, he just feared letting down his fellow troops.

Whatever it takes!

Jock grabbed one of the soldiers, heaved him over his shoulders and hauled him across open ground and into Hell's Halfpipe, looking up at the ridgeline to check on the enemy, hoping in that split second when everything becomes crystal clear that his compatriots' suppressive fire would save all their lives.

Bullets snapped past his ears but miraculously missed their targets, making a dull *phffft* when they hit the hard clay of the bowl. Some ricocheted off the rocks. But Jock was on a mission to get his soldier brother out of the line of fire to the casualty collection point where the injured were being treated. He was out of breath, his chest heaving, but he managed to lay his wounded patient down gently and safely.

'Thanks, buddy,' said a medic.

'No worries, mate,' Jock replied.

The company's medics, who had worked with the paramedics in New York City after the World Trade Center attacks, had set up an emergency triage section and soldiers were being assessed for treatment. It was a bloody, moaning mess, but nothing the medics couldn't handle.

Jock wiped the blood from his hands onto his camos, grabbed his M4, stood up and raced back into the line of fire to help the last of the wounded to safety. There was no thinking, no worrying – just doing.

'He saw there was a need there to go out and pull some of those guys to safety and dress their wounds. And he put himself in harm's way; under fire he moved out, collected some of these wounded and dragged them back to safety in the ditch they were in,' Lieutenant Colonel Tink would say later.

Someone helped Jock into the last few metres of Hell's Halfpipe, but he didn't stop to exchange names and phone numbers as if it were a civilised car crash. He got down low, monkeyed back to his position and hooked right into his radio to put in a call to the SAS Regimental HQ.

It was near to 10am local time. Staff in the HQ could hear the fire fight coming over Jock's radio, but the commanders in the TOC at Bagram could not see how chaotic it was in the valley because the Predator was still locked on the compound at Sherkhankhel further north. 'We were advised that 25 personnel in black were moving west from a compound, essentially up into high ground where they had earlier shot at the Americans,' Tink says now, referring to the Predator vision.

Jock Wallace couldn't believe that no one had been killed in the torrent of gunfire and kept his eyes on the ridgelines, calmly informing his liaison officer, Clint, when he spied an enemy target, updating the sitrep for the brass at headquarters. It was crucial information, and with other reports coming in from around the valley, it let the commanders know just how far off the mark the intelligence had been about al Qaeda and Taliban numbers in the Shahi Kot.

According to Major General Hagenbeck, Jock's radio work was vital.

'The Aussie SAS soldier there was instrumental because he had direct communications right back to us [via the Regimental HQ] and he, in essence, could talk us through what was actually happening on the ground and give us an even better sense of how the fight was going,' Hagenbeck said.

Sergeant Pete and Sergeant Tommy Oldham were taking fire outside Hell's Halfpipe and bringing their weapons to bear on al Qaeda. Most of the mortar platoon had got to safety, but Sergeant Pete found himself on the back slope of the bowl, receiving indirect fire.

'This is probably where I've said the dumbest thing I've ever said in my life,' Peterson says now, laughing at the memory. 'I crawled to the lip of the bowl, and we're receiving a lot of indirect fire, and I get up on the lip and I can see all my Charlie Company and I can see my commander in their sanctuary. But I still have to run through a hill of fire to get to these guys and here's the dumbest thing I've ever said.

'I yelled out "mortars inbound", meaning we [he and Sergeant Oldham] were inbound. I only wanted them to lay suppressive fire, but everyone in that bowl thought [mortar shells were inbound] and everyone gets down and we come flying over the hill.

'All hell breaks loose and I get to the bottom of the hill and I look at Lieutenant Colonel LaCamera and go, "And here I am." And he goes, "And here you are."

'And I'm like, holy cow: we got there, everyone's alive and all the wounded are in a good location.'

Grippe's right-hand man, Healy, was surprised that the soldiers had managed to get through the morning for so long before any casualties occurred. A seventeen-year veteran, he knew the realities of war.

'I can't explain how or why no one was injured up to that point, because the fire was so intense. But after you've been there for a while you get used to it, so you'd get up and move around and you'd have bullets zinging right by you,' Healy says now. 'But you had to get up and do your job.

'We had some guys that had some pretty good bleeding wounds: arms, legs, facial wounds … The Doc obviously wanted to get them out of there, but the first casualty report made a decision not to send a medevac [helicopter].'

The commanders at Bagram received the first casualty report indicating that several soldiers from Charlie Company were injured, some seriously. None of the injuries, however, was considered life threatening and the highly skilled Army medics had the situation under control. A decision was made to delay sending a medical evacuation chopper until more was known about the enemy numbers, weapons and locations.

The decision was frustrating, but Healy had been in the Army long enough to know that decisions like that had to be made.

'It does really hurt that your guys could die, but you don't want to see them get on the helicopter and it get shot down and kill four more people,' Healy says now. 'It's hard for us but I am sure it's harder for the guys making the decision.'

The decision that they weren't getting out any time soon added to the fear in the halfpipe. But the fear sat well with the thumping adrenaline that kept the young soldiers going. Healy saw that the GIs who had been tossed in at the deep end had a determination and resilience that could only be born of war. Of 'kill or be killed'. The will to survive.

'It was real scary. When you get in a situation like that, when you know you are outnumbered real badly and they've got the high ground, you feel kind of desperate,' Healy says.

'And once you get over that, you're fine. And I think another thing that motivated the [young soldiers] was, like me, whenever I'd see one of our guys get wounded, I'd get so pissed off that I'd want to – not really get even – but make sure the enemy are not going to do that again. Our guys fought like they were veterans. Ninety per cent of them were just amazing.'

CHAPTER 11

*'Lying on your back, looking ten kilometres up
in the air, you can see the B-52s overhead and see the
bombs drop, and you hope you've got more than a
few seconds to live.'*

JOCK WALLACE

Jock grabbed the sleeping bag from his pack and did a
monkey-run over to the casualty collection point, placing it
over one of the more serious casualties from Sergeant Pete's
mortar platoon while medics attended to other wounded soldiers.
They could use the bag more than Jock could. It could ultimately
mean the difference between life and death for those with limbs
torn open, and would stave off hypothermia for the soldiers in
danger of going into shock.

'One guy had shrapnel up the side of his body, cut straight
across the eye, shrapnel chopped his eye in half. He was about
nineteen, a young American kid,' Jock recalls. 'They were just
kids. They were lacking skills and lacking tools but they were not
lacking courage, they certainly were not – they did their best, the
poor little bastards.'

He thought back to last night – a time that seemed so long
ago now – when Colonel Frank Wiercinski had revved up his
troops. Standing next to Wiercinski on the Humvee had been a
chaplain with the US Army, who had led the troops in prayers.
The Ballad of the Green Beret played over the speakers, as did
the anthems for the Rakkasans and the 10th Mountain
Division. Once the final amens were said, the young men and

women of Anaconda who chose to, dispersed to their multi-denominational padres for blessings and last rites.

Those without religion in their lives headed straight to the chow line at the back of the hangar for a feast of crayfish and other delicacies rarely found in an army mess. *Battles came with a different menu*, Jock had noted wryly. It was a repast fit for the Last Supper but the soldiers heading out in the morning didn't think of that then. They were thinking of their stomachs, which had become accustomed to the challenging and mysterious flavours of MREs, otherwise known as Meals Ready to Eat, single-ration combat food. And they were thinking of victory ahead. Jock didn't treat himself because he had had to recode his radio equipment. Plenty of time for a feed later.

By ten o'clock the next morning, after five hours under ambush in the Shahi Kot Valley, Jock wished he'd hoed right in. He rummaged through his all-purpose lightweight individual carrying equipment pack – his ALICE pack. Cold-weather gear, H_2O, equipment to protect his comms gear, and nothing to eat but three lousy cut-down MREs. This was going to be a long day.

Jock was joined by two US Air Force troops whose job was to call in close air support for Charlie Company.

Senior Airman Stephen Achey had been separated from his unit within minutes of alighting from the Chinook and had come under direct fire from al Qaeda. He crouched behind his rucksack, but the rounds found their target. Three bullets tore into his PRC-117F multi-band tactical radio, knocking it out of action. But Achey was determined to live and somehow managed to get out of the open valley floor and into Hell's Halfpipe with another airman, Technical Sergeant Vick McCabe. Armed with his AR-15 rifle, he also braved running into the line of fire to retrieve another radio that had been left in the open. They hooked up with Jock, whose radio was alive. Major bonus.

The men introduced themselves as if they were at a back-yard barbecue at Swannie, not under fire in Afghanistan.

Achey and Vick were members of the Tactical Air Control Party, and were tasked with calling in every asset flying in the sky above, regardless of whether the aircraft were on reconnaissance missions or flying in a holding pattern waiting for a bombing raid. They worked by directly calling the Bossman in the Air Force's E-3 airborne warning-and-control system (AWACS) aircraft who coordinated the joint air power and deployed fighter planes on their individual missions. And on some occasions they were able to call the pilots without the assistance of the Bossman.

Even though they had joined the US Air Force, they spent all their time on the ground with the Army, working side by side with the grunts in the most dangerous of conditions. Achey, who was a bit younger than Jock, and Vick were right at home with their new Aussie mates.

They began radioing in to the Bossman but came up against a hurdle. The frequency bandwidth for the satellite-based communications system used by the Americans had been largely dedicated to the Special Forces who had arrived in-country within days of the September 11 attacks, leaving only a single frequency – or channel – for the forward air controllers to coordinate target bombings close to friendly forces.

'It's like being in an AOL chat room with 36 other people and you're trying to have a conversation with one person,' an air officer would later tell Elaine Grossman of InsideDefense.com.

'Can you get us CAS, any way you can?' Achey asked Jock, who started to call the Bossman on a different frequency.

No joy. But Jock didn't give up. *Failure under fire was not a fuckin' option*, he thought.

Jock could see that al Qaeda had pinpointed the casualty collection point and begun walking fire in on Hell's Halfpipe. Things were not looking good. *The bastards*, he thought.

Jock tried a different tactic and radioed the Regimental Headquarters. Clear as a bell.

You beauty. Jock's radio was a lifeline. He had a direct link back to his HQ and it rarely went down. The information was subsequently filtered and calls for CAS were radioed to US pilots in the region who flew in to send a rain of fire down onto enemy targets.

'One Oscar this is Niner Charlie,' Jock said. 'Over.'

Clint was beside him, writing up a sitrep in his notebook.

'One Oscar, over,' came the reply from one of Jock's fellow chooks back at the HQ.

'We are getting smashed by mortars. We need CAS. Over.'

It was tough getting messages out over the radio because the battlefield was loud and soldiers were running around, yelling and answering calls for fire, helping their brothers in arms.

'There was a lot of noise and tension, pandemonium – not pandemonium as in people freaking out – but people trying to do the right thing, people trying to see something that needed to be done, screaming it out,' Jock says now.

His fellow chooks at HQ could hear the gunfire. Al Qaeda were ripping mortars along the front and sides of Hell's Halfpipe where the men were huddled. Shells exploded all around. For those on the ground the noise was earsplitting, and explosions reverberated through the troopers' bodies.

'One Oscar, this is Niner Charlie, over,' Jock said again, as calm as ever. 'We are being bracketed. We need CAS urgently.

'We have just taken multiple casualties. We can't move from our position. We need it now or you won't be speaking to us in a minute. Over.'

The next voice Jock heard was that of the squadron's commander, Major Dan McDaniel.

'What kind of CAS? Over.'

'Any kind. Over,' Jock said.

Jock says now: 'I don't want a tick in the box for calls for fire, I want an aeroplane that drops bombs. But we got the plane eventually. That was a pretty hairy moment.'

Senior Airman Achey was on the radio and in the middle of attempting to call a B-52 when his signal went down. He looked at Jock who instantly opened a line of communication. Achey jumped on Jock's radio, giving the location of the al Qaeda targets on the eastern ridgeline for another run. Pure synchronicity.

But the wrong grid references were being read back. Clint, with eyes like a hawk and ears like a bat, abruptly and with authority cut into the transmission.

'Wrong coordinates,' he bellowed quickly and clearly, correcting the references.

Clint asked for a read-back to make absolutely sure they were right the second time around. They were.

'Roger. Out.'

Clint had averted a potentially fatal error. Given the circumstances of the full-blown battle, it was nothing short of a miracle, not to mention a sterling example of soldiering. Had Clint not been as alert as he was, a bomb would have taken out the entire company in Hell's Halfpipe.

You can always rely on Clint to get it right, Jock thought, well pleased that he wasn't the lone Aussie out there.

Jock and Achey were putting in call after call for CAS when they got the alert that CAS was inbound. The American AWACS radioed Achey telling him they had a B-52 in the air. It was manna from heaven, loaded as it was with Mark 82 bombs and JDAMs – the joint direct attack munitions bombs that could wipe out a small village in one fell swoop.

The B-52 was twenty minutes away. Jock hoped it was on course. He was looking through his binoculars, searching the sky for the plane when it came into view.

'Lying on your back, looking ten kilometres up in the air, you can see the B-52s overhead and see the bombs drop, and you hope you've got more than a few seconds to live,' he says now.

Jock was looking up and watched as the bomb bay doors of the B-52 opened. *Bombs away*, he thought, knowing it wouldn't be long before he found out if the deadly delivery would find its mark on the eastern ridge about 400 metres away.

'Everyone was holding their breath. It's a very tense moment from bombs away to explosion,' Jock says now.

Jock put his head down in the dirt and covered his ears, waiting for the bomb.

Boom.

A sonic boom reverberated throughout the valley sending shockwaves through the soldiers' bodies as the ordnance found its target and obliterated al Qaeda bunkers and weaponry.

You bloody little beauty, Jock thought. *That'll teach you to fuck with us.*

'You are feeling shockwaves from the RPGs and mortars, and from your own air strikes going in – the big shockwaves from when the B-52s drop their guts. Every molecule of your body moves, every single atom is hit by the shockwaves – the sound. First you see the light, the vision, then the shockwaves, the sounds, and then the shrapnel snivels in overhead.'

Jock kept his head down as shrapnel tore through the air just centimetres away – another potentially fatal moment. About ten seconds later, he looked up and saw that a shard of hot metal had landed about half a metre away from him over the lip of the halfpipe. He reached out and grabbed it, burning his hand in the process. He wanted it as a souvenir, a reminder of the awesome power of the B-52 and the accuracy of the pilots and bombers overhead.

'I thought, "You're mine." I keep it with my medals,' Jock says now.

'It's a comforting feeling, once you know that they can drop a bomb from that height. You know those guys are backing you up. It was pleasing that they were that accurate. It was a helluva bang. There was nothing else all day that was as big as that.'

It was all over in a couple of minutes.

Soldier on, Jock thought.

The bombing was unequivocal, but it didn't stop the hail of ordnance from other enemy positions in the valley and more AQ would filter in.

Doc Byrne was trying to get round to the back of the halfpipe where the most seriously wounded had been taken. The medics had done all they could for the kid with the shrapnel chest wound who now needed more specialised treatment. The Doc was trying to navigate a steep gradient about five metres high to reach him.

Referring to the Doc, Jock says with a laugh: 'He's not in the best shape physically, he's a little bit older, with thick glasses and a big mouth that I'd previously encountered. He just grabbed his bag and started running up the hill with his escort who had come to get him, and the ground just started dancing all around him.'

'Get down, Doc,' the soldiers yelled at him.

Jock watched as the Doc made another three attempts to get over the rise but he kept getting shot at and had to scramble down.

Grippe was watching, full of awe and respect, for the Doc was as brave as any of the war-scarred grunts in the halfpipe.

Grippe stood up, typically ignoring the lethal rain of ordnance, and began walking down the bowl again.

'Give me suppressive fire up on the hill,' he hollered at his troops.

Jock recalls: 'Everyone just jumped up and started shooting shit out of the eastern ridge, which was great. Got the doctor over, saved that guy's life, but chewed up a hell of a lot of ammo at the same time.'

Twenty-year-old Private First Class Jason Ashline from the 120mm mortar platoon was lying prone on the dirt providing security when the order to shoot reached him. As he lifted himself up on his left knee, he got hammered by a hail of bullets and was knocked flat on his back.

'I really wasn't thinking at that point,' Ashline recalls. 'I thought I was injured, but it didn't hurt. It just felt like someone smacked me really hard in the chest with a baseball bat. I remember feeling a lot of pressure and that kind of threw me off balance. I didn't really feel anything and everything went really quiet and I remember lying there and I looked at the sky and snapped back to it.'

Ashline was lucky. His bulletproof vest had saved him and while mortar rounds had injured some of the Americans, the al Qaeda bullets didn't have the power to puncture the Kevlar lining provided by Uncle Sam. Two bullets lodged in the front of Ashline's vest, about three centimetres from the edge. Ashline said a quick prayer of thanks to his Lord and then got back to work.

After the battle, he claimed the vest as a lucky charm and keeps it on his dresser alongside pictures of his two children. But Uncle Sam made him pay the cost of it!

Jock and Clint continued calling in sitreps to the SAS HQ, and the information was passed through the chain of command to Lieutenant Colonel Tink in the TOC at Bagram and ultimately on to Anaconda's overall boss, Major General Hagenbeck.

Jock had detailed at least two Priority One casualties, meaning that unless the wounded were evacuated as soon as possible, they could die. Battle statistics paint a grim picture of wounded in combat. On average, one out of every four soldiers injured in the line of duty will die. Combat commanders know the statistics and those at HQ knew that the all-important so-called 'magic hour' had long passed. The magic hour is the first hour after a soldier has been hit. If a seriously injured casualty makes it from the battlefield to the operating table in those crucial 60 minutes, his or her chances of survival are exponentially higher than if they don't. But the men in the Shahi Kot had already been bleeding for more than an hour, and they would be lying out there all day.

Jock's sitrep also included several Priority Two and Three casualties which, while less severe than the Priority Ones, were serious.

Jock's stoicism on the radio was noted in the ops tent and his and Clint's actions would be commented on by the Commander of Special Operations, Brigadier Duncan Lewis, days later in Australia.

Out in the field, Jock distinguished himself with his ingenuity.

He had a Special Operations Group Babyseal knife, about 30 centimetres long, and began digging a trench in the clay in which to lie, out of the line of fire. Unfortunately, Clint had left his small hand shovel back at base and started to dig in with his bare hands, promising himself never to forget his entrenching tool again.

Eventually, Clint's hole would be big enough to fit three men. It was backbreaking work because they had to dig where they were lying. If they stood up, they'd get shot. *It's fucking hard to dig a hole you're lying in*, Jock thought to himself.

Some of the Americans were surprised, but the Aussies' SAS training was superior to that of the grunts in the US infantry and they understood that a soldier in a battlefield stood a better chance of survival if below ground level. So they dug. They didn't get the name 'diggers' for nothing.

Known as diggers' graves or shell scrapes, the trenches would be life-savers later in the day.

CHAPTER 12

Shortly after 11am, an F-15 roared overhead on a bombing run and a blinding light erupted from the ridgeline. A Stinger missile had been launched and was chasing the fighter plane.

When the Soviet Union's 40th Army delivered its highly trained airborne troops and Spetsnaz commandos to the Afghan capital, Kabul, on Christmas Eve in 1979, it also delivered a sense of unity to the fiercely independent people in the fractious landlocked nation. Afghanistan has long been a geopolitical prize sought after by empire builders, for it provided the one thing that growing nations desire and need: trade routes. Afghanistan had them running to the east and west and therefore serving the rich economies of Europe, the Middle East and central Asia.

As such, the rugged, remote country, nestled in the heart of central Asia just above the 30th parallel, has had a long history of war dating back to at least the sixth century BC, when it was part of the Persian Achaemenid Empire. A series of conquering forces subsequently claimed the forbidding landscape that for a time had been ruled by Alexander the Great and for hundreds of years thereafter was divided, back and forth, between the Persian and Indian empires, until the nineteenth century when the British arrived. And so began another struggle for dominance in central Asia, this time between Imperial Russia and Britain, then one of the most powerful colonisers in the world. The battle would lead to the subsequent creation of

Afghanistan proper. By then, Islam had been the country's religion for more than a thousand years.

The internal politics of modern Afghanistan has echoed the region's history and been marked by bloody coups, insurgencies and takeovers. The country is a complex mosaic, with bitter and enduring tribal, clan, family, ethnic, religious and feudal rivalries that are as much a result of thousands of years of invasions as they are ancient blood feuds and enmities. Known as *badal*, the Pashto word for vengeance, the feuds are treated as if they are new battles to be fought and won, whatever the provocation. 'The Afghan will never turn the other cheek,' writes Mohammad Yousaf in *Afghanistan, the Bear Trap*, noting that a killing must always be avenged.

Afghanistan is a country in which homage has long been paid to the tribal warlords or village elders, and clan is everything. Traders, subsistence farmers, shepherds who herd goats and sheep in the high country or desert plains, all pay fealty to the local chieftain.

The official language of Afghanistan is Dari, also known as Farsi, and about half the population speak various dialects of the Persian language. Almost as many speak Pashto, the native tongue of the Pashtuns, who are the dominant ethnic group in the country and come from the Durrani tribe in the south or the Ghilzai tribe in the east.

Ethnic Uzbeks, Tajiks, Turkmen and Shi'ite Hazara make up the rest of the population. Effectively, Afghanistan comprises five quite distinct nations within its borders and five very distinct peoples. Some are nomadic, while others are urban.

The repressive Taliban regime, which seized control of Kabul in 1996 under the leadership of the one-eyed Mullah Mohammed Omar, was mostly ethnic Pashtun. Its fierce opposition, the Northern Alliance, consisted of Uzbeks, Tajiks, Turkmen and Hazara. According to the anonymous author of *Hunting al Qaeda*, the Pashtun warlords are most interested in their own personal power and wealth. 'If it's advantageous for them to support the Americans they will, but if it looks like the Taliban is winning, you'll see a lot of people who had just vowed to fight them to the death switch sides in a blink of an eye. Pashtun warlords have spent the last 25 years of civil war betraying each other on a daily basis.'

Geographically and physically, Afghanistan is a breathtakingly beautiful place. Dominated by the Hindu Kush mountain range, it is often the victim of violent earthquakes and both floods and droughts. Smaller than the Australian state of New South Wales and almost as big as the American state of Texas, the Afghan landscape is vast and varied, from spectacular mountains snowcapped all year through to high-altitude desert regions that change with the winds and shifting sands.

It shares borders with six countries. Pakistan runs along the eastern and southern sides of Afghanistan for 2430 kilometres, while China shares 76 kilometres of an almost unnavigable peninsula of land known as the Varkhan Corridor in the far northeast. Iran is on the west, and to the north are Turkmenistan, Uzbekistan and Tajikistan.

Just as the locals have remained independent of each other, so have they remained defiantly independent of the succession of governments in Kabul.

Despite its tumultuous history, Afghanistan had in its own way been functional. Surprisingly, the country refused to choose sides during the Cold War and was blessed with aid and friendship from its neighbour the Soviet Union and, to a lesser extent, the United States – a continent and an ocean away. Both wanted to dominate the strategically located Afghanistan, which by the end of the 1970s was ruled by a struggling communist government.

But things changed when the Red Army stormed into Afghanistan. A common purpose united the disparate people, who answered the call to jihad – holy struggle – and fought the invading forces with a ferocity for which they'd become known throughout history. They called themselves 'mujahideen', or 'soldiers of God', and the soldiers of the Red Army in turn called them *dukhi* or *dushman* – ghosts or bandits – for their fierceness and ability to disappear into the mountains. Their battle cry was, as it had ever been, 'Allahu Akbar', God is great.

Physical courage is central to the Afghan character and to be without courage is considered abhorrent. People without courage were despised, according to Mohammad Yousaf, a Pakistan Army brigadier who witnessed the Afghan spirit while coordinating mujahideen operations against the Soviets in the early to mid 1980s.

A month after the invasion, a Soviet reporter, Gennady Bocharov, was holed up in a hotel in Kabul when the mujahideen leaders put on a terrifying show of psychological warfare against the Soviets. As recounted in George Crile's compelling book *Charlie Wilson's War*, a turbaned elder in Kabul sounded out a cry that was picked up by thousands of Muslim faithful.

Allahu Akbar, he sang as dusk settled on the capital, God is great.

A rising crescendo of *Allahu Akbar, Allahu Akbar* echoed across the city in response, from men and women alike. It was soon joined by *Marg, marg, marg bar Shurawi* – death to Soviets, death, death, death.

'Each of us knew that the fanatics take their time about killing you,' Bocharov reported, his terror writ large. 'We knew that the first thing they do is pierce your forearms with knives. Then they hack off your ears, your fingers, your genitals, put out your eyes.'

It took a certain kind of courage to be so brutal, and the Afghan people were renowned for it.

Jock Wallace was a keen student of history and had a scholar's thirst for knowledge about the places the Australian Army had taken him. An avid reader, he knew something of Afghanistan's past and had paid close attention to the traditions and tactics of the mujahideen, who had been hailed at home and in the West as heroes and anti-Soviet crusaders during the long war. *Ironic, given the circumstances now*, he thought.

The Soviet invasion in 1979 was seen through the prism of the Cold War, and immediately extended beyond its country's borders.

The American president who witnessed the global creep of Soviet communism, a Democrat and former peanut farmer from

Georgia named Jimmy Carter, declared the Soviet invasion of Afghanistan 'the greatest foreign policy crisis confronting the United States since World War II'. President Carter subsequently authorised the Central Intelligence Agency to take action against the Soviets' 40th Army.

As a result, the tribal chieftains and warlords who led the mujahideen became the beneficiaries of covert arms and money from the CIA, as well as from a few other anti-communist nations with geopolitical interests in the primitive but resource-rich Afghanistan. CIA spooks funnelled billions of dollars' worth of weapons into the country to arm the freedom fighters in their war against the Soviets, initially via Pakistan, whose government lent to the cause the efforts of its formidable intelligence service.

Satellite intelligence maps, anti-tank guns, thousands of the Czech- or Russian-made DShK machine guns, which the mujahideen called the '20 shooter', and thousands of surface-to-air (SAM) Stinger missiles originally built for the US infantry, were smuggled over Afghanistan's six borders. The arsenal arrived the old-fashioned way, on the backs of camels and donkeys, or hidden in rickety trucks that rolled along a highway known as the Salang Pass. In another twist, the Russians had built the highway during their years of neighbourly friendship with Afghanistan. It was an impressive engineering accomplishment and featured a 3.2-kilometre tunnel cut through the Hindu Kush, granting access through the difficult mountainous terrain.

The mountains belonged to the mujahideen and those who came before them. Over hundreds of years, they had carved a labyrinth of caves in the cliff faces, which provided refuge to the freedom fighters during the brutal winter months and a hiding place from enemy forces.

By 2000, with Afghanistan under fundamentalist Taliban rule, the caves would be taken over by al Qaeda and used by Osama bin Laden, who had moved to Afghanistan after being expelled from Sudan in 1996.

There were about 100 caves on the eastern ridgeline above the

Shahi Kot Valley, with dozens directly overlooking the 10th Mountain's position. Hidden by concealed entrances, the interconnected caves had been tunnelled deep into the mountains and ranged in height from one to several metres, and were up to 30 metres deep. Many had been reinforced with concrete for added protection against the Soviets' powerful birds of prey, the MIG fighter planes.

After al Qaeda moved in, they positioned mirrors on bends in the tunnels to reflect sunlight to the deepest corners of the caves.

With the collapse of the Taliban, the conquering coalition forces and their Afghan partners swept through the caves, uncovering cache after cache of weapons and munitions. Each new discovery revealed a treasure trove worthy of Aladdin's Cave and gave a fuller understanding of al Qaeda's operations.

The terrorists had stockpiled, by the tonne, mortars, cannons, RPGs, Soviet- and US-made Manpad and anti-aircraft missiles, and AK-47 ammunition. Mortar base plates had been cemented in, allowing al Qaeda fighters to easily move mortars in and out of the caves on tracks, while ducking for cover from the coalition fighter planes swooping in for a bombing raid. Among the ordnance, US soldiers and SAS troopers found cell phones and bomb-making manuals with detailed descriptions of the most effective methods to attack people and vehicles and to destroy bridges.

Some caves had been lavishly carpeted and decked out with comfortable bedding, all of which was illuminated by hanging light bulbs powered by solar energy panels set up at the cave entrances. Walls were covered with dog-eared pictures of the world's most wanted man, and the terrorists' hero, Osama bin Laden. Soldiers found other necessities for long-term living, including food supplies, bags of wheat flour, wood-fired stoves for heating and cooking, water, punching bags, foreign passports, and makeshift intravenous fluids bags and racks on which to hang them for medical emergencies.

A former CIA chief who covered the region, Milt Bearden, would later tell *The Los Angeles Times* newspaper that the valley 'was always the last redoubt [for al Qaeda]. When all else failed, guys would fall back to there. It really is the home-field advantage drawn out to some exponential degree. There's not a square kilometre that hasn't been used for an ambush of somebody.'

Jock Wallace looked up at ridgelines that concealed al Qaeda and Taliban sniper and machine-gun hides and artillery posts and was aware of the bitterest of ironies. Charlie Company was being attacked not only by weapons provided by the Soviets, but also by those provided by the Americans to the mujahideen *dukhi*, to fight the Soviets.

Once upon a time the mujahideen had been the United States' close friend in fighting the Soviets, and now many of them had become its most vehement enemy.

The enemy had the soldiers surrounded and, as Bearden said, they were capably exploiting every nook and cranny of the valley and mountains.

Fortunately, the men in Hell's Halfpipe had support – albeit disappointingly occasional – from the skies above. The responses to calls for CAS had been sporadic and often came after long delays, as fighter planes and bombers flew in stacks at different altitudes, unloading strings of bombs and missiles on the AQ hotspots, called in by Jock, Vick, Achey and other soldiers in the valley.

The B-52s were stacked the highest and therefore were safest from the enemy. The fast movers – the F/A-18s, F-16s, F-15Es, F-14s and the Marines' AV-8 Harrier vertical takeoff jets – flew lower and, while they had the advantage of terrifying speed and even more terrifying 21st-century weaponry, they had a major vulnerability – the SAM, or surface-to-air missile.

Jock wondered whether the enemy in the valley had managed to import the missiles. The CIA had given the mujahideen up to 2500 heat-seeking Stinger missiles during its ten-year-long munificence. In the following decade, as the political landscape of Afghanistan changed, the CIA began an ambitious program to buy them back, offering between US$80 000 and $150 000 per missile.

The program was first authorised by President George Bush Snr and re-endorsed by his successor Bill Clinton, but it had largely failed. By 1996, about 600 of the missiles were known to be in circulation. The warlords and local Afghan commanders were not giving up their weapons easily. By then the ruling authority in Afghanistan was the repressive Taliban, yet another virulent enemy of the West and a regime that provided safe harbour to Osama bin Laden and his terrorist training camps, and the US commanders had no way of knowing if they had secured any of the circulating SAMs.

Soon after Jock had arrived at the US Marines' forward operating base at Camp Rhino in southern Afghanistan the previous December, two shoulder-fired Stingers had been targeted at US warplanes. It gave the air component command full warning that air support was vulnerable to attack from the Stinger.

So far that morning, the terrorists had unleashed a mother lode of weaponry and Jock was thinking al Qaeda would be just as likely to have the odd SAM stashed away in a bunker. *Sneaky bastards had everything else*, he thought. In fact, they even had the ubiquitous Garmin global positioning system (GPS) equipment and Northface tents and parkas, as had been discovered earlier that morning by the Mako Three One patrol.

'In case anyone was guessing as to whether they did or didn't have SAMs on site, it was soon confirmed about mid-morning,' Jock recalls now.

Shortly after 11am, an F-15 roared overhead on a bombing run and a blinding light erupted from the ridgeline. A Stinger missile had been launched and was chasing the fighter plane. Forward air controller Stephen Achey radioed the pilot who instantly took evasive action and corkscrewed his aircraft straight up, throwing 'chaff' as the missile followed in a similar corkscrewing manoeuvre.

From their position further north in the bowl, Grippe and LaCamera were watching in awe at the pilot's skill in outrunning the SAM.

'What the hell is that?' LaCamera said out loud, before answering his own question. 'That's a surface-to-air missile,' he exclaimed as the SAM chased the fast mover.

The pilot's counter-manoeuvres saw the plane spiral higher and higher, straight up in the sky, while his 'chaff' counter-measures hit the missile, detonating it in a shower of flames and smoke.

'That made it very hard to get air [support] after that,' Jock says.

By then, the fast movers had unleashed a string of 27 MK-82 weapons set for airbursts, the better to attack enemy firing positions and troops in the open. Several fighter planes had also launched more precision-fired JDAMs, which ripped into targets, blowing them to pieces.

Forward air controllers called in CAS non-stop, some of which was answered. According to a US Air Force report on Operation Anaconda published in 2005, *Operation Anaconda, An Air Power Perspective*, a B-1 bomber dropped several JDAMs on the ridgeline where al Qaeda had been pinpointed. The bomber immediately responded to another call for CAS from soldiers on the valley floor who had located an al Qaeda lair, onto which the bomber fired several more.

Between 10am and 12.30pm, a total of 25 JDAMs were fired in Operation Anaconda. *Boom, boom, boom.*

Jock felt every bomb. Each explosion felt like a charge had gone off inside him. He just hoped like hell the SAS patrols were in the clear, especially after Vick had finished explaining the finer points of the JDAM to Jock; how they never go off target. Vick told a good story and his new Aussie mate was convinced.

'The JDAM is a 2000 pounder that's been modified. It was produced around World War II, and instead of throwing them away, they built a computerised, motorised tail fin [that] bolts on the old back and guides them in on target,' Jock says. 'Supposedly, JDAMs never go off course and if they do, won't detonate. They are meant to be harmless to us.'

Jock saw a plane overhead and knew it would be searching out its targets on the high-tech electronic system in the belly of the beast. He waited, nervously, and watched in disbelief as a JDAM soared over the hill near them.

Jock looked over at Frank Grippe.

'Have you guys got men over there?' he said. 'A bloody JDAM just landed over there. You better check if they're alright.'

The JDAM had landed not far from where Sergeant Pete's mortar platoon had been before they got taken out earlier.

Again, fortune smiled on the men in the Shahi Kot Valley, and no one was injured. The bomb did not detonate. God only knows why, but no one was asking God.

The bombing runs didn't stop the enemy and the soldiers were still under fire. It felt to Jock as if there were at least a thousand al Qaeda and Taliban hidden throughout the virtually impenetrable mountain ridgelines and in the caves and villages in the valley.

As soon as the planes had gone, AQ and Taliban fighters emerged from cover and began firing. The fast movers were gone before they could be called back and the troops on the ground knew there would be a long wait before the next lot arrived.

'The fast movers didn't stay over target long enough, that was the problem,' Jock says.

But they couldn't. The constricted theatre of operations – eight nautical miles by eight nautical miles – didn't help. The fast movers simply did not have the manoeuvrability of the Apache gunships.

The problems with the CAS were later acknowledged by the Air Force.

'The unexpected demand for close air support coupled with the deficiencies of the theatre air control system was a jolt,' wrote Dr Rebecca Grant in the US Air Force report that documented the lessons learned from Operation Anaconda. 'With the tight airspace crowding aircraft closer together than ever before, many of the aircrews had hair-raising stories to tell about near misses. Others ran out of time while the aircraft ahead of them worked targets.'

The objective language of the report did not mirror the reality of war for Jock Wallace, although the words 'hair-raising stories' gave a hint.

Injured soldiers were moaning in Hell's Halfpipe. The Americans' ammunition was running low. Al Qaeda had employed the mujahideen tactic of attack-and-take-cover to great effect. And all landing zones in the valley, including those further north, were under intense fire. In between bursts of digging in, Jock manned the radio. He was not aware if any plan to relieve them was forthcoming. Not yet.

'By lunchtime, the casualties are starting to mount, the Americans have got no idea, nobody's going anywhere,' Jock says now. 'There's no plan to get out of there, we can't even get the wounded out ... I've got my best-case scenario [which is] we all get out of here alive. Or at least *I* do, at the bare minimum, and I'll get as many of you out as I can.'

A pragmatist by nature, Jock wasn't kidding himself or bolstering his confidence with false hope. *You can't bullshit a bullshitter*, he thought.

He had spent nearly six hours in the valley now and somehow he was still drawing breath. Eight men had been injured and were out of action. He couldn't explain it. Despite being deeply irreligious, Jock began thinking that maybe, just possibly, it wasn't his time to die.

'Slowly, this idea started coming into my head that somehow or somewhere there was something there protecting me,' he says. 'When I say protecting me, that's only for want of a better word. There was something else, there was some force or something on that battlefield that was a governing or guiding hand. I liken it to fate, as in fate was standing there tossing the dice on the people who were there. You saw people side by side – one would walk away, one would go down. Why was it that one, why wasn't it the other one? Why was one lying in the bottom of a trench, when another was getting belted by shrapnel? Just to test us, I suppose.

'I'm pretty sure that, on the day, there was this thing that came over me ... I still don't attribute it to a god, but more a chakra or karma, perhaps; even the Buddhists have it as reaching an epiphany or enlightenment. [But I] don't know that those magic mushrooms exist.'

Signalman Wallace knew what was going on. Command Sergeant Major Frank Grippe was in constant communication with Jock's liaison officer, Clint, and Jock was passing the information back to the SAS HQ.

Grippe was an optimist and believed wholeheartedly in the ability of his boys and the staying power of the 10th Mountain Division. And he was also counting on the Command's strategy. 'We had about 125 people, 85 or so in our position, 45 or so just to the north, just a couple of clicks away,' Grippe says now, recalling the manpower in their part of the Shahi Kot Valley.

'We had another blocking position set up. Some of our scouts – you know, hunter-killer teams – were out and about by themselves just gun-fighting with all these al Qaeda. And then another platoon had set up a blocking position on a small canyon out in the hills and they whacked a whole bunch of people that day. They got a watch on Marzak and they were sniping people in Marzak, putting machine-gun fire into Marzak.

'There were a lot of close-in fights, a lot of long-range shooting going on. I saw my guys shoot guys at 500 metres and knock [the enemy] over, which I know surprised the hell out of the al Qaeda when they were off in the distance like that. All of a sudden, *bang*, then you hear a snap and the knucklehead bodies are down.'

After all, Grippe believed in the 10th Mountain's motto, 'To the Top'. Nothing was going to stop his men.

CHAPTER 13

'I've got a 5.56mm fully automatic M4 and a 9mm
pistol on my belt, and a killer stare in my eyes.'

JOCK WALLACE

It was lunchtime in Hell's Halfpipe and the only thing delivered was four JDAMs, courtesy of the US military. From his position Jock had no idea what or who had been taken out, but the fiery explosion and cloud of smoke that billowed into the sky rose higher than the towering mountains, and that gave him an immense feeling of satisfaction. But it didn't ease his hunger. Jock hadn't had a good feed for 24 hours, having missed the Last Supper spread of lobster and lasagne the night before.

His ALICE pack held three days' worth of cut-down rations – Meals Ready to Eat – and ten litres of water. The ciggies, which eased an appetite and quelled the nerves earlier, were gone. Stock depleted. Despite a gnawing feeling in his gut, Jock didn't feel like tucking in. He wasn't a finicky eater. He'd dig into just about anything as long as it wasn't rancid, didn't move, and didn't look like it had an experimental scientific project growing out of it. Years in the Army had taught him to dull his palate and heighten his imagination. MREs were not known for their culinary virtuosity.

Besides, Jock figured that the way the fighting was going – to hell in a handbasket and fast – he could be stuck in the valley for days. His rations would have to last and he'd need them at night, when the temperature nosedived to below freezing and energy was at a premium. And there was too much going on to take time out for a feed. Jock couldn't quite work out how to hop into an MRE while digging in, manning the radio and calling in CAS and sitreps – *Where are your manners, son, didn't your mother teach you not to speak with your mouth full?* – and keeping an eye on the surrounding ridgelines for enemy on the move. It also seemed somewhat callous, perverse even, for him to be chowing down while the bloodied and wounded moaned right beside him, with bullets zinging by and mortars and RPGs howling overhead.

Some of the wounded who had been seen by the Doc and were in a stable condition had been moved from the casualty collection point and were lying a few metres away from Jock. They were in a dried-out creek bed that, over time, had cut into the earth and was the lowest – and therefore safest – part of the halfpipe. Their wounds had been bandaged and some had been pumped with morphine to mask their pain. Other soldiers spread out along the sides of the bowl, taking up firing positions, laying down preventive cover as they maintained a vigilant watch over their stricken comrades, while checking for al Qaeda and Taliban snipers and mortars. The way Jock saw it, there was too much going on to take a lunch break or step outside, so to speak, for a ten-minute breather.

Yeah, ya insensitive bastard, real nice time for a smoko, he thought.

The last time Jock had really enjoyed an MRE was a few weeks earlier: Menu No. 7, Chicken with Salsa. Almost as wide and long as a sheet of A4 paper and about five centimetres thick, MRE meals are packed with a miniature bottle of Tabasco sauce and disposable moist hand-wipes for hygiene. And they are sealed in a brown plastic wrapper stamped with the improbable warning, 'US Government property. Commercial resale is unlawful'.

Jock always got a laugh out of the jumped-up caution. Who in their right mind would want to resell an MRE? Jock hadn't actually removed the chicken with salsa from its packaging, nor had he tasted it, but he had used the wrapper to write a line to his mum back home using thick black smudge-proof Texta. She'd love his ingenuity.

> Hello Mother,
> Ran out of paper here so I'm using my initiative. Happy N Year 2 U. Have you been paying my credit card? Hope so.

As if he'd be belting the plastic in a war zone. His mother would appreciate the irony. His note went on:

> Hope you are well. I am fine. Not sure how much work we have left here, but sounds as if Bougainville & the Philippines are about to go off. Had the last 2 days back in base camp – nice, good rest, food, warmth, etc. Spoke to you yesterday. It's good to be the patrol sig. Not really meant to test the phone in that manner, but hey, what are they going to do? Send me to war – ha, ha. Go to a net cafe, they will show you how to send me a message, okay. Cheap, instant and a lot easier for me to use compared to voice calls. U can even contact me in the field.
> Love 2 U,
> Take care,
> Martin

Funny how things go in war, he thought.

The last truly decent feed Jock had had was weeks earlier at FOB Kandahar, where he had noticed a group of Afghans hanging around outside the perimeter of the compound. The rugged-up locals were as curious about the allied forces as Jock was about them.

Dozens of Afghans with connections to the ruling clans – including many of those in the recently installed temporary government under Hamid Karzai – had been given jobs on the base cleaning out the latrines. It was putrid work but they were getting paid handsomely for it – as much as US$100 a day, which was more than they had been earning under the Taliban. Groups of about ten locals were escorted on and off base by armed soldiers in the course of doing the dirty work.

They also brought with them a wide social circle. Jock suspected there would be a few among them who still had a strong allegiance to the ousted Taliban and al Qaeda fighters, and so did the brass, hence the armed escort. But they did not seem overtly threatening – they were unarmed and smiling most of the time. The children, particularly, hung around hoping for a bit of American largesse, grabbing a soldier and posing for photographs and asking for candy. Jock didn't really trust the adults – *well, this is a war and they are Afghans*, he reasoned – but it didn't stop him making the most of their hospitality.

The locals weren't afraid of the coalition war effort. Quite the contrary; they'd decided to exploit it as much for their own commercial gain as for anything else, and if they could make a quick buck cleaning the crappers, then so be it.

Aged mud huts across the road from the old Kandahar airport had been turned into a makeshift kitchen for the Afghans, complete with barbecuing facilities. The Afghans set up huge aluminium pots on burning wooden piles over which they cooked rice pilaf, and stewed vegetables with chicken and tomato and *nan*, the unleavened bread, a staple of the Afghan diet.

At lunchtime, the men were escorted by American soldiers onto the base and into a carpark at the front of the airport terminal where they rolled out long mats. The cooks dragged the pots of steaming food to the gate where the food was loaded on a Humvee and driven the hundred metres to the mats. It was a bigger, badder version of meals on wheels.

Lines of Afghan men and young boys shuffled into place, sitting cross-legged on the ground, shoulder to shoulder, while a couple of Afghans walked behind them throwing pieces of *nan* onto the carpet in front of them, followed by small bowls of rice and stew. With a solicitous bow and a generous sweep of the arm motioning them to sit if they were not already, kitchen staff welcomed whoever chose to dine with them, including the uniformed and heavily armed soldiers who worked inside the security fence.

Jock dubbed the daily ritual the 'muj feed' and noted that the happy social atmosphere contrasted with the wartime backdrop of Hercules, Chinooks, Apaches and Black Hawks thundering down the nearby runway. It didn't seem to matter to the locals. Jock put it down to the ever-present inconsistencies and surprises of war, not to mention the fact that the Afghans had been living with civil war for the better part of three decades. They had got used to the *snap*, *crack* and *boom* of bullets and bombs. And they had long lived in terror of the lethal firepower of the Soviet's MI-24 Hind helicopter gunship that the mujahideen had dubbed the 'devil's chariot'. In contrast, the sight of a non-firing Apache gunship coming and going was benign. At least there on base.

'The muj feed was pretty popular with me and Ando, the SAS's water operations man. We worked it out after the first couple of days ... you could sit down and have a feed there and then all the Yanks worked it out as well. That sort of style of cooking is not uncommon in that they [Afghans] all do bulk feeds. There's no snacks or little yoghurts or individual portions,' Jock says.

'You just go and if the mats are there, sit down, and they start filling up. Once they say "Sit down", you had to get in quick and jockey for position. If you came in late, you'd just tap them on the shoulder and they'd squeeze around.

'You just smile, "Thanks, mate." You could say anything you want to them.'

Even though Jock was suspicious of the Afghans outside the base perimeter, he didn't feel any danger once they were inside. They were under escort the entire time. And Jock was locked and loaded with his superior and ubiquitous firepower. It was his American Express card. Jock never left home without it. And he was also with Ando, who was as tough as they come.

'I've got a 5.56mm fully automatic M4 and a 9mm pistol on my belt, and a killer stare in my eyes,' Jock says. 'They didn't ask for any money, but they wouldn't anyway. They were getting paid handsomely by the Americans. That was a good deal for them and they probably never had it better in their lives. Christ knows what their jobs were before that, but monetarily I would say they were remunerated quite substantially and there was talk of $100 a day – which is shit-loads for them.'

Shit-loads for shit loads.

Jock also didn't give a damn about the possibility that he was breaching any official protocols by fraternising with the locals. The Aussies were nothing if not anti-authoritarian and Jock, particularly, was nothing if not an amateur anthropological adventurer.

'It's easier to ask for forgiveness than ask for permission,' Jock says now, chuckling. 'Telling Ando to do something? I don't think so. They [the Command] are more likely to deny a request like that because they can't be bothered looking into whether it's feasible.'

It was 12.13pm in the Tactical Operations Center at Bagram. The Predator vision was still rolling on the main video screen at the front of the room. The operations staff were compiling sitreps and intelligence was being sifted to determine the extent of the enemy's position and the likelihood of reinforcements. Major General Hagenbeck pulled his Aussie counterpart aside.

'LaCamera has it pretty much under control right now,' the two-star told Lieutenant Colonel Tink after hearing from LaCamera's position. 'It's pretty much a stalemate.'

At 12.20pm – 0750 zulu – Hagenbeck picked up the phone and asked for close air support elsewhere in the valley. The battle was not confined to the men in Hell's Halfpipe and the general, who had control over the entire region, was constantly receiving information from the frontlines. Tink recalls that Hagenbeck had already decided to bomb the small town of Marzak later that day. Marzak was teeming with enemy fighters whom the soldiers from the 10th Mountain and

Rakkasans had been sniping at with some success from nearby positions. He also planned to conduct a last-light attack and was revisiting the second airlift to be flown in on the Chinooks that evening, as previously scheduled in the original OpOrd, but the second wave of reinforcements depended on the situation on the ground and so far it had been too volatile to air-assault them in.

Last light was still several hours away; the sun wasn't due to go down until 5.50pm local time. A lot could go wrong, but equally, a lot could go right and elsewhere in the Shahi Kot, it already had. Despite the battles, most of the blocking points, Hagenbeck said, had been secured.

But Hagenbeck and Tink knew the commander of the Rakkasans, Colonel Wiercinski, was under fire on the Finger and that his two 101st positions on the valley floor were engaged in close-quarters combat. Though the soldiers were taking a pounding, they were winning. Wiercinski had flown his tactical command post into the war zone for an hour to get a feel for the heat of the battle, to see what was going on. His UH-60 Black Hawk came under direct fire as it tried to navigate a landing spot just outside AO Down Under, Tink's area of operation. An RPG exploded under the nose of the chopper and an al Qaeda fighter with a Kalashnikov AK-47 scored some direct hits on the tail and rotor. Lady luck dealt the crew a decent hand, though, and neither attack was able to stop the helo. After dropping the colonel and his team, the Black Hawk took off in a cloud of dust and raced back to Bagram. But the hour that Wiercinski had planned to stay in the Shahi Kot stretched into several.

'We had high ground. I think the enemy thought we were just another element, not a brigade headquarters,' Wiercinski later told Colonel Austin Bay for a report on The Strategy Page website. 'My C2 bird took hits. I told him to leave us. I had nine guys with me. Then the al Qaeda tried mortars. But we were located on such an acute point it would have had to be a direct hit, with the mortars, to get us. Their fire kept getting closer and closer but we just stuck it out.'

To Tink it seemed that only piecemeal reports from parts of the battlefield were filtering back to Hagenbeck in the TOC.

'One of the problems was that Wiercinski is up here [on the Finger] fighting his own war, his guys are down here [in the valley] fighting their own war and communications between LaCamera and Wiercinski and us are not good,' Tink says. 'Limited information was getting back from LaCamera through Wiercinski to Hagenbeck, and I don't know why, to this day. I can only assume that this was probably because Wiercinski was fighting his own war.'

Jock had maintained lines of communication all day – except for a ten-second moment when he had had to change batteries – and his connections never once failed. His signalling gear was a lifeline, especially when the few radios still held by the Americans went down.

Wiercinski told Austin Bay that the enemy didn't think the Americans had the 'stomach for a big fight' and made bad assumptions about the US strategy.

'The AQ did stupid things in Shahi Kot Valley. Very early on I could tell there were no civilians in those three towns,' Wiercinski told Bay, referring to Sherkhankhel, Babukhel and Marzak. 'There were no colours, no smoke, no animals, no hanging clothes, nothing to identify it as a populated area, with people living there. I looked down and asked, "What's wrong with this picture?" There were no civilians in there. They had moved them out.

'Well, what did that do for us? It helped our ROE [rules of engagement] incredibly. We went in there with good tight ROE. We went in with an initial intent to screen people, but it was very obvious in the first ten minutes there was nothing but bad guys there. The place did not have the look of anything else in Afghanistan. It had the look of a battlefield. I thought, "This is going to be a fight." And I honestly think they didn't think we had the guts, the chutzpah, the ability to get in there and duke it out with them.'

Tink came to a similar conclusion about the operational status of Marzak and the other two villages in Objective Remington.

'I remember, as Jock's aircraft came in, the Predator came up to the village of Marzak and you could see the people in the village come up,' Tink says. 'There was no running around at the time, it was all very organised; and what we subsequently learnt days later, we knew they knew we were coming, they just didn't know *when* we were coming. And they had obviously decided to fight and, because they knew we were coming, they moved the women and children out. This became obvious in quick time that there were no women and children in these villages. And once we knew that, a lot of the restrictions placed on us – having to be excessively careful not to kill civilians – were really removed. Those villages were flattened at the end of the day.'

The restrictions Tink referred to came under the Australians' rules of engagement.

Australian soldiers abide by certain international conventions and take their ROE seriously. Each war comes with a different set of political, geographical and cultural circumstances, and thus its own ROE. The soldiers don't have carte blanche to shoot at or attack anyone or anything.

Instead, the Aussies deployed in Operation Slipper were all given a general ROE card covered in heat-sealed plastic that clearly and precisely outlined what they could and could not do in war. It was small enough to fit into their fatigues and had to be carried with them at all times. The rules of engagement stated that their mission was to conduct ground operations in Afghanistan to fight international terrorism.

The rules of engagement were prescriptive. Jock and his fellow SAS soldiers had them drummed into them repeatedly. The ADF would not tolerate cavalier cowboys and indiscriminate behaviour among its personnel. The ROE were restrictive but standard for the Australian forces, and to breach them was to risk a court martial and charges under the Australian Defence Act.

The Americans abided by similar ROE. As well, US troops were schooled in search methods to ensure they would not offend the faithful in the Islamic country. According to Sean Naylor, one innovative commander told his troops that the best way – the most sensitive way – to ensure that a person wearing a head-to-toe *burqa* was a female, and not an enemy fighter trying to disguise himself or conceal potentially lethal weapons, was to check the size of the person's feet. The enemy would do whatever it took to defeat the infidel Westerners; a pair of gnarly men's feet under a *burqa* were unmistakable. It was wise to check them out, the US commander warned.

Hagenbeck was studying the sitreps and revising the plan. Men from the 2–187 had come under fire while trying to take an al Qaeda compound at the northern LZs. Inside, the soldiers found a teapot on the boil, half-eaten breakfasts and bedding for about fifteen men. The enemy had taken off into the hills as the choppers landed, leaving their munitions behind. Prayer beads were found in a Nike bag that was stuffed with blasting caps. Soldiers found night-vision goggles, sniper and assault rifles, binoculars, hand-held radios, 50 alarm clocks, Casio watches and books on digital electronics. But as Colonel Wiercinski told Sean Naylor, 'these guys weren't taking an electrical engineering exam in that compound'. They were making bombs.

Other blocking positions had also been secured. The biggest problem was in the south at LZs 13 and 13a, right where Jock and Clint had landed with LaCamera and Grippe and their men.

'We felt very good about the initial landing and then some of the reports began to come in that there was small-arms fire, but all the reports I was getting from Colonel Wiercinski was that they could handle them and take out the bad guys. And that proved to be true in six out of seven incidents,' Hagenbeck told me, sitting in his office in the Pentagon.

'And the fight, the momentum, from where I sat ... just seemed to grow over the first two hours, just bigger and bigger and bigger down in the south. And I didn't know if we had literally flown into a hornet's nest or whether some of the al Qaeda that had been up in the northern part, the east ridgeline, were trying to escape and had headed down there coincidentally. I never knew and never had a sense of it. I just knew that the fight was getting bigger and bigger over the first two hours.'

CHAPTER 14

Each round that exploded out of Jock's chamber was
for one of the wounded blokes lying a metre or two away,
patched up and morphed up to their eyeballs.
Pfffat, pfffat, pfffat, pfffat.

Jock Wallace was digging into the blood-soaked and snow-covered clay of Hell's Halfpipe with his Babyseal knife like a man possessed, tossing the frozen earth out as he dug a deeper shell scrape. The tips of his fingers were scraped raw from clawing at the sharp rocks buried in the icy dirt and his knuckles were bloody and hurting, but he'd blocked out the pain in pursuit of protection. Pain was not an option. They were eight hours into the fight and, despite the thunderstorm of firepower from the skies that the coalition was directing at the enemy, al Qaeda and the Taliban hadn't let up.

And they were gloating. *Jesus Christ, the fuckers are gloating!* Jock thought. Every so often after launching an RPG or another mortar at the men from Charlie Company, the ninja-clad AQ would dash out of their hiding places high on the ridge, yell something in their native tongue, grab their balls and gesticulate at the men down below, taunting the soldiers in Hell's Halfpipe. They had no fear; the soldiers' 7.62mm ammo had run out hours earlier and the smaller 5.56mm rounds had trouble making the distance.

Yeah, real religious, Ahmed. Jock decided he was not going down to these smart-arsed bastards.

'We could hear them laugh at us. They were laughing every

time we shot at them. They were 2000 feet above us. Our small arms could not reach them up there,' said Private Wayne Stanton, a young soldier from Tennessee.

Some of the al Qaeda and Taliban threw stones, an impotent act the soldiers found comically medieval, given the more modern firepower they had at hand. A chorus of foreign words punctuated by *Allahu Akbar* rang out down the valley when one of the US troops missed his target.

The enemy did the same thing after an air strike roared over. As soon as they heard the incoming fast movers, the enemy ducked into their caves and waited for the bombs to explode before emerging in a vulgar display of triumphalism, grabbing their crotches and dancing around.

'Before the dust had settled they were out shooting at us again. They were even waving at us. It was a little disappointing,' SAS Warrant Officer Clint said soon after the fight.

It pissed the soldiers off, but at the same time the taunts only served to rev them up more.

The enemy was so close that Jock could almost smell them. He and Clint had been having a deadly serious but friendly shooting competition – aiming their M4 carbines at the enemy 200 metres away and seeing who could get off the best shot. Jock's finger was on the trigger, the weapon locked on semi-automatic to conserve ammunition, spitting out well-aimed shots at targets in range. Each round that exploded out of Jock's chamber was for one of the wounded blokes lying a metre or two away, patched up and morphed up to their eyeballs. *Pfffat, pfffat, pfffat, pfffat.* It was near on impossible to tell if he got any direct hits with the amount of ammo pounding the ridges, but pulling the trigger was satisfying nonetheless and seeing the enemy duck for cover meant they weren't trying to kill him.

Jock wasn't superstitious but, like most soldiers going into battle, he had mentally written his name on a bullet and put it in his pocket for luck. It meant that he, Jock, had the only bullet marked for himself and there wouldn't – couldn't – be another one like it in the bowl of death in the Shahi Kot Valley that day. Myth, superstition, old wives' tale – screw it. Everything helped.

He maintained his position on the southern end of the bowl, keeping his hand and ear on the radio and his weapon fully cocked. He was still digging in, creating a deep shell scrape for safety and peace of mind. It was impossible to get comfortable or complacent; to do so meant certain death. Jock's view was southeast, and most of the enemy were burrowed into positions on the eastern ridgeline higher up and further north; that is, in front of him and over his left shoulder. He could hear the fight hammering his eardrums and he felt the hard spray of dirt and shattered stones ricocheting off the ground when bullets and shrapnel landed nearby, but his job was to watch the backs of the 10th Mountain in Hell's Halfpipe. Their troops needed cover from the rear as they manoeuvred into position to take aim.

'It was quite unnerving because I had my back to them [the enemy], basically. And if I turned around, then no one was watching *our* back. Had it all gone to shit, you would have had to turn around and make the best of the situation,' Jock says.

Jock was vulnerable in his position but his fellow soldiers were in a direct line of fire and he stood his ground, keeping his focus and maintaining his communications network.

The enemy inched closer towards the ambushed men. Jock eyeballed al Qaeda creeping along the narrow jagged ledges in his sightline.

He reacted immediately. 'Single enemy. Moving left to right,' he yelled over the roar of death. 'Reference: large rocky outcrop.'

A couple of shooters raised up on their elbows, lifting their heads and shoulders over the lip of the halfpipe, took aim, and fired a barrage of bullets from their weapons. Bingo. The enemy was cut down. Gone.

Hoo-ah!

'If you see the enemy you give a target indication,' Jock says now. 'That's distance, direction, description – you describe the enemy. You always give your range so people will look at that distance. If you say "lone enemy", people will look around anywhere, but if you say 200 metres, *bang*, people's eyes will go out to 200 metres. It becomes second nature.'

In war, second nature was paramount.

Fast movers screamed overhead, answering calls for fire further north at one of the six other coalition positions that had been established successfully during the first two hours of Anaconda. LaCamera and Grippe at the northern end of the bowl conferred over their internal field radios with the Rakkasan commander, Wiercinski, at his command post on the Finger.

A thousand things were going on at once. Each man was engaged in his own personal war and battle for survival. The confined kill zone had men cramped into the bowl, but several squads from the 10th Mountain had managed to combat-crawl up the sides of the halfpipe to secure a better firing position. But in doing so they came under fire from enemy hidden in crevices and crags on the ridge.

The enemy was creeping in closer, trying to surround Charlie Company.

'We had to shoot them off the rocks, morning and afternoon,' Jock says now.

It was chaos. The troops were being attacked by al Qaeda and Taliban fighters dug into positions higher up the ridge behind Jock; he couldn't see the enemy but he could hear their gunfire. 'At that stage I don't know that there's not twice as many coming from the other end,' he says.

Back in the TOC, Major General Hagenbeck listened intently to the battle raging more than a hundred kilometres away. The racket of explosions and gunfire had turned into a white noise of war – ever present; unceasing. And it was being broadcast in real time over the radio and accompanied by almost surreal Predator vision from the kill zones. Hagenbeck's liaison officer relayed the updated sitreps from the various positions in the Shahi Kot Valley.

The battle plan had changed, significantly. Hagenbeck had

spent two weeks mapping out the AO and strategising Anaconda with the commanders from various arms of the US military, including the Special Forces, the US Air Force, the Navy and the Marines, as well as the commanders of the international coalition forces. But war is organic and human responses are unpredictable.

Surprise is the best weapon; without it, you're done.

By early afternoon, things were increasingly fluid for the planners in the Tactical Operations Center. Hagenbeck had the whole valley and all seven blocking positions to consider. Wiercinski's command post was under fire, but holding its position. 'We survived three mortar barrages during the day, and at one point, we had nine to ten al Qaeda coming to do [kill] us. But instead, we did them,' Wiercinski later told reporters at Bagram Air Base. 'They had been building this place and this defence for years. We definitely put a spike through their heart.'

General Zia Lodin's Northern Alliance forces – the main effort in Anaconda – were slowly withdrawing from the valley. The Afghan warlord had lost three soldiers and 24 were injured. Almost all of his trucks had been destroyed. They would not return to Gardez until much later that night and would not get back into the fight for a couple of days.

Other US Special Forces patrols that had infiltrated into the mountains were feeding reports back to the TOC, describing enemy hideouts at other locations.

About 200 enemy fighters had launched a barrage of accurate mortar and machine-gun fire on 45 men from Charlie Company with the 2–187 in the northwest soon after they exited the Chinook. It was another version of the same story: al Qaeda had the valley direct-fired and the American soldiers copped a hiding, but they fought on.

More al Qaeda forces were sighted travelling into the valley in a convoy of nine beaten-up old trucks mounted with machine-guns. Coalition aircraft responding to a call for CAS spied the convoy and took aim. As one soldier on the ground later told reporters: 'Luckily, the 200 people were neutralised from the air.

They weren't holding back. We gave them every chance to surrender. They had their minds set on killing Americans.'

The combat order was changing, minute by minute. The coalition supporting effort – the Anvil to General Zia's Afghan Forces' Hammer – was now the main effort in Anaconda.

Hagenbeck had decisions to make.

Colonel Mulholland, who headed the 5th Special Forces Group, had previously told him that this would be a different kind of fight; that if the enemy were Arabs they would stay and fight rather than try to escape through the rat lines. But others in the intelligence community had the opposite view and believed that, once cornered, the enemy would try to escape.

Hagenbeck's battle strategists had briefed him on several courses of action including how to capture and kill escaping enemy fighters and how to deal with their surrender. But he had assumed Mulholland's worst-case scenario; that they were going to be in for a pitched battle. His assumption was right.

'So early afternoon the discussion that went on back at the headquarters was, "What do we do?"' Hagenbeck says.

He knew he had to medevac the wounded soldiers out of the Shahi Kot Valley and he wanted to maintain and continue the momentum further north where other soldiers had secured their blocking points.

'We decided – to describe it doctrinally – to reinforce success,' he says. 'So the decision in early afternoon [was that] when the sun went down, we would fly in medevac helicopters to the south to pull those guys out. And we would take that second lift of six helicopters and fly into the north, instead of the south, and we would reinforce the north and they would move down the ridgeline towards the south. So we thought it was going to go pretty good from that aspect.

'And we also began that afternoon to pick up, for the very first time, indications [al Qaeda] might be reinforcing. But we can tell you now, the signal intercepts that we had, they thought that they had us where they wanted us ... The Russians had fought two major fights there and been hurt badly and they thought this would be a repeat. They were calling this the jihad against America and its allies, and they were calling every able-bodied person to come into the fight.'

Al Qaeda were preparing for a bigger showdown and kept coming into the valley in small groups spread out over the treacherous terrain, making them a more difficult target. They moved in during the daylight knowing that the American forces had superior technology at night.

'We had all the night vision advantages, from satellites all the way down to the soldiers on the ground with night-vision goggles, and if they moved at night they were killed and they knew that,' Hagenbeck says.

'But days later when they tried to escape to the south, that's when the Aussies lit them up – the SAS.'

It was 1.30pm local time in the Shahi Kot Valley. The fog, which had been playing havoc with the Predator vision during the morning, had cleared well and the sun was burning through the thin air and into the faces of the soldiers in Hell's Halfpipe.

Sergeant Robert Healy, Bob to his mates, was at the command-and-control point for the 10th Mountain and put his sunglasses on, tucking the arms under his helmet, looking every bit like the rock star soldier.

Lieutenant Colonel LaCamera walked by, clearly amused. 'Hey, is it Cool Guy sunglasses time?' he asked and quickly whipped his own shades out and put them on as well.

The sergeant laughed. It was a much needed moment of levity. But the sunglasses didn't last long.

'I figured out, boy, I'm getting shot at real close here,' Healy says now. 'I figured out my glasses were giving off a nice glare and I was a real nice little target. Put my sunglasses back away for the day.'

He got another laugh soon after when Major Jay Hall got caught in the cross hairs of a sniper and came barrelling down the bowl, skidding in on his arse.

'Saaaaaaaaaaaaaaaaaafe,' he called, baseball style.

Rowan Tink was in the TOC with Hagenbeck, paying close attention to the reports coming in from the battle. Tink, a country boy from Dubbo, had graduated from the Royal Military College, Duntroon, in 1977 at the age of 22, and in 1996 was made a Member of the Order of Australia (AM) for services to his country in the field of reconnaissance and surveillance.

He understood the mercurial nature of war, having commanded Australian and New Zealand SAS forces on operations including Operation Desert Thunder against Iraq a few years earlier. He had also been out on a couple of SAS patrols in southern Afghanistan in the preceding weeks, meeting the troopers and strategising with the SAS squadron commanders about the Aussies' roles in Anaconda.

Tink had a direct pipeline to Hagenbeck in the TOC. He asked the general about a blocking requirement to the west of the Whale, in a crucial position that had been left unsecured when General Zia's Afghan Forces began to withdraw earlier that morning after three soldiers were killed. Hours earlier, Tink had briefed his 1 SAS Squadron and ordered that a patrol be prepared to move in and act as a blocking force to cover for Zia's exit if need be. Tink's strategy turned out to be prescient.

Hagenbeck gave Tink the thumbs-up to establish the position. 'It was clear that Zia's forces weren't around there,' Tink says now.

Tink wanted to plug the hole – '"a gate was left open" is the best way to describe it' – to ensure that any escaping forces would not rush between the Whale and 1 Squadron's position. It was a strategic manoeuvre.

Tink spoke again to the officer in command of 1 Squadron, Major Dan McDaniel, and told him to pass the assignment to a small SAS patrol. The troopers had been prepared and instantly swung into action setting up an ambush at a place inside AO Down Under that they named Papa. All up, at that point, there were about 50 Aussies in the AO under Tink's command, including Jock and Clint who were still taking fire and fighting, quite literally, for their lives. Tink was well aware of the danger his men were in and the exceptional job they were doing defending their positions.

Thirty minutes later, reports filtered into the TOC that Zia's forces had broken to the rear on the north–south highway, having totally withdrawn from the valley. Tink noted that Zia was taking his troops back to Gardez.

The mood in the headquarters was sombre.

'This is a bitch,' said someone in a thick American accent.

No one disagreed.

CHAPTER 15

The pilot misjudged the chopper's height from the ground and slammed the aircraft into the runway, coming in on its side like a Hollywood stunt. Booooom. A huge orange fireball exploded and the chopper caught fire.

Until Anaconda, Jock Wallace had been having a busy if bullet-free war. After a brief refuelling stopover at a beautiful atoll in the middle of the Indian Ocean, he had landed in Kuwait towards the end of November, ten weeks after the September 11 attacks which were still fresh in his mind. The SAS Regiment arrived on a Royal Australian Air Force 707 and hit the ground running. As the commanding officer's signaller, Jock formed part of a small advance party that set up in Camp Doha. The group was top heavy with colonels, captains, majors and warrant officers. Jock was the only digger. The boss was the SAS Regiment's Lieutenant Colonel 'Gus' Gilmore, who went to work on securing a role for the 150 SAS troops the Australian Government had sent to the War on Terror.

Jock set up the communications network back to Australia in a room in a shed also used by an American Marine Expeditionary Unit (MEU) under the control of James N. Mattis, who was the brigadier general in command of the 1st MEU and Task Force 58 in Afghanistan.

Doha was a forward operating base left over from the first Gulf War. It was manned by a skeleton crew of Americans in case Saddam Hussein decided to have a second crack at invading

Kuwait, after being successfully repelled by Western allies in 1991 in the war known as Desert Storm.

Jock was flat out, running around like a blue-arsed fly, meeting with the Yanks, establishing relationships and securing equipment and codes from them. As the CO's chook, he had to ensure that everything was ready for when the SAS boys known as Task Force 64 arrived. The Aussies set up in a huge hangar in which they installed ATCO huts for offices. There was room enough to sleep up to 300 soldiers. The Yanks, who had money and were armed to the teeth, generously built a wall in the hangar which Jock and his mates dubbed the '$40 000 wall'. It provided the Australians with privacy.

It was short-term. Gilmore received word that the entire Aussie contingent was heading into southern Afghanistan to FOB Rhino.

This was a coup. The Australians operated under their own control and command, unlike Special Forces from other countries who were attached to Task Force K-BAR.

K-BAR was officially known as the Combined Special Operations Task Force – South, and was located in southern Afghanistan under the control of US Navy SEAL Commodore Robert Harward. (Task Force Dagger was its equivalent in the north of Afghanistan.) Made up almost entirely of special operators from the SEALs, US Army and Air Force, as well as SF soldiers from various coalition forces, it was charged with a series of high-risk roles. The primary job for K-BAR commandos was to destroy the al Qaeda and Taliban infrastructure and disrupt their ability to conduct terrorist strikes. In short, the mission was to find the enemy hiding in the southern and eastern parts of the country, and capture or kill them. (The Americans were big on naming most of their task forces after some mean mother of a weapon, usually a knife, as in K-BAR, Dagger and Sword.)

Jock was stoked about the move. This was the real deal and Rhino was in the thick of al Qaeda country, just a couple of hundred kilometres south of Kandahar, heartland of the Taliban.

The Australians exited in the pitch black of night on board a huge

C-17A Globemaster III cargo jet, courtesy of the US Air Force. The flight to Afghanistan would take about two hours and the men were fully prepared. This was no joy flight. Fearsome 'devil vehicles' – the Aussies' LRPVs – sat in the guts of the aircraft behind several surveillance-and-reconnaissance vehicles. Closest to the rear exit ramp were Polaris four-wheel motorbikes known as quads, and some 'sixbies' – six-wheel motorbikes used for patrolling and transportation. The vehicles were all chained to the floor to prevent any mid-flight accidents.

Jock was sitting on a sixbie. *Beats walking*, he thought. He had his night-vision goggles (NVGs) draped around his neck and wore his Kevlar-lined body-armour vest with front and back ballistic plates over his brand-new MK1 desert camouflage gear. He had his 60-kilogram ALICE pack loaded on the back of his bike, his fifteen-kilogram ammunition webbing slung across his chest, bandolier style, and his M4 slung in the opposite direction to the webbing across his front, barrel pointing down. His helmet was where it should be – protecting his noggin.

As on the trip to Shahi Kot Valley, the plane was blacked out – standard operating procedure flying into a desert runway in the middle of enemy country – but a couple of dull red lamps glowed, creating what would have been a romantic ambient mood in any other circumstance. The USAF crew all wore night-vision gear and noise-cancelling earphones.

Most of the Australians, including Jock, had never flown on a Globemaster before and were impressed with the show the American aircrew put on. Thirty minutes out from landing, the wartime hosties revved up the action, signalling to the troops to check their equipment and chains. Crew members manned the weapons systems and countermeasures in case al Qaeda fired a missile at the aircraft, although there was absolutely no way the USAF would be flying a fully loaded operational aircraft into a hot landing zone.

Ten minutes out from Rhino, the crew began barking out orders. Jock put his NVGs on and removed half the chains pinning his sixbie to the floor. Almost ready to roll. The rest would come off once the plane hit the dirt runway.

'Five minutes,' the crew hollered.

Each soldier at the front turned around to the man behind and held up his hand with five fingers clearly splayed and displayed. The message was passed down the line in the same way.

Two minutes. Two fingers. Weapons were cocked. Jock's 9mm Browning pistol had fourteen rounds in the magazine instead of the fifteen it could take. He believed in safety precautions and missing a round meant there was less chance the pistol could jam. Jock was meticulous about safety and always kept his weapons effectively combat-ready. He was renowned for never going anywhere without them. Even when manning the radio in the communications tent, or the chook pen as the signallers called it, he would have had his M4 slung across his back. *You never know*, was his private motto.

Jock could feel the plane banking and knew it was almost showtime. His heart was pumping a couple of thousand beats per minute. There was no messing around.

'You have to be more switched on than any time in your life,' Jock says. 'If you don't have everything turned on and running at high speed, then you are not going to be doing your best. And your best is the only thing – that's all you've got. You don't get a second shot and your mate might not either. So if you are not going to do it for yourself, at least do it for him.'

Jock was focusing on his own job and the blokes with him. There was no point in worrying about what might occur once the Globemaster hit the runway in the middle of al Qaeda country. At that point, the soldiers couldn't do a thing about it and worrying about hypotheticals got them nowhere.

'All you can do is react to it and make sure you're 100 per cent good to go and those around you are, too,' Jock says. 'You are just going to take it as it comes on the ground, and if your shit is all ready then you are going to be able to better deal with it than if you're still trying to put your socks on.'

Bang. The C17 hit the dirt and the engines screamed as the pilot set himself up for a short landing, braking hard. Jock strained against the pressure of being thrown forwards off his sixbie. The back ramp came down.

'Go, go, go, go, go,' the air crewman roared, swinging one arm in the direction of the blackened desert outside while chopping the soldier sitting on the quad on the arm with the other hand.

The quads raced off, kicking up a cloud of dust behind them as the wheels found traction with the ground.

Jock revved the handlebar on his sixbie, got the chop on his arm, sucked in a huge gutful of Afghan air and hooned down the ramp and into the sands of Afghanistan, not knowing what to expect. Would Ahmed the camel driver be there to greet him with a hail of bullets from a Kalashnikov or an ancient World War I Lee Enfield rifle? Or would it be plain sailing?

He was in hostile country. Thousands of al Qaeda and Taliban were reported to be in the region. Anything was possible. But the men needn't have worried. The welcoming committee consisted of a couple of Australian SAS who had flown in an hour earlier and a bunch of Americans who'd set up a defensive perimeter along the dirt runway. They were inside fortress Rhino within minutes and joined Mattis's MEU.

So this is Afghanistan, Jock thought. *Nothing to it.*

FOB Rhino is a walled white-brick compound that runs about 200 metres long and 200 metres across and sits in the middle of a flat desert plain of shifting sands in the middle of nowhere. Depending on which way the wind blows, the wall either towered above the soldiers on the ground or came in around chest height, thanks to the mountains of sand that collected against the bullet-riddled compound walls. Guard towers were on every corner, standing sentry over a mosque, workshops, sheds and shower facilities.

According to the accepted history that gets rolled out with every new arrival, a rich emir from the United Arab Emirates originally owned Rhino and used it as a falconing lodge. But there are those, like Jock, who favour the alternative and possibly more accurate version: that it was a heroin processing plant in a country notorious for its production and trafficking of heroin.

Soon after the war began, an American Marine unit overran the compound and an AC-130 gave it a thorough hammering. Whoever had been there previously was long gone.

'There were 40mm and machine-gun holes all through it. It had been well pasted,' says Jock.

The Marines set up a perimeter wall 100 metres out from the compound to act as the first protective barrier against al Qaeda. Humvees with Stingers mounted on them were parked inside the walls, and some were armed with TOW (tube-launched optically tracked wire-guided) anti-tank missiles. The Marines' vehicles were also armed with state-of-the-art radar and infrared capability that could sweep out up to sixteen kilometres and detect things coming in.

The atmosphere was electric. The Marines were another example of can-do men, and it resonated with Jock and the Aussies' SAS creed of 'Who Dares Wins'. With their motto of *Semper Fidelis*, Latin for 'Always Faithful', the Marines were as patriotic as Jock had ever encountered.

'Everyone was fully anticipating heroic deeds and all that sort of stuff – big battles,' Jock says now. 'Everyone was really fired up to go because this was the first big battle. Everyone cut their teeth in Timor ... and so everyone knew this was the big chance. We were already on the stage and we were waiting to join in. Everyone was in very high spirits and looking forward to getting on with the job. Champing at the bit. And the Americans loved it.'

When Jock had first laid eyes on the Marines' top dog, Brigadier General Mattis, he had been unimpressed. Mattis was a small, wiry bloke who could have slipped by like a shadow. To Jock's way of thinking, he was Mr Nobody, but that was nothing new. It was what he thought of most officers. That changed, though, when Mattis opened his mouth and addressed the Australians.

'I don't care who you are; I don't care if you're a cook, a cleaner or a commo guy. You will get on that wall and you will fight,' Jock recalls Mattis saying.

Jock is a Gen X pop culture soldier and, as Mattis spoke, Jock instantly thought of the crusty Marine played by Jack Nicholson in the movie *A Few Good Men*. 'You want me on that wall, you need me on that wall,' Nicholson's character, Colonel Nathan Jessep, said in one particularly ballsy scene.

Mattis had the same powerful delivery.

Jock remembers Mattis saying gung-ho things like, 'These people will not treat you decently. They are not the same as us. It's a big embarrassment [to them] for us to be here and they are going to try and dislodge us out of Afghanistan. These people killed my relatives. We appreciate you being here, and you have got to be here for the right reasons. You can't be here and not kill.'

The SAS Regiment's 1 Squadron all bunked in with the Marines, including the squadron's deployable signal troop and support staff such as the mechanics, armoury and electronic sight technicians. They worked, ate, slept and shat right alongside each other.

On the first night, an al Qaeda patrol probed the camp. A white Toyota Hilux truck – favoured by al Qaeda and Taliban forces in Kabul and Kandahar – drove through the desert with a herd of camels. The sentries spotted the truck and called a stand-to, a drill that has all soldiers man the post on full alert, ready to fight. The soldiers set off illumination mortars that lit the night sky like daylight, followed by a string of flares that hung in the sky for minutes illuminating a huge slice of the desert. For the next hour, night was day as a quick-reaction force in light-armoured vehicles with big chain guns drove out to engage the truck. Helicopters also swept the desert in search of al Qaeda.

'Elusive Ahmed disappeared into the dunes, and unfortunately he was never questioned as to why he was in the vicinity. Amazingly he got away,' says Jock now.

After 90 minutes, the soldiers were just about to receive the 'stand down' order to leave the perimeter wall when an old Huey helicopter came in to land about 200 metres away. The downdraft from the chopper's rotors was churning up the dust from the runway, browning out the landing zone and blinding the pilot.

The pilot misjudged the chopper's height from the ground and slammed the aircraft into the runway, coming in on its side like a Hollywood stunt.

Booooom. A huge orange fireball exploded and the chopper caught fire.

'What the fuck was that? Was it shot down?' someone yelled.

'Nah, mate, it was just landing,' came the reply.

'Ah shit, no poor bastard is getting out of that.'

Jock just felt sick in the stomach. For fifteen minutes he watched as the ammunition rounds and rockets on the Huey exploded, shooting out everywhere. It was too dangerous to get anywhere near the downed chopper. The troops on stand-to were gutted; the Marine chopper had just completed a desert sweep looking for the Hilux.

'We were just thinking, those poor bastards, they were dead for sure,' Jock says. 'The next day there was a little bit of the tail rotor, the rest of it was a blob of dust and twisted metal and ash; hardly anything recognisable.

'But we found out that they actually all survived! That was the good bit. They all got out a bit battered, they all got out alive – probably three or four of them.'

Jock was at Rhino for several nights, during which time SAS men were tasked with patrols in the vast flat desert region around the base. They were often out for several days at a time – the longest of all the Special Forces – acting as Mattis's eyes and ears and providing intelligence on the enemy, and building a reputation as some of the finest soldiers around.

Shortly after arriving at the FOB, the Americans brought in the infamous 'American Taliban', Johnny Walker Lindh. The twenty-year-old US citizen and Muslim convert had been captured by the Northern Alliance while fighting with the Taliban.

During interrogations by agents from the CIA and FBI, Lindh

revealed that he'd trained at al Farooq, an al Qaeda terrorist training camp in Afghanistan, and had met Osama bin Laden. He was moved to Rhino after an uprising at the prison near Mazar-e Sharif, where he and other Taliban fighters were being held. During the uprising, a CIA agent, Johnny Michael Spann, was killed. It would not be repeated at the base.

The fact that an American traitor was on camp was of no consequence to Jock or the 400-odd Marines and SAS troops.

Jock says: 'It was just like, "Oh, you know Johnny Walker is here?" "Oh, is he? Stiff shit." No one really cared too much. We were looking for real enemies, not some little dickhead idealist or misguided fool.'

The sojourn at Rhino came to an end four days before Christmas. Gilmore had been invited to deploy his SAS squadron further north to secure the Kandahar airport and prevent the Taliban from regrouping in their region.

'This was a calculated move to basically prevent any Taliban force from re-forming, if they hadn't already done so,' Jock says.

The coalition needed to take the airport so they could get troops and supplies in-country.

Before they left for Kandahar, Brigadier General Mattis gathered the troops for an impromptu farewell and motivational speech. The Commander of CentCom, General Tommy Franks, had flown in to greet the soldiers from the MEU and the SAS. Fully armed Marines and Aussie troopers, most of whom hadn't had a proper shower for weeks, crowded into a huge shed or spilled outside under the warm afternoon sun – one of the wonders of being in a mountain desert with winter approaching.

Mattis stood on a raised platform at the front and once again left the Aussies with no doubt about what he thought of them.

'You added great firepower to my unit and I was more than happy to have you on board when I saw that you were looking for a job,' Jock remembers the brigadier general saying.

Mattis also addressed the gathered Americans.

'We wouldn't be here standing so strongly without allies like this.'

Jock was impressed. The American general was truly polished and sounded as if he'd been born with a sound bite in his mouth.

'He thanked everybody very much and got it through to his boys how important his government and his bosses saw the Australians on the ground in Rhino – as invaluable,' Jock recalls.

'Mattis reiterated that we were there, in no uncertain terms, to fight al Qaeda and Taliban; that they would have no mercy on us; they will not treat prisoners as we understand prisoners are to be treated; they are not good people; they are going to do bad things to you if you get caught or your mates are caught.'

Before leaving, Mattis had one last gift for the troops. Cheerleaders!

It was coming up to Christmas and the US Army traditionally provided entertainment for the troops abroad as a way to lift morale. They'd been doing it since World War II, when a volunteer group called the United States Organization – USO – sponsored visits to war zones by entertainers like Bob Hope and the Andrews Sisters.

The troops at Rhino had to make do with the television comedian Drew Carey and lounge-crooner Wayne Newton.

General Franks kicked off the show. Flanked by a team of heavily armed soldiers who provided close personal protection, the four-star general thanked the soldiers for their personal sacrifices in serving their country in Afghanistan, and then launched into what seemed to Jock like a pretty good stand-up routine.

'He was just so funny, he was one of the better entertainers on the day,' Jock recalls.

Franks' team, though, didn't crack a smile. They were there to do a job; protect the boss, not laugh at his jokes.

Carey was a former Marine, a jarhead, who stood on stage telling blue jokes and swearing, much to the amusement of the Yanks. Rhino was a Marine base, and once a Marine always a Marine. Brotherhood. Jock thought he was a dickhead.

Newton belted out a couple of classic standards that only the geriatrics among the troops would know, and there weren't too many of them. But they loved him just the same. Jock recognised Newton when one of the Americans obligingly pointed out that he was in the movie *The Adventures of Ford Fairlane*. A showman from the old school, Newton mingled with the soldiers, asking questions about their hometowns and how long they'd been away.

Newton grabbed Jock's hand.

'G'day, mate, how're you going?' Jock said.

Newton instantly recognised the accent.

'Hey, you Aussies —'

Jock cut him off. 'Look, mate, I haven't got time to talk, but you're the worst fucking Elvis impersonator I've ever seen. Keep working on it.'

Jock was having a lend of the singer, but the Yank didn't fully appreciate or understand the idiosyncratic Australian sense of humour which centres around taking the piss.

Not that it mattered to Jock. He was on a mission to meet all of the five beautiful cheerleaders from the Miami Dolphins. He didn't know a thing about the football team that the women led the cheers for, but he was happy to see them doing a dance routine in their aqua-green and orange colours just the same. He had twenty minutes before they left.

'There was a big buzz and we all stank,' Jock says with a laugh. 'We were unshaven and filthy. Everyone was tooled up; we've got guns on, bristling everywhere. We're walking around with Minimis and M4s.'

The soldiers had all been through basic training and knew how to move in large groups. Shoulders first. Jock drew an imaginary bead on the cheerleaders and made his way through the crowd, pushing Marines out of the way.

'I'm making good ground on these cheerleaders who are giving out free cuddles to all the smelly Marines – I wanted to save them from that fate,' he says. 'And this immovable uniform suddenly appeared in front of me and it wasn't getting out of the way like all the rest of them.

'And I'm like, *right, smart arse*, and as I looked up, about to react to this show of force, I've seen four big silver stars about eye level.'

It was General Tommy Franks.

He looked Jock in the face, registered that the soldier had recognised him and the silver stars, and smiled.

Jock recalls: 'He's gone from a look of "He's going to hit me" to "Oh, you dickhead, you didn't know it was me, did you? See the effect I have on people."'

'G'day, sir,' Jock said.

'Soldier,' Franks replied.

Jock slid by and, *whooshka*, got his first cheerleader.

'She had just finished freeing herself from a stinky little Marine and I'd pushed the next one out of the way, so I was first,' Jock says. 'She said hello and asked me my name and where I was from and gave me a big cuddle, and I wouldn't let her go. Held her for longer than what she probably thought was necessary. And having pushed it as far as I could, I said goodbye.'

The cheerleader moved on to the next bloke and Jock tracked her move, jockeying into position for another cuddle, pushing another Marine out of the way.

'I did it about five times till she worked out it was the same smell and said, "Hey, haven't I seen you?"'

'The Yanks were more than accommodating,' Jock says now in recognition of the Americans' hospitality that had provided the cheerleaders and their free cuddles.

'Those Marines, they were awesome.'

With the fresh perfume of cheerleaders cutting through the manly soldiers' smell, Jock and the Australians exited Rhino bound for Kandahar.

Living with hundreds of brawny, bearded blokes in a tent-and-Portaloo city in a foreign country crawling with al Qaeda and

Taliban fighters who want nothing more than to kill you in the name of Allah does something to a man's psyche. If that man is Jock Wallace, it makes him resourceful.

Jock spent most of the War on Terror in southern Afghanistan at what was once known as Kandahar International Airport but was now called FOB Kandahar. In its heyday the airport was a thing of beauty, its terminal an architectural adventure reminiscent, in some abstract way, of the Sydney Opera House, with a row of huge arched windows several storeys high overlooking the main runway. And it was all encircled by a spectacular mountain range off in the distance.

But those days were long past and until recently the airport had been occupied by the Taliban, who captured Kandahar in 1994 and turned it into the new power centre for Afghanistan before embarking on a violent program to conquer the rest of the country, finally seizing Kabul in 1996. The Taliban's leader, Mullah Mohammad Omar, had established the fundamentalist regime's top decision-making body, the Supreme Shura, in Kandahar. As a result, he rarely left the city that was settled on a fort originally built by Alexander the Great. The airport was key to protecting the regime as it was within striking distance of the ancient city.

A paved road led up to the terminal whose external side walls were covered with murals of passenger planes and fighter jets, marking, of course, the country's most recent history of war. The Taliban's days were seriously numbered, though, and it had been living on borrowed time since Mullah Omar's most notorious international guest, Osama bin Laden, launched the September 11 attacks. Almost exactly two months later, coalition forces secured the airport and removed the Taliban without a single shot being fired.

The damage, though, had been done already. The airport was the scene of previous heavy fighting and parts of it had been blown to bits. Windows were shattered, doors had been kicked in, and anti-Western graffiti was scrawled everywhere. The walls were pockmarked with bullet holes, and some offices inside the terminals that once housed Taliban forces had been left booby-trapped.

The Americans were the first troops to arrive, followed soon after by the Australians, and the airfield went from housing 400 soldiers in the first months of war to almost 5000 by the time Jock rotated out of the country for home at the end of March.

The Americans had commandeered the prime real estate in the terminal, overlooking the runway, leaving the Australian SAS Regiment to set up its HQ inside a small office looking out over the carpark where taxis would, in peacetime, drop off fare-paying passengers and where, during this war, the locals had set up their 'muj feeds'. It was also directly opposite a beautiful rose garden which Jock was happy to see still in bloom despite the rapid onset of winter.

The terminal was located 200 metres behind the forward perimeter of the airport, opposite the main road that was ably guarded by vehicle patrols from the US Marine Corps. For accommodation, the headquarters set up three old Vietnam-era green canvas tents better suited for the steamy climate of a South East Asian jungle than the bitter cold of an Afghan winter.

'Everybody else's tents have got liners and built-in heaters and all these other filtration systems, et cetera, and we've got the old jungle tents,' Jock says now. '*You beauty*. We looked like the St Vinnie de Paul-dressed kids at a private school, but we could hold our heads high.'

The fighting Sabre squadron under the command of Major Dan McDaniel set up a hundred metres down the road, past a mosque and near the Germans and a small contingent of Kiwi Special Forces troops.

'On the other side of the road was what we called The BC – The Body Club – The British Columbians – Canadians – who would sit round in their jocks all day rubbing suntan oil on each other and pumping up at the gym,' Jock says with a laugh. 'These cats were at a holiday resort. They didn't give a shit about their guns, they didn't care where they were as long as the coconut oil was on and they were punching 300 on the bench press.'

Despite being driven out of their spiritual homeland, Mullah Omar's Taliban had not given up the prospect of re-forming elsewhere in Afghanistan and reclaiming what they believed was rightfully theirs, especially Kandahar.

'There was a real air of trepidation and expectations of something really big. It was still early days,' Jock says of the Australian contingent's arrival. 'We thought, "Cool, we're going into Kandahar, we're not waiting for the Taliban, we're going in." And I got off at the airport and it just fizzled. It didn't keep building.'

The SAS patrols worked the surrounding countryside in the Helmand Valley, searching for remnants of the fundamentalist regime and al Qaeda terrorists, but Jock was stuck at the regimental HQ at the FOB, sorting out the communications traffic to and from Australia for the chain of command. Being bound to the HQ and the commanding officer, though, had its advantages. It allowed Jock to hone his diplomatic skills. He made new friends with valuable members of the US Marine Corps with whom he engaged in improvised trade negotiations.

The Aussie regimental staff including the chooks quickly became known as a hospitable bunch of blokes who always kept a coffee pot on the boil. The only country that could outdo the Australians for coffee was Turkey which, at that time, had a single liaison officer stationed in a small office next to the SAS HQ. He became snakey if his brew wasn't up to scratch, something the Aussies loved to rib him about.

The Americans drank some foul-tasting mass-market brand that the US Government dutifully shipped in and, despite its less than smooth taste, it soon became the preferred accompaniment for the GIs who also had a habit of chewing a particularly nasty type of tobacco called Copenhagen and Skoal. The dip, as the chewing tobacco was known, came in a wonderful array of flavours, including cherry, bourbon and wintergreen, and rotted the men's gums and gave them a stinking, foul breath. The long-cut variety of tobacco was wadded up and stuffed between the front lip and teeth of the bottom jaw. Experienced dippers, though, would chew the fine-cut blend, which had a tendency to make a mother of a mess in the mouth of a newbie dipper, who invariably ended up looking like he'd had a couple of front teeth knocked out.

Some of the soldiers who chewed Copenhagen and Skoal, including some of the Aussie SAS troopers, wore small bottles tied around their necks into which they spat the rancid mix of tobacco and saliva once it had lost its flavour and high-octane kick. It was a disgusting habit but, despite its obvious drawbacks, the dip had its advantages, ones that Jock would see in Operation Anaconda.

'If you are out in the field and you're a smoker, the dip is the perfect thing,' he says. 'If you do it silently and spit it into a bottle then you can keep your mental chemistry at its normal level and not go off on a nicotine withdrawal rage. The alternative is to have a cigarette and leave a scent as a signal for the enemy. That would be one of the advantages of the dip over smoking, and it doesn't affect your lung capacity.'

Jock could get his hands on the dip and coffee or anything else, for that matter, thanks to his connections with Jeremy, a three-toed banjo-picking Marine from West Virginia. Jeremy was the go-to man on base.

Jock met Jeremy while on one of his customary recces around base. Jock referred to this habit as a little bit of anthropological exploration. He toured the base and scavenged objects that took his fancy, including bits of shrapnel, Afghani *pakhul* hats and even discarded Osama bin Laden propaganda sheets written in Arabic, Chechen, Dari or Pashto.

He also bought and traded items with the local friendlies. Luckily for Jock, the local Kandaharis were renowned traders, taking after their ancient forebears who'd plied the trade routes almost since the beginning of time, and they lined the streets leading to the base hoping to find like-minded souls among the coalition forces. They hit pay dirt with Jock, who in turn struck gold with Jeremy. Jeremy liked Jock's 'Ossie' accent and Jock liked Jeremy's unorthodox entrepreneurial vigour. Together, they were a formidable, if incongruous, team.

The Yanks, Jock found out from Jeremy, were exceedingly generous when it came to outfitting their beloved troops. Just about every item marked for the Quartermaster Store in Afghanistan had been written off as a capital expense as soon as it was loaded on a US cargo plane and shipped out of contiguous USA. The brass expected nothing to return and, generally speaking, little did.

Jeremy, says Jock, was as dumb as the proverbial and could barely spell his own name. His accent was so thick hick hillbilly that Jock couldn't really be sure his name was Jeremy. The vowels rolled into the consonants like molasses and Jeremy could have been Jeremy or Jamie or Jeremiah, Jebediah or Jimmy. Or even Jonathan.

'He was illiterate, but he had a way with people. He was a salesman. We had this hell racket going on, it was poetry in motion,' Jock says now. 'But it was not for personal gain. I would get stuff for other people in the contingent and trade it. They all wanted the American boots. I couldn't understand it. The Australian Government had just spent millions of dollars reinventing the wheel and made its own army boot. They did it, and in my opinion they did a good one. But all these blokes wanted to go and swap them for a pair that's about a hundred dollars cheaper. There's nothing flash about the Yank boot.'

Soldiers also wanted the American uniforms, badges and emblems. Weaponry was also popular, particularly the K-BAR knives, M16 bayonets, and the American Benchmade flick knives. 'They are cool knives,' Jock says.

Whenever the grunts saw Jock and Jeremy walking down a path together after sunset, they knew it was trading time. Soldiers lined up to swap boots for badges and knives, or cold-weather gear and blankets for the souvenirs Jock had found littered around base. Some of the Yanks would trade the more expensive

GORE-TEX items, knowing they could always report to the Q Store and get a new one courtesy of Uncle Sam. The Aussies, on the other hand, kept a tight watch on inventory.

The Americans had another tradition of striking coins to commemorate their wartime endeavours. A coin might be struck to honour the commander of US Central Command, General Tommy Franks, or the 5th Marine Expeditionary Unit or the Rakkasans from the 101st Airborne. The Yanks used the coins as a type of currency and traded them for desired items. The practice amused Jock, who thought the big hulking troops in their camouflage gear were more like pre-adolescent schoolkids playing with their swap cards in the playground.

'There's a big trading thing with them,' says Jock. 'They'd go, "Do you want coins?" "Nah, mate." It's not like it can be redeemed. It's just a gay thing the Yanks do. Basically that became currency around there; everyone got into swapping these Yank coins. It was just funny watching the personalities. They were hoarding this one, or they wouldn't declare that they've got one of the other ones so no one would nick it. It kept them entertained. Me? I was too busy getting sleeping bags and tents and stuff like that – the legit sort of stuff.'

After two months of steady trade, Jock's kit was first class, and he'd done a pile of favours for his mates, too.

He didn't know it then, but his enterprise would stand him in good stead in the Shahi Kot Valley.

CHAPTER 16

*'I remember thinking how much enemy fire
was going into Jock's position. I have never heard
so much firepower.'*

TROOPER JOHNNY, B TROOP, 1 SAS SQUADRON

Command Sergeant Major Frank Grippe decided to take a stroll down Hell's Halfpipe to see how his men were coping under the intense pummelling they were taking.

'G'day, Digger,' Grippe said to Jock humorously, the way Americans do when they try to pronounce the unique Aussie greeting and know they haven't quite pulled it off. 'You having a good day, soldier?'

Jock had to laugh. *This guy is unfuckin' believable*, he thought as bullets bounced into the bowl.

'It could've been better, sir,' Jock replied, typically understated. Grippe laughed. There was nothing like a bit of humour to keep morale up.

Despite the sun, which was high overhead and had mercifully warmed the valley a couple of degrees, it was still freezing. Jock was still digging in. His little trench was almost deep enough to lie in. He hadn't spoken to the Australian headquarters for at least an hour and now radioed in a sitrep, getting a bloke called Ben from the chook pen.

Ben asked Jock where he'd been.

'Digging in, over.'

Jock updated Ben, who passed the information through to

193

Tink, who in turn passed it to Hagenbeck's people. Tink had been watching the battle unfold, ensuring all the SAS patrols were safe and in contact, keeping informed of the situation and liaising between the Australian HQ and the TOC. Six JDAMs had been dropped over the valley but al Qaeda and Taliban elements were still shooting. Jock's information was vital. He relayed the condition of the wounded soldiers: some were critical, others less so but most were coping with their injuries and several had received pain medication.

'It's funny, human nature,' Jock says. 'There's one guy and he's been wounded pretty badly up and down his side and he doesn't whinge at all. And this other little prick, he's got a few nicks and cuts and he's obviously hurt, but he's whingeing and carrying on enough so they just shoot him up with morphine. "Shut up, you little bastard." He went down. This other guy, I'm pretty sure he wouldn't take the painkillers and they didn't even know he hadn't had any. I remember asking him, "Have you had any?" and he said, "No, no" and he'd been there for a couple of hours already. "Do you want any?" "No, no." I'm pretty sure he wanted to be compos, switched on – he managed his pain.'

The fact that al Qaeda didn't inflict greater damage on the men they had pinned down in a bloody ambush continued to amaze Jock, especially as the Americans' ammunition was running low. Much of it was sitting in the rucksacks out in the open. Sitting ducks, just like the soldiers in the halfpipe.

'I can't really explain how such a big force in such an advantageous position didn't manage to do more damage. I really can't explain it,' Jock says now. 'It seemed like at times on the battlefield there was just so much shit flying around you that it would be impossible not to be hit.

'And you're watching guys with bullets landing right up the side of them, both sides of them, all the time, all bloody day. You're thinking, *what*? Almost four guys simultaneously with rounds lighting up both sides of them for what seemed like ten,

ɔck Wallace in the early hours of D-Day defending his position in the southern
nd of Hell's Halfpipe against al Qaeda and Taliban fighters hidden on the eastern
dge of the Takur Ghar. US soldiers are in the background immediately behind
ɔck and on the slope in the distance.   Photo by SAS Warrant Officer Class 2 Clint

Top: Standing beside their much envied LRPVs – otherwise known as 'devil vehicles' by the enemy – SAS patrols review the situation in Afghanistan.

Courtesy Australian Army

Middle right: Jock Wallace and two fellow Australian SAS Anaconda veterans at Bagram in March 2002. The SAS contingent received a Meritorious Unit Citation for their outstanding contribution in Afghanistan.

Courtesy Martin Wallace

Below right: As night approaches, and with Jock and Clint still in Hell's Halfpipe, SAS Commander Lieutenant Colonel Rowan Tink (centre) was inside the TOC discussing Anaconda's progress with US Army Major Lundy (left) and Hagenbeck's chief of staff, Colonel Joseph Smith (right).

Photo by John Berry, courtesy
The Post-Standard

Top: SAS troops on patrol in the badlands of Southern Afghanistan.

Courtesy Australian Army

Middle left: A few days after his harrowing eighteen hours on D-Day in Operation Anaconda in March 2002, Jock Wallace relaxed outside the main hangar at Bagram Air Base.

Courtesy Martin Wallace

Below left: SAS Patrols operated in all conditions and terrain in Afghanistan. When travelling on foot, they occasionally relied on old-fashioned techniques to transport equipment, including using donkeys the troopers named Simpson, Murphy, and Roy and HG.

Courtesy Australian Army

Above left: Jock and Clint were at the gates at Bagram to welcome back the SAS soldiers from their fourteen-day-long patrols in the Shahi Kot. The Australian troopers, including Jock's mate Johnny, stayed in the field longer than any other Special Forces operators.
Courtesy Australian Army

Above right: The 10th Mountain Division's Lieutenant Colonel Paul LaCamera (left) and Sergeant Major Frank Grippe (centre) attend the Bronze Star medal ceremony for US soldiers inside the hangar at Bagram soon after Anaconda was declined a victory.
Courtesy Sergeant First Class Michael Peterso

Below left: Sergeant Pete from the 10th Mountain Division's 120mm mortar platoon after receiving the prestigious Bronze Star for Valor for his actions in Operation Anaconda. CentCom commander Tommy Franks flew in from Florida to present the medals.
Courtesy Sergeant First Class Michael Peterso

Below right: One of the many Bronze Stars awarded to soldiers who took part in Operation Anaconda.
Courtesy Sergeant First Class Michael Peterso

Above: Jock Wallace's gold Medal for Gallantry has pride of place on the left, alongside his campaign and service medals. Above the medals are Jock's Unit Citation, Chief of General Staff Commendation, and Returned from Active Service badges.

Photo by Frank Violi

Below: Nine months after Operation Anaconda ended Margaret Wallace received this invitation to her son's investiture ceremony for the Medal for Gallantry to be held on 27 November 2002.

Photo by Frank Violi

Martin 'Jock' Wallace stands outside Government House after receiving one of the nation's highest decorations for bravery in perilous circumstances, the Medal for Gallantry. He reluctantly removed his royal-blue beret for the photo, thereby robbing his Corps of Signals of the recognition he felt they deserved.

Photo by John Fedes, courtesy News

fifteen seconds ... *tttt, tttt, tttt, tttt, tttt,* all around them, without getting hit and you think, "How the hell did that happen?"

'We're watching this one guy. We were screaming at him, "Get down, get down, get down, you dickhead." He didn't understand. "What? What?" "*Get doowwwwwwwn*, you're about to get shot." And he did. Whack, fair in the arse. He knew what we were talking about then, slipped two steps down the bottom of the hill.

'I don't know if he was confused, didn't realise what was happening, but the ground was alive, *boom*, dancing around him. Four or five of us were screaming at him.'

Jock thought the soldiers would have learnt from past experience. Earlier, another soldier got caught in the free fire lane about 50 metres from Jock's position. Al Qaeda had the GI directly in their cross hairs.

Ya bastards, Jock thought.

The enemy were taking well-aimed shots at the bloke, firing all around him, and he just stopped for a split second before he began running in a zigzag.

Jock couldn't believe it.

How the fuck could you be so stupid, mate? Run one way; don't keep turning and doing circles backwards and forwards across this tiny little space at half speed, crouched, thinking you're hiding from someone.

The soldier was like deer in the headlights. He had bullets landing at his feet, cracking overhead, and people were screaming at him to get one way or the other. He was completely stunned by the volume of fire.

'I just thank Christ I have never reacted like that – except in the presence of a woman,' Jock says. 'That's the most intimidating of forces.'

At 2.32pm, the Tactical Operations Center received the word that General Zia Lodin and his battered Afghan Force was definitely en route to Gardez and would come back to fight another day once they had recovered and reinforced. One

American special operator would later tell *The Los Angeles Times* newspaper that Lodin and his men were extremely resilient throughout the rest of Operation Anaconda despite the beating they took on D-Day. 'He got knocked down and then he got back up and he came back into the same place where he'd lost about ten per cent of his people. And then he did it a third time.'

But for now, al Qaeda's promise to fight to the death as a test from God had temporarily stalled Task Force Hammer.

Jock knew how they felt, so did his SAS mate Johnny, who was on a hill further south with his patrol, sighting al Qaeda positions and calling in grid references.

Johnny could hear the amount of firepower going into the valley and was worried about his mate Jock. He hadn't heard Jock's voice over the radio for a while. An SAS veteran, Johnny could tell who was firing by the sound of the bullets. The coalition forces were using 5.56mm and the Taliban had the 7.62mm heavy weapons that make a bigger punch. A bigger *whoomph*.

'I remember thinking how much enemy fire was going into Jock's position,' Johnny says. 'We are not on any kind of death wish, but you always prefer yourself to be in that kind of position because I know how I would handle it.

'I have never heard so much firepower, I bet my bottom dollar that I've never heard so much firepower go into an area, as where Jock was.'

He knew the GIs with Jock were well trained, even if many of the younger soldiers had no battle experience, and that some of the command were former Rangers and Navy SEALS who had undertaken similar training to the SAS troopers. But he would rather have been there himself.

The men from the 10th Mountain had brought in a battery-powered, shoulder-fired AT4 anti-armour rocket that has a maximum effective range of 300 metres and can penetrate 35 centimetres of armour. Lieutenant Colonel Paul LaCamera looked over at Frank Grippe.

'Who's our best shot, Sar Major?' LaCamera said.

Grippe called out to a private who ran over.

Jock says, recalling the moment: 'They've brought this poor bastard forward, and it's, "Right, son, we've only got one round. You confident you can do it?" What's he gonna say – "Ah, no sir"? This is LaCamera talking to the best-shot private soldier. "And don't you miss, boy." And of course, what happens?'

Jock was furious, not at the poor bastard who'd just missed an al Qaeda nest with the last rocket they had, but at the entire situation the soldiers found themselves in and the way it had unfolded. A control freak who ranks safety and preparedness as his top priorities, Jock was frustrated at the poor intelligence that had clearly underestimated the enemy positions and numbers. And he was frustrated that they were still under attack with no apparent way out, and vexed by the long delays for CAS.

'Why didn't you train your men not to drop their fucking packs – especially when they're not even getting shot at,' Jock says now. 'Why weren't you doing em-plane and ex-plane drills getting on and off the helicopter the day before, instead of going for a two-hour famil [familiarisation] joyflight? Let's do the real shit, then it would have worked out.'

Jock didn't blame the soldiers – 'most of them were young' – but he did blame the brass. The one thing he was thankful for was Grippe and Sergeant Robert Healy, who kept a firm hold on the show. 'What prepped us for this was just watching the September 11 attacks,' Healy told reporters during a press conference four days later. 'We knew we were going to be called up and go into combat and rid the world of this evil here. And all the boys are ready to do that.'

One member of Healy's 1-87 wrote on all of his hand grenades the names of two friends who perished in the September 11 attacks. This was personal.

Healy had a handful of guys including tactical air controllers and radio operators and forward observers in his position. Before flying out, he had ordered half a dozen of his troops to bring in empty sand bags in case they needed to make a secure fighting position around the control element. It would soon turn out to be a fortuitous move.

'They were worth their weight ten times in cold piss, they were bloody brilliant,' Jock says of Grippe and Healy.

'These guys were, at the time, making the calls and coming up with the decisions that were effective – and *required* essentially – for our survival. They were the ones who had the initiative. They were the ones who stepped up to the mark. That's the shit you can't buy.'

Sergeant Michael Peterson's eight-man mortar platoon had turned into an infantry squad. With their massive 120mm mortar out of action, they had nothing better to do than help each other stay alive. LaCamera had asked Sergeant Pete to liaise with Captain Nelson Kraft to find a position up on the slope of Hell's Halfpipe and pull security for the men in the bowl. Kraft directed him to a position and Peterson instantly knew why none of the other troops had occupied it until now. It was a bad spot on the northeastern corner, completely barren and with no covering protection. But the position was vital.

An order is an order, he thought.

Peterson started up the hill and turned to his young soldiers.

'Who's got the balls to follow me up this hill?' he yelled over the racket.

Sergeant Pete reckoned he sounded like an egotistical jackass but sometimes you've just got to say stupid things, he thought, and this was one of those sometimes.

He looked back over his shoulder; his men were stunned. His comments were totally out of character.

'Get the fuck up the hill,' Sergeant Pete yelled, and as one, his platoon fell in and started moving up behind him.

'They were brave, they were just awesome kids. They were looking at me like, "You've just gone mad",' Sergeant Pete says now.

Peterson's men got to position and instantly a young buck private named Ryan got pinned by a sniper. Each time the soldier tried to manoeuvre into a safer position a couple of centimetres in either direction, the sniper traced him, winging bullets right next to his head. Ryan was trapped.

'Sergeant Pete, Sergeant Peeeeeeeeete,' Ryan yelled.

'We just kind of reached over and grabbed him and pulled him away,' Peterson says.

Sergeant Pete's men were shooting at the enemy as fast as the enemy ducked out of their hideouts. The firepower was terrifying and would have paralysed lesser men. Sergeant Pete looked over behind his position and saw four al Qaeda fighters with weapons raised running towards his men, ready to shoot.

'There is a rule that you never fire over the heads of any of your guys – you never want to do that, it's called flagging,' Peterson says. 'You just don't do that. But at this point I just don't have a choice so I just start firing. I engage these guys and, alright, one of them is down, and that's when [Raul] Lopez came in with the two-oh-three and he just kept dropping rounds in there. I don't know if we got all of them but I tend to think we got a few. And I start to wonder if those are the guys who inflicted all the gunshot wounds later on that night, because somebody was back there.'

CHAPTER 17

*Down in the bowl, Jock had dragged some of the
injured men into his shell scrape and was lying over them,
taking shots and firing at the enemy, leaning on the injured
for leverage. They were safe and out of the line of fire
but Jock had made himself more visible and
increasingly vulnerable.*

IT HAD JUST GONE 3pm in the Shahi Kot Valley and the sun was starting to sink in the western sky. Someone was quietly saying a couple of Hail Marys and a few Our Fathers. 'There's no atheist in a foxhole,' Paul LaCamera would say later. Luckily for him, someone upstairs was listening to the prayers.

Up on the hill, Grippe was engaging the enemy on the opposite ridge with small-arms fire. After a lull in fighting, the battle was back on. When it rains it pours.

'Incoooommmmming,' came the warning call.

But it was too late. A mortar screamed in.

Booooooom.

Al Qaeda's aim had improved significantly and the mortar exploded in the bowl, about three metres away from LaCamera's battalion's command post at the northern end of Hell's Halfpipe, the battlefield TOC, blasting his most senior men off their feet. Six men were wounded. Healy and the colonel's operations officer, Major Jay Hall, were tossed over like rag dolls. Shrapnel cut through their uniforms and tore shreds out of their muscled bodies. Healy, who had been based in Alaska and was one of the few soldiers used to the high altitude and cold conditions, and his men had dug small ditches in the ground and filled their sandbags to build a perimeter, but it did not protect them when the mortar exploded. Healy was hit and had shrapnel holes behind his right ear. Blood was pouring out of his leg and shoulder where the jagged metal had ripped into him. Hall, too, was brassed up but not seriously wounded.

A piece of jagged shrapnel had torn through Sergeant Andrew Black's knee, almost blowing it right off. Black, who was Healy's radio operator, was losing blood fast.

A piece of shrapnel deflected about five metres, up the slope, tearing into Grippe's right hamstring and torso. He felt as if he'd been body-slammed by a wrestler. Blood poured out of his wounds, staining his torn fatigues.

'I'm hit,' Grippe yelled down to the command post as he kept firing.

Grippe didn't have time to worry about his wounds. Healy had his head down, fully expecting another mortar – where one lands, another surely follows – when LaCamera charged past and banged on Healy's helmet. The lieutenant colonel ordered the men to move position.

'Let's go, let's go,' LaCamera yelled.

Healy lifted himself up and raced about ten metres up the slope, ignoring the pain in his leg and swatting his bleeding ear like it was a mosquito.

He turned around and saw Sergeant Black in the hole where he'd been blasted. He had gone into shock. Healy charged back down and grabbed him, dragging him up the hill. It was just in time. A second round came in, exploding in the exact position where Black had been.

Healy hauled Black to cover and looked down at the wreckage that had been Black's knee. Most of the 10th Mountain soldiers had been trained as combat life-savers and all the drills told Healy that Black's injury was bad.

'Hey, bud, you're probably going to lose your leg,' he said to the fallen soldier.

'I don't care, just get me out of here alive,' Black replied.

Healy called the medics. One jabbed a syringe full of morphine into the sergeant's thigh and another placed a tourniquet above where his knee had been to stop the femoral artery from haemorrhaging.

'The medics did a good job to keep him alive,' Healy says now.

Peterson's position on the slope of Hell's Halfpipe turned out to be better than he'd first thought. The wounded were located at the casualty collection point down in the bowl, near where Jock was manning the southeast corner, and al Qaeda had begun shooting at them, zeroing in on their position.

'It was crazy. At one point you just get mad,' Peterson says. 'I'm trying not to [but during] a particularly intense mortar barrage, we're getting nailed and I was infuriated. I was mad. I wanted to just kill all those guys because they would not stop and I'm watching our guys get hit left and right and they're hitting the CCP – the casualty collection point – and re-injuring people.'

Sergeant Pete's men were running from one side of the bowl to the other, firing with their weapons on automatic burst. The return enemy fire tossed them around, but the young soldiers got right back up and returned fire. The shooting would be intense for two or three minutes, then go quiet for a couple of minutes. *What the hell's going on*, Sergeant Pete thought in the brief silence between each barrage. And then it was on again. Volley for deadly volley.

'There may have been a couple of wuss boys out there, but you know what ... the kids were awesome,' Peterson says. 'Those guys – they're buck sergeants and privates – win all wars, you know. It's not leaders like Sergeant First Class Peterson at the time.'

Staff Sergeant Randal Perez had also risen to the occasion and was continuing to lead by example, doing the job of a lieutenant. As Mark Thompson would write in *Time* magazine six months after Anaconda: 'Perez kept in touch with his men over the radio or by going helmet to helmet.' Thompson recounted how Perez ran from one soldier's firing position to another in and around the halfpipe. He was checking on his active troops as well as the wounded and would be recognised for his courage later.

Healy couldn't speak more highly of the soldiers' bravery.

'About five of the guys from Charlie Company stayed up on the ridgeline and they were receiving sniper fire and machine-gun fire, rounds were bouncing all around them, but they stayed there to cover our movement,' Healy said four days after the ambush. 'None of them faltered. They knew they could get hit at any time but they stayed there and held their ground and made sure we got out of there.'

Down in the bowl, Jock had dragged some of the injured men into his shell scrape and was lying over them, taking shots and firing at the enemy, leaning on the injured for leverage. They were safe and out of the line of fire, deep in the Afghan dirt, but by manoeuvring the soldiers Jock had made himself more visible and increasingly more vulnerable.

Jock was well aware of the dangers and knew that a ten centimetre shard of shrapnel with torn edges could cut a man in half, but the wounded needed to be protected. At all costs.

Incooommmming, came the warning again.

And a nasty fucking wait for the boom, Jock thought.

The seconds between the warning and the explosion were sheer terror. Jock didn't know if the mortar would make its destination and wipe them from the face of the earth in an explosion of blood and guts, or if it would be a dud.

Booooom.

'Mongrels,' Jock thundered.

Frank Grippe was astounded at the amount of fire, and later reflected on the injuries. 'When a mortar came in ... Sergeant Black just about got killed. We had a mortar land right in the middle of the TOC. Healy took some shrapnel, Jay Hall took some shrapnel. I was returning fire up on the hill and we had mortar rounds landing right in the bowl, I mean right in the bowl. It was pretty interesting,' Grippe says with usual understatement.

'It's like someone hitting you with a sledgehammer. It's just weird the way explosives deflect. And for whatever reason I got hit here in the upper hamstring and it put a hole in my side. That's all. I yelled down to the TOC that I'm hit, and to the guy next to me. I kept returning fire and the guy next to me just put a gauze over the wound. It wasn't till a couple of hours later that I got in the mode of looking at it.

'If I take the attitude I'm out of the fight and go and sit on my arse and feel sorry for myself ... you're not setting an example for the troops. And you need every gun available, plus I'm just another pissed-off New Yorker. And when you meld the three together you just drive on.'

Healy took the same attitude. As former Rangers, he and Grippe had survived the toughest of the tough training to graduate from Ranger School, and they understood the value of true leadership.

'You can't sit down and do a time-out or get on the disabled list,' Healy says now. 'That's one more weapon that would be out of commission if you didn't keep fighting ... You are not going to lead troops if you basically give up and let them do the fighting. If you are able to still do stuff then you need to do it, and most people did that.'

Two more mortars landed in the spot vacated by the US soldiers.

Jock's Australian colleague, SAS liaison officer Clint, was close to the command post when the mortars walked in but was luckier than Hall, Healy, Grippe and Black and had the relative luxury of more cover. It was all relative.

'Clint nearly got nailed by a mortar big time,' Jock recalls.

Clint was about two metres at the absolute maximum from the centre of the blast. His personal radio took the brunt of the shrapnel which ripped through its speaker.

The mortar rounds that nearly took out the entire command of the 10th Mountain got the adrenaline pumping. Jock was amped. He could see how Sergeant Pete and Sergeant Major Grippe charged their men to great heroics and he was going to do all he could to keep them in the fight.

Mortars raged on. Doc Byrne threw himself over one of the

injured when incoming was called – 'probably one of the bravest things I saw,' says Sergeant Pete.

Jock saw it too. *Fuck this*, he thought. *This is beyond 'Do no harm'*.

Jock got on the lifeline and radioed in to the chook pen.

He spoke firmly and clearly. 'One Oscar, this is Niner Charlie. We are taking casualties from mortars. We need CAS.'

Jock was calm but the intensity of his voice conveyed the message.

He ended his transmission with a stab at irony. 'Back to digging in. Out.'

There was nothing he could do but wait.

Sergeant Robert Healy was at the new command-and-control point in Hell's Halfpipe when one of his privates yelled down to him. The kid was up high on the slope of the bowl, out in the open, lying flat on his guts, his rifle propped on a rock, as he looked through his binoculars.

'Sergeant Healy, come here,' he yelled.

Healy raced up the slope. If a young private calls for help, you don't leave him wanting or waiting, especially not when bullets are bouncing all around him.

'I think I see where the guy directing mortar rounds is,' he said, pointing up at the eastern ridge and handing Healy his binoculars. The snow on the mountains had turned black from the bombs, changing the complexion of the Takur Ghar.

Thunk. A bullet ricocheted off Healy's helmet, nearly knocking him over.

Healy collected himself and searched through the binos, spotting the dirty big mortar tube sticking out of a cave. The private was right. *Hoo-ah!* Healy slid down the slope to the radio and ordered the forward air controller to call in an air strike, while the kid held his position up on the slope.

A fast mover screamed in and fired at the coordinates that the FAC had read out to the pilot.

Booooom.

The al Qaeda hide went up in a puff of smoke.

'I was very impressed with the young privates. I am in awe because those kids were amazing,' Healy says now.

The youngest soldier in the battle, Daniel Menard from the 120mm mortar platoon, was shadowing Sergeant Pete's every move, never letting him out of his sight.

At one point during a particularly intense mortar barrage Menard crawled up to Sergeant Pete and lay there, staring him in the face.

'What the hell are you lookin' at?' Sergeant Pete yelled.

'I'm scared, Sergeant Pete.'

'Man, we're all scared, just keep fightin'.'

'And he did and he performed. I can't imagine a seventeen-year-old going through what he did. He was a boy. He should have been going to the high school prom, but now he's a sergeant. He's awesome.

'Here is a seventeen-year-old kid – in my personal opinion he has got no business being out there,' says Peterson, who has since retired from the US Army. 'My son is seventeen now and I can't imagine him going through the hell that Menard went through.'

Sergeants Grippe, Peterson and Healy were showing true leadership in what had indeed turned out to be a sergeant's fight, showing their younger troops how to fight and survive by their own actions. For Grippe and his fellow non-coms, the concept of 'do as I do, not as I say' was a personal and absolute canon.

'There was a lot of times during that fight when I probably should have been down instead of up, but you have just got to go out there,' Grippe says. 'It's not like you are big and heroic and full of bravado. You have got to go out there and do a little inspiring. That's all it takes. Get up on the line and shoot some rounds, put a couple of rounds down; show the guys where your suspected enemy targets are and advise the commander on tactics, where people should be positioned; go talk to the wounded and keep them motivated and so forth.

'And shoot the breeze with old Digger while he's putting rounds down the range, go joke around with Clint and Wallace.'

Grippe's actions were the stuff of military legend. Jock calls him 'the ace in the American deck'.

'When it came down to it, Grippe was the one making the calls, Grippe was the one giving the right ideas and he was the one making the plays – basically he had the reins on the day. He was very good. Grippe inspired people just by his presence.

'He was walking past me and I'm shitting myself looking out, and he's, "Oh Jock, you having a good day?" And he's just walking past. Bullets landing up and down, all around, and Grippe would walk right through. It keeps your level of morale high, or picks it up again if it's dropping. Snaps you out of it. Gives you confidence. Everyone was shitting themselves – especially the wounded. They're feeling defenceless but they are still conscious. They don't know what the hell is going on.'

After Jock's last message to the communications tent, Lieutenant Colonel Tink was getting a stronger feel for how perilous it was in Jock's immediate vicinity in the Shahi Kot Valley. For 30 minutes from 3.45pm, the coalition commanders met in the Tactical Operations Center at Bagram for what was described as a 'critical meeting'.

Major General Hagenbeck and the commanders once again discussed the options as the battle moved forward, including withdrawing the soldiers who were under ambush in Hell's Halfpipe or leaving them in position to continue fighting. Hagenbeck had a lot to discuss, including the other positions that had been established successfully around the Shahi Kot Valley by the US troops who had been sending back up-to-date sitreps to the TOC.

When it came to Jock's position with the 10th Mountain, Rowan Tink noted in his green war diary: 'Hagenbeck did not make a decision to withdraw or reinforce the 1-87th. He chose to leave his decision till later with a view of implementing a new course of action at 0300 zulu.'

That was 7.30am the next day – fifteen hours away.

The men in Hell's Halfpipe could not wait that long.

Out in the battle zone, Jock was thinking if they didn't get out of there fast, they'd be dead and the reinforcements would have the privilege of extracting 82 men in body bags.

CHAPTER 18

*'The contingent was a little bit emotional at
Christmas time. I did see a few grown men cry talking
to their kids. No one batted an eyelid.'*

JOCK WALLACE

Jock wasn't always a soldier. Exactly seven years after enlisting
as a seventeen-year-old he discharged because he got jacked
off with the way the brass did things. The digger's lament. Then for
six years from January 1994, he was a regular civilian who went to
university, studied for a science degree, moved house, fell in love,
had his heart broken and fell out of love. Just like a regular civilian.

He moved through an assortment of jobs while studying at
university, including working as a doorman at a strip joint, as a
ranger on Rottnest Island, and unloading boxes from big interstate
rigs. Upon graduation, he began growing *Pleurotus ostreatus* –
oyster mushrooms. Even though Jock wanted to experience life in
Civvy Street, his connections and mates were mostly Army and he
still drank with the boys from the sig squadron, keeping up to date
with their antics. It helped, too, that he was in the Army Reserve,
ready to be called to action if need be.

But six years of living vicariously was enough. In October
2000, right after Sydney congratulated itself for putting on the
best ever Olympics, which was protected by the SAS Regiment's
counter-terrorism squadron, Jock Wallace rejoined the
Australian Army. He headed straight back to the Royal Corps of
Signals at the SAS in Swanbourne. East Timor was unravelling,

211

fast, and he wanted to be in on the action. It was what he had trained for.

'The sigs are obviously more intelligent than a grunt, that's how they ended up in the Sig School – they had more ticks on their green sheet in the aptitude testing,' Jock says now, with a laugh at the inter-unit rivalry in the Army.

When he transferred to the elite Special Forces unit in 1989, the signal squadron used old radios that his predecessors had plugged away on in the Korean conflict and the Vietnam War, punching out Morse code on valve sets as base and patrol radios. When he rejoined in 2000, the highly trained signallers had become digital natives working with new deployable and secure multi-band data and other advanced networks. Morse code was out and Jock Wallace was, officially, a communications dinosaur. Jock, being Jock, easily adapted; after all, he was a quick student who had a natural feel for comms.

The first year back in uniform went by in a blur of activity. After several years out of the regular Army, Jock was getting back into the swing of Army life. His first mission took him to South East Asia for six weeks. The time out of Australia was just the ticket and Jock loved being back in the Army – loved the camaraderie, the tall stories, the profanity, the ribbing, the excitement and the achievement. Those six weeks and the following counter-terrorism Olympics in Darwin, reminded him of what he'd missed and how much he'd missed it.

Then on 29 August 2001 Jock found himself involved in the take-down of the Norwegian container ship MV *Tampa* in one of Australia's greatest political and diplomatic crises of the year. The *Tampa* had rescued 438 people from a sinking people-smugglers' boat in Indonesian waters about 140 kilometres away from Australia's Christmas Island. The unauthorised boat arrivals (UBAs), as the Australian Government called the people, had nearly drowned when the wooden boat named KM *Palapa 1* sank. They asked the captain of the *Tampa*, Arne Rinnan, to take them to Christmas Island but Prime Minister John Howard refused the ship permission to land on Australian territory.

Rinnan steamed ahead nonetheless. A diplomatic stalemate ensued as the *Tampa* approached the island. An elite team of SAS troopers had set up there in a local gymnasium. As Rinnan steamed toward the island, the SAS team were called in to board the ship. They had to stop the *Tampa* reaching Australian territorial waters.

Jock was with the signal troop attached to a fighting squadron specialising in counter-terrorism and established the comms link back to Australia.

The mission was an atypical SAS assignment and, for five days, the troops on board the *Tampa* gave much needed medical aid and cooked and cleaned for the mostly Afghan asylum seekers. It wasn't all pleasant; some of the troops contracted scabies from the illegal immigrants and others fell sick from diarrhoea after an outbreak spread through the wretched human cargo. After days of political negotiations and front-page headlines around Australia, the fate of the *Tampa* and its unconventional cargo was decided. Had they landed in Australian territorial waters, they would have been able to apply for asylum. Instead, at the end of the standoff, the illegal boat arrivals were transferred to Nauru and New Zealand for processing. Many, ultimately, would be granted asylum in Australia.

Jock didn't buy into the politics of the situation but was proud of the work his SAS colleagues performed during the *Tampa* crisis. And he was mightily pissed off at the swell of public criticism from the bleeding hearts who had no idea of what the SAS men had done or how they provided urgent medical attention to the UBAs. Or how they'd cleaned up the latrine when they boarded the *Tampa* rather than let the desperate people – including four pregnant women – wallow in their own excrement every time they used the makeshift toilet facility the *Tampa* crew had set up in an empty sea container.

You got a beef, talk to your local politician. Don't blame us, he thought.

Jock hadn't been back at base for more than a week when the murderous attacks of September 11 occurred, and the SAS were back in action once more.

Leaving home was easy. The boys were fired up and Jock was a single bloke, which helped. He knew this from experience. Years earlier when he was part of a 45-man contingent of radio operators and drivers deployed to the Western Sahara with a United Nations force in Operation Minurso, Jock had been involved in a long-term relationship. The troops were sent to provide logistical support to the UN mission whose job was to monitor the fragile ceasefire between Moroccan forces, the Polisario and Western Sahara independence fighters while they implemented a referendum on their political future.

The tour of duty would last nearly ten months, and having a girlfriend made leaving rough and the time away more difficult. Pining for girlfriends and wives while on active duty was an unavoidable occupational hazard and, while tough, it was just as bad if not worse for the person at home, waiting and worrying. Soldiers had to steel themselves to make phone calls home, knowing how hard it was to hang up on the voice of a loved one thousands of kilometres away. The hours afterward were frequently the darkest.

'It's very hard for the man on the ground to actually make that call and then accept all the emotional backwash that is going to be there after the phone call; whereas the family is saying, "Oh, thank Christ." It's probably more of a relief for them. There were a lot of good family men with their arses on the line,' Jock says of SAS colleagues.

Being single was better; it meant there was no personal or emotional baggage attached, no worrying if the girlfriend or wife was straying or the kids misbehaving. That was the upside but, of course, there was a downside. To a single bloke, going home to nothing, no warm welcome, was tougher still.

It wasn't always easier for the entangled soldier returning home. For some it was a breeze. Walking off a troop transport plane and away from the stink of dozens of deployment-jaded men into the outstretched arms of the missus had its attractions. Knowing they'd be getting some action was one of them. But for some married soldiers, returning home was just as tough as it was for the single trooper. Some felt irritable and out of place, isolated from their wives and kids after so long away.

'I went away [while I had] a girlfriend I was very keen about,' Jock says now. 'I went to Western Sahara; that was a nightmare.'

When he went to Asia, Afghanistan and later Iraq, Jock was single and unattached which was great while he was away because he didn't have to worry about a girlfriend at home. But nearing a return home, being single was 'bang in your face. And everyone else is like, "Great." They've weathered the storm. You are counting your false blessings.'

Birthdays were hard, but Christmas was worse. Jock spent Christmas of 2001 at the forward operating base at Kandahar International Airport. Some of his chook mates got into the festive spirit and fashioned a metre-high Christmas tree from an antenna and stuck a cardboard star on the top. They placed white boxes tied with red ribbon underneath alongside a couple of MREs as gifts. It was the best they could do but it didn't alter the fact that some of the men – there are no women in the SAS – were feeling desperately homesick.

'The contingent was a little bit emotional at Christmas time. I did see a few grown men cry talking to their kids,' Jock says. 'No one batted an eyelid – just winked at 'em and kept walking, you know. It was mutual support in being allowed to express yourself in a way that I think soldiers aren't meant to, at least in the perception of the public.'

Without girlfriends, wives, partners or regular playmates, some soldiers developed a strategy to deal with moments when fellow troopers asked about the loved ones back home. It didn't take too long before they got sick and tired of having nothing to say or show for themselves.

Jock had a plan to stave off any such potentially fraught moment with the Americans, who seemed to want to show everyone pictures of their girlfriends. He had ripped a picture of a pretty brunette out of a magazine, folded it neatly, put it in his wallet and tucked it in his backpack with his other stuff. She was something to look at and he often bullshitted to Jeremy, the *Semper Fi* US Marine at Kandahar with whom he set up a lucrative trading business, that the beautiful babe was his girlfriend. Jock didn't know if Jeremy ever believed his story of love and romance, but he didn't care. It helped pass the time in the long, boring stretches that come with war.

Pictures and letters from girls back home helped take the soldiers' minds out of the battlefield, however briefly. They could make a combat-weary trooper think he was anywhere other than in some stinking hole in the middle of a desert waiting for angry al Qaeda to cruise by and present themselves as a hostile target.

Jock Wallace might have been footloose and fancy-free going to Afghanistan but he certainly wasn't joining the monastery. War didn't turn virile young men into chaste eunuchs, far from it.

While at FOB Rhino, Jock spied a good-looking officer whom he thought looked hot. He was also impressed because she could do chin-ups. 'I thought that was pretty cool,' he says. The woman was a Marine aged somewhere in her mid-twenties and, in Jock's thinking, she had a way of making camouflage gear look sexy, especially when working out. The fact that she was an officer meant she'd been to officer school, which meant she had brains. Jock liked smart women.

Handsome and charming, Jock had a way with the ladies, something he'd been finessing since his days as a fresh-faced seventeen-year-old digger during basic training at Kapooka. On Valentine's Day the first year away from home, Jock sent a single red rose each to a handful of teenage girls on the cusp of womanhood back in Tamworth. The girls had gone to school with Jock, and a red rose from a strapping soldier on Valentine's Day was about as romantic as you could get. In the weeks after Valentine's Day, Jock's mother Margaret ran into several of the girls, each of whom exclaimed with girlish delight how touched she was at Jock's amorous gesture. Margaret laughed to herself and thought, *cheeky bugger, how many more?*

Roses and romance were Jock's signature.

Just before Christmas, the regiment's commander, Gus Gilmore, had to make a trip to Kandahar where he was negotiating the SAS's ongoing role in Operation Enduring Freedom. Being the CO's signaller, Jock went along as part of the advance party. They flew to Kandahar in a Marine CH-53E Super Stallion helicopter, and as well as taking his signal gear with 'CO's Sig' written across the top, Jock took an empty ammunition box. He'd been to Kandahar a couple of times to scout out a location for the squadron's eventual move and had noticed the well-tended rose garden near, ironically, the crappers that were cleaned by the local Kandaharis. It was incongruous to see such a thing of beauty at an army headquarters, but such were the ironies of life.

Jock had decided to exploit the trip in his campaign to woo the Marine officer back at Rhino, whose surname was Perez, first name unknown.

In the middle of the night, he snuck out of the Kandahar sleeping quarters and walked over to the rose garden, picked about 30 red roses, and laid them in the ammo box. *Mission accomplished, ya smooth bastard.* The next morning, the US Marines flew the Aussies and Jock's floral cargo back to the sandblasted outpost of Rhino.

'As soon as I finished what I had to do with the CO, I broke free and went over to where [the woman] was working. She wasn't around and I said to one of the boys, "Where's Ma'am Perez?" He said, "I'm sorry, she's gone back to the ship." She had left that night. I was spewing – I was left with this box full of roses and no one to give it to.

'I went away, and came back after writing a note with some

instructions on the box, and asked them to be forwarded to her on the ship. I'm not sure if she got them, because I never heard from her.'

In the meantime, Jock had told some of his fellow diggers about his plan and while they thought it was a good scheme, they took the piss out of him because it didn't work.

'Ya dickhead, Jock.'

'Just trying to do my bit for the ladies at war,' he shot back.

CHAPTER 19

Jock didn't want to think ahead, but he knew what would come next. Guerrilla warfare was ugly and its fighters often left their most fearsome assault to the last light of day.

Late afternoon in Hell's Halfpipe, Jock's radio squelched to life. 'Niner Charlie, this is One Oscar. Update on sitrep.' The voice belonged to another chook at Bagram.

Jock looked at Clint. 'They want a sitrep, mate,' he said with a laugh.

Clint looked at Jock with a face that said, *Are you kidding me?*

'No fuckin' change,' Clint deadpanned.

Jock felt like a bit of a dill. 'It's obvious to me we haven't gone anywhere so there's no change and I didn't really need to ask him that question,' he says now.

'This is Niner Charlie, sitrep no change. Digging in, over.'

'Keep up the good work, you're doing good. Over.'

Yeah, like I need you to tell me that, Jock thought. *Patronising prick.*

'Back to digging in. Out.'

In the Tactical Operations Center, Major General Hagenbeck had two long conversations with Colonel Wiercinski who was still in the valley with his men. Both discussions focused on getting the medevac helicopters into the Shahi Kot to evacuate the wounded. The major general dispatched the choppers but an hour into the flight he turned them around. Sitreps from the battle reported that more al Qaeda and Taliban fighters were infiltrating the valley and it was too dangerous to attempt an evacuation mission. He could hear the gunfire over the radio – the noise was unrelenting – and Hagenbeck was convinced the choppers would be shot down if they went in.

'I could talk to Wiercinski, and Wallace was ... calling in close air support.'

Reports of Jock's transmissions were being passed to Tink in the TOC who informed Hagenbeck.

Hagenbeck, a considerate and educated man, was relying on Wiercinski's judgement and a number of transmissions from the field, including those from Jock. The two-star could also hear other calls for fire coming into the command centre over the American networks, including from LaCamera who was about twenty metres away from Jock.

Wiercinski and LaCamera were in contact from their two positions in the battle, and the special operators were radioing in with reports from their observation posts in the valley, updating their commanders who were in the TOC next to Hagenbeck. As the commander of Operation Anaconda, Hagenbeck carried a very big stick and had spent the previous two weeks meeting at least once a day with the commanding officers of all the units involved in the fight, seeking their situational awareness of the enemy locations and listening to their suggestions about how they would contribute to the battle. Nine countries had provided small contingents to the US-led operation, and Hagenbeck met with all of the commanders as a matter of course, as well as his fellow commanders from the US Marines, Navy, Air Force and Special Forces. This approach was typical of his management style.

The day before the operation, immediately after the battle update brief, Hagenbeck's chief of staff, Colonel Joe Smith, had invited all the commanders to a meeting in the major general's office.

The meeting was followed by tea and cake. Official invitations were distributed. Lieutenant Colonel Tink attended, as did

Colonel Mulholland, Colonel Wiercinski and a liaison officer from Task Force K-BAR.

Tink found the tea party to be a 'most quaint formality'.

'To this day it still blows me away that we sat around and had tea and cake,' Tink says. 'It almost had a surreal feeling of the Last Supper. It was only a small table, and we all sat around it with tablecloth and proper cups and saucers, and small bread-and-butter plates with slices of teacake.

'There were a couple of jokes being made, but overall there was an upbeat sort of mood to it all. We had been going flat out for a long time, and there was pressure on Hagenbeck from behind to get this thing going. This was the first time to sit down and have tea and cake together and all the work has been done and all we can do now is do it tomorrow. Showtime.'

The afternoon tea was typical of Hagenbeck's well-mannered and collegiate approach.

'Here's how I approached it,' Hagenbeck says now, referring to the way he planned Anaconda. 'We've got two weeks to go into this fight; everybody wanted to be in the fight. We had the smart guys lay out concepts, we had them lay out courses of action, and every day I met with my commanders, just us in my office ... just once a day, sometimes twice. And I let them have their say about what they thought they could do and about what they could bring to the fight.

'And part of it was to get to know each other, to develop expectations. Now, I made the decisions on the play, ultimately, but I let all of them have a say in the development of this fight and we went from worst case to best case.'

Hagenbeck wanted the commanders of the conventional forces and special operators to have a complete understanding of the task and purpose of Operation Anaconda and how each other thought. He wanted each of the main players to be full bottle on their missions so that, when and if separated, they would all be singing from the same song sheet.

Hagenbeck knew his top brass and how they thought, and he also had absolute faith in Jock and Clint and the Aussie SAS troopers in the field. Years earlier, Hagenbeck had spent time at the Singleton Army barracks in New South Wales as part of the US Army's exchange program with the Australian Army. When the 10th Mountain moved to Bagram, Hagenbeck reacquainted himself with the commanding officer of the SAS Regiment in Afghanistan, Rowan Tink. The veteran soldiers shared old war stories from Hagenbeck's days in Australia in the 1980s, when the two career soldiers had known each other. Tink had attended a course at the School of Infantry in Singleton where Hagenbeck was serving at the time.

The US–Australian exchanges were common and other soldiers in Operation Anaconda had also benefited from a visit Down Under. Sergeant Robert Healy spent three weeks at the Australian Army's parachute school on the south coast of New South Wales in 1989. Healy, a US Ranger instructor, loved the laid-back Aussie lifestyle and even managed to guest-star on one of the *Crocodile Hunter* shows with Steve Irwin.

Hagenbeck's experiences in Australia filled him with confidence about the SAS's contribution to Anaconda. 'I knew an awful lot of the Australian SAS, having lived down there and having trained with them,' he says.

'They don't get any better. They are superb. I mean, they are true professionals in every sense of the word,' Hagenbeck says of the troopers involved in Anaconda.

'I knew what they could bring to the fight. I had seen what they were able to do already, and at that point I felt very comfortable. I knew how tough they were physically and mentally, and they were very straightforward and candid. I knew quite well that they would tell me what they thought they were capable of doing, and if they said they could do it I knew they could.

'In a bit of a scuffle, they don't let go till they win.'

As the information came in from the battlefield, Hagenbeck and his operations and intelligence officers in the TOC processed it.

'I went to great extents to keep my mouth shut, because I did not want to be guilty of trying to fight the fight on the ground when I didn't really know the specifics of that sort of thing,' Hagenbeck says, explaining his tactics on the day. 'My conversations were with Wiercinski only, and you can count them on one hand. He called back and made reports and we'd get a 'Roger, out'. Wiercinski had called me and told me that all the soldiers that had been wounded had been stabilised and there were a handful of them that were in very bad shape, but he thought that they could hold on for a while, so I went with his recommendation.'

Around 4pm, the calls for CAS were answered when an AC-130 gunship armed with a 105mm howitzer roared overhead and ripped into the countryside. A B-1 bomber followed soon after and delivered several 1000-pound JDAMs in a box pattern on the mountain, razing a Zeus (ZSU–23) 23mm anti-aircraft artillery piece that was spotted jutting out of a cave on the ridgeline.

According to the official US Air Force report released in 2005, the crew of another B-1 later reported that it dropped fifteen JDAMs on six targets in six bomb runs. Around 4.30pm, stacked higher in the sky above the B-1s, a B-52 dumped several 1000-pound JDAMs on Marzak and repositioned to launch 27 free-fall MK82 bombs which exploded along a string of targets.

The afternoon bombing raid was a double-edged sword for the men in Hell's Halfpipe. Jock was lying on the hard ground of the halfpipe watching the bombers drop their load.

'I hope they're on target. I hope they're on target. I hope they're on target. I hope they're on target,' he said over and over.

'It's a real mongrel feeling because you know they are there to help you, but one slight stuff-up and the help will be the opposite,' he says now.

'They dropped their guts. It felt like 60 000 kilograms. It didn't feel like three 2000-pounders, let's put it that way. They landed about 400 metres from us. I had my fingers in my ears and I was just waiting to die, basically.'

By late afternoon, Hagenbeck's command had received more intelligence from the special operators and soldiers in the valley.

According to the USAF report, Hagenbeck's Coalition Joint Task Force Mountain informed the Coalition Forces Land Component Command, or CFLCC, that 'hardcore elements, sensing success against coalition forces, perceive no need to exfiltrate at this time'.

It was bad news and confirmed that Colonel Mulholland's prediction that al Qaeda would fight to the death was spot on. Not that any of the blokes in the bowl doubted it.

'Around mid-afternoon, [al Qaeda] were [so] confident that they would stand outside the cave entrance and grab their genitals and flip us off, wave to us,' Jock says now, 'because by that stage they realised we only had 5.56mm [weapons] and we didn't have enough and we couldn't reach out to them. They could shoot down into us but our weapons didn't make it back.

'I felt useless, ripped off. You just felt frustrated and it's a sinking frustration.' Jock was armed with an M4 but would have preferred to have an SLR (self-loading rifle), which had a longer range. 'I would have been shooting those little pricks off rocks all day with one of those. They will go twice as far as an M4,' he says of the SLR.

The old SLRs had a range of 600 metres and would have put the majority of the enemy in Jock's range. His M4 had a laser sight aimpoint but it was only good to 360 metres.

'Even at 300 metres, the red dot of the aimpoint nearly covers the whole body so you could be shooting him in the tip of his toe or parting his hair, you don't know,' Jock says.

The M4s are versatile weapons and good for operating in cars and jungles, but lousy in the open when the enemy is more than a few hundred metres off in the distance.

Lieutenant Colonel Tink was in the TOC for a 1200 zulu briefing – 4.30pm local time. The briefing confirmed that the Americans had taken fourteen casualties and reiterated the one KIA (killed in action) – Stanley Harriman who had been killed earlier that morning. At that point in the TOC no one knew for sure that friendly fire had claimed the first American life in

Operation Anaconda. The harsh reality would come later. Tink also recorded that 21 Northern Alliance soldiers were wounded, with one KIA.

The 'stalemate' mentioned by Hagenbeck earlier did not accord with the information Tink's staff were pulling together from the SAS patrols in the field and Jock and Clint's sitreps.

Tink's operations officer (OpsO) also informed him that he believed the communications between Wiercinski and Hagenbeck were intermittent and lacking detail. Tink tasked the OpsO to seek what is known in military terms as 'ground truthing', or more detailed reports from the scene of the battle. Tink wanted to supplement the Americans' information.

'The 1200 briefing ... was the point at which it became apparent to me that Hagenbeck and I were receiving differing reports about the gravity of the situation,' Tink says now.

At 4.44pm Tink further noted: 'Raiders taking heavy mortar fire.'

The raiders were Jock and the 10th Mountain Division. The tension in the TOC was palpable.

At 5pm Hagenbeck's command contacted CFLCC with another message. CFLCC fell under the leadership of the US Army's Lieutenant General Paul Mikolashek. Hagenbeck's newest estimate for the situation in the southern end of the Shahi Kot Valley was that there were still between 200 and 300 al Qaeda in the three villages, with at least another hundred in the surrounding hills. Not all were Afghans, and some were foreign fighters who had joined the jihad.

'The enemy positions on Takur Ghar and Marzak are presenting robust defences,' CJTF Mountain reported.

Back in the valley Jock's ears were ringing from the sustained bombardment. He felt like he'd been held up by his ankles and shaken. He simply could not believe the number of enemy fighters in the valley.

As he looked south, he could see them manoeuvring in closer, inching their way along the precarious goat tracks on the rocky ledges a couple of hundred metres away. He checked on the wounded in his shell scrape, made sure they were covered, and pulled the trigger on his M4. *Ttttt, tttt, tttt, ttttt.*

And again. *Ttttt, tttt, tttt, ttttt.*

'How'd you go, buddy?' asked one of the injured American kids.

'Yeah, not bad, mate,' Jock replied. He had to remain positive so the kid wouldn't give up hope after lying in that hellhole for the past eleven hours with a chunk ripped out of his body and pinned down by the enemy. Another young fella crammed in next to him was morphed up, feeling no pain at all, the lucky bastard.

Jock still had a bit of confidence in the firepower that was coming in to back up the troops. Even so, he felt at a serious disadvantage. They had the best troops and the best equipment but they weren't able to use it in the best possible way to gain ground. The troops couldn't put the firepower down range to attempt to gain ground, and because they were using close air support it was too dangerous to send soldiers forward because the US bombs could have taken them out.

'That's the compromise of using air – you have to take a tactically inferior position in that situation.

'Guys were pissed off and there was a realisation – you definitely knew they knew they were in the shit,' Jock says. 'I'm not saying that the individuals there on the day did a bad job; I'm saying they were let down by the system that put them there. They were told one thing and given another.'

Jock believed also that the soldiers couldn't successfully fight their way out of the valley if they had wanted to. 'As a group we could have made a concerted effort to fight out, back south down the valley, but we couldn't because we didn't have the weapons or the bloody terrain to do it.'

Jock figured the air assault had gone in half-arsed but he wasn't blaming the troops on the ground for the situation they now found themselves in. Instead, he was dirty on the REMFs – the 'rear echelon motherfuckers' – who, he'd lay money on it, couldn't organise a piss-up in a brewery.

'You felt betrayed; there had been a breach of agreement

basically,' he says. 'I will go in and fight for your cause, I'll give my life, but I'm not just going to walk up to the block and surrender it. I'm going to fight for it. But as a soldier I anticipated if you are going to go off and fight in someone else's country you may as well make it a good bloody effort ...'

The sun was sinking slowly in the western sky, and with it the temperature. It was positively freezing. Jock's bloodied knuckles had crusted over, a mix of dirt, blood and, he was sure, ice. He looked up at the majesty of the landscape and marvelled at how it had all come to this.

Jock didn't want to think ahead, but he knew what would come next. Guerrilla warfare was ugly and its fighters often left their most fearsome assault to the last light of the day.

These jokers would be no fuckin' different, he thought.

'Things had sort of gone quiet for a little bit, that's the calm before the storm,' he says. 'Have you ever heard the expression "things are too quiet"? Well, they bloody were, that's because these little mongrels were doing all their manoeuvring to get into position. And then all of a sudden, *bang*, all hell broke loose again.'

CHAPTER 20

Gently, he shifted his torso and placed the grenade under his chest. The weight of his body kept the safety bail down, preventing the fuse in the grenade from being lit and detonating under him.

B*oom. Boom. Boom. Boom.* The thunderous explosions announced the onslaught and broke the deceitful silence that had fallen on the Shahi Kot Valley while the al Qaeda and Taliban fighters covertly negotiated positions for their last-light attack. Jock didn't look at his watch – no need to when you're living each minute according to someone else's battle plan – but a gentle darkness had started to shroud the valley and long shadows from the Whale blanketed Hell's Halfpipe. He guessed it was around 5.30pm, maybe a little later – almost half a day since they landed at the foot of an al Qaeda stronghold.

Boom. The fifth rocket, like the ones before, smashed into the eastern bank of the bowl; all in quick succession, all fired from the eastern ridgeline. Once the dust had settled, a wicked torrent of machine-gun fire rained down from the western side high above a precipitous cliff that dropped straight to the valley floor.

The barrage was full-on, the most intense fire of the day and there was absolutely nowhere to hide.

'How the fuck did the motherfuckers get over there?' Jock said under his breath, using the soldier's preferred profanity in almost every possible grammatical combination.

The enemy was less than 200 metres away on the west. Perfect sniping position. The rockets and mortars from the east, *bang, bang, bang, bang, bang,* were the signal to terrorist elements on the west to open fire. Al Qaeda had the men from the 10th Mountain pinned down, surrounded on two sides, east and west, and closing in from Marzak one kilometre north, zeroing in on the ambushed soldiers with mortars and RPGs and giving it everything they'd got. Which was a shit-load.

Machine-gun rounds cracked like bullwhips overhead, smacking into the halfpipe, kicking up dirt and rocks on all sides of the bowl. If a trooper got up, he'd be caught in the crossfire.

You're not going to get me, Ahmed, not tonight, not here.

Jock thought of Johnny on patrol further south in the valley, hoping that he didn't decide to lead his men up to Jock's position to save his mate. Soldiers are like that. In the Army, mateship is king. Your fellow soldier isn't just a fellow soldier, he's your brother. *You'd bloody well die for him.*

Jock was on the southeast corner with his radio, his backpack and a handful of wounded piled into his and Clint's shell scrapes. Grippe's men were combat-crawling in and out of the line of fire, trying to find protection on the eastern slope of the bowl where they had positioned themselves to shoot into the eastern ridgeline. But now they were getting their arses shot off from the western side. Sergeant Pete thought the whole world was shooting at him personally.

'Where the hell are they comin' from, the sky?' he yelled at Grippe.

The soldiers spun around, returned fire at the western sniper positions and somehow avoided getting killed as they manoeuvred up and down the bowl, taking effective countermeasures by scrambling up the western slope. But that put them directly into the line of fire from the bad guys who had been there all day on the eastern ridge. It was a no-win situation in a confined kill zone, which is what the enemy wanted. There was bugger-all cover.

230

'Get down, get down,' Jock screamed.

Bang. One soldier copped a bullet in his buttocks and crashed to the bottom of the bowl on top of the wounded, screaming in agony: 'I'm shot, I'm shot.'

Still, it was a miracle he was alive.

The soldiers couldn't cover either side without getting shot at. It was about to get worse.

Al Qaeda launched their ground assault from the north, out of Marzak.

'At this stage we are completely surrounded. They weren't friendlies shooting at us,' Jock says. 'They were trying to sneak up on us and at the same time they were dropping mortars on us and hitting us with rockets. The guys who were up on the ridge were pouring all their small-arms fire down on us in order for the guys on the western ridge to sneak right up on us. They came up to about 50 metres from us when they were coming out of Marzak. They came up pretty close – 50 to 100 metres.'

Jock, prone, looked to the southeast. Small-arms fire buzzed by his ears. He had a clear view.

Jesus fuckin' Christ.

Two hundred metres away he spotted an al Qaeda terrorist crouched behind an RPK light machine gun. All of a sudden, the air opened up as an AQ fighter began punching rounds straight at Jock. There was no cover. The terrorist was higher than him and had the advantage. Bullets sprayed in front, beside and over Jock's head.

'They were on target; they were ripping into us,' Jock says. How the hell they missed him God only knows and Jock wasn't inclined to stop for a quiet chat to find out.

The 10th Mountain force was now surrounded on all four sides. The enemy had a clear shot right up the guts of the bowl, straight into the back of the soldiers fighting up the northernmost slope, where Grippe and LaCamera had re-established their command post. Al Qaeda fired over the wounded who were at the casualty collection point, lined up shoulder to shoulder, trying to keep warm and stay alive as Doc Byrne attended to their wounds. Jock and Clint dragged more of the wounded into their shell scrapes to keep them out of the line of fire.

'We were lying on top of them to fight. Treading on them, crawling on them, crawling over them; we threw them in our own holes,' Jock says now. 'With fire from the west as well as the east, it was even worse, so you are crawling on your hands and knees at best.'

Sergeant Pete bolted for the western slope with his riflemen to lay down suppressive fire on the new al Qaeda positions. It was kill or be killed. The soldiers didn't dwell on it.

'We got some folks up there and they started suppressing, but [the enemy] were really making a mess of where Jock and where some of Charlie Company was at – they were hitting those guys pretty good,' Sergeant Pete says now.

The machine gunner was aiming at the men of Charlie Company who were countering the assault out of Marzak. Jock knew he had to silence it straight away. It was either that or they'd be doing a body count in Hell's Halfpipe before the day was out.

Jock was with the only other able-bodied person in the southern end of the bowl at that moment – a young American soldier. Clint was in the guts.

Instinct. If he didn't react, neither of them would be there much longer.

He dropped the radio handset, ripped his M4 to automatic and squeezed the trigger to engage the enemy, firing half a magazine's worth of 5.56mm bullets. The Yank arced up, too.

That's mighty neighbourly of you, friend.

The enemy machine gunner dropped like a sack of shit. Jock emptied the remaining half of his magazine – another fifteen rounds – into the crumpled heap just to make sure he didn't get back up again. There's no second chance in a war zone.

Jock and the young American GI were facing south, aiming and shooting. Mortars and bullets were landing to the left and right of them, coming from the eastern and western ridgelines and now the south.

'Most of the available bodies were engaged in a gunfight trying to stop the assault from the north, so the machine-gun bullets from the south were ripping right past me and into their backs,' Jock says. 'The rest were pinned down in the middle of the pipe unable to return fire. There was literally only two of us holding the entire southern end of the pipe.'

Seconds later, four or five al Qaeda fighters began creeping around their fallen comrade, firing directly at Jock and the Yank.

'Stupid fucks,' Jock roared.

He slammed another magazine into his M4, released the working parts, and pulled the trigger, throwing lead down range. He picked off the enemy one by one, split second by split second, with brutal and lethal efficiency. *It's us or them.* Two mags depleted. Eight to go.

'They were really stupid, they popped up over this rise like they were invisible and creeping along, and we're just *bang, bang, bang*, "Get out!" I gave them a couple of bursts of automatic. Engaged it, knocked it and got a few more of the bastards who were coming up on the left and the right of it. We never saw them again,' Jock says. 'And they weren't a problem.'

Jock and his new buddy had dispatched the enemy machine gunner and his comrades with skilled efficiency that reflected the urgency of the situation. Mortars, rockets and machine-gun fire were coming in from the eastern and western ridges, and a ground assault was creeping down from the north.

'We were now reduced right down to the bloody bottom of this creek bed in a sea of wounded, injured soldiers just littered everywhere,' Jock says.

The insane amount of fire lasted about twenty minutes, then stopped for a minute. Jock knew the score. The enemy were regrouping. Typical mujahideen tactics. They'd been doing it for hundreds of years.

Pffat, pffat, pffat, pffat. Rat a tat tat.

Bullets landed at Jock's prone body, blasting dirt and rocks into his face with the fury of a gale. He was lucky he had closed his shooting eye, otherwise he would have been blinded. He copped a mouthful of dirt, but not an eyeful.

'They were really trying to wipe us off the face of the planet and they did a pretty bloody good job considering they didn't have air power,' says Jock now. 'They exploited the situation quite well. The bloody Americans walked into the biggest ambush I've ever seen – or put us into it.

'In retrospect, I think that the [first five] rockets at last light were the signal for the assault to commence from the west, and that was the first time we knew that these little mongrels were around on the western side. Up until that stage, we had fought off any assaults coming from the north to get around behind us on the west. Apart from the fact that we thought there were forward observers up there, there was never any indication of any kind of significant force attempting to dislodge us on the west. But once they had the west and the east, it was quite clear that they were going to try and pin us down from those ridges and try and sweep through with a ground assault, which is what they tried to do from Marzak.'

Jock had been glued to the radio all day and knew that Marzak was a hotbed of activity. Even though his view was south, he could hear the enemy getting ready in their calls and cries and the intensity of the shooting.

The situation was getting worse, if that was possible. Soldiers shot over each other's heads, firing east and west, while those who could looked north toward Marzak, waiting for the ground assault to arrive. The noise was horrendous, and Jock thought if anything would make you succumb to fear the noise would be the trigger. That and a frightening lack of visibility. But the soldiers had a job to do, fear or no fear. No one was succumbing to anything, not the least these AQ fighters screaming *Allahu Akbar* while trying to kill him – Jock Wallace – and the men from the 10th Mountain Division.

But they were still taking casualties. The Yanks used tracer fire, which gave Jock the utter shits because it was a double-edged sword. Dusk had settled over the Shahi Kot Valley and the tracer gave away their precise position, enabling the enemy to zero in with their mortars, but it could also help pinpoint enemy targets for CAS and other soldiers.

Jock grabbed his handset.

'One Oscar, this is Niner Charlie,' he said. 'We are surrounded. Enemy are now active on western ridge. We have a ground assault occurring on our position from the north and enemy have just established machine gun in the southeast. Wait, out.'

Minutes later, Jock was back on the radio.

'This is Niner Charlie. We are being bracketed. We have just taken casualties. If we do not get CAS, we are not going to be here in a couple of minutes.'

Jock wanted to convey exactly how precarious their position was. The rounds ringing out in the background helped.

'I was using every subtlety that I could to enhance the point to the chook on shift – he would have had a gaggle of Ruperts behind him listening in,' Jock says now. 'He is sitting on the radio and behind him on a little U-table are the Ruperts.

Jock told the chook: 'This is Niner Charlie. I'm going back to the fight. I'll get back to you when I can. If I can. Out.'

Jock then radioed the Bossman, the call sign for the US Air Force's E-3 AWACS plane flying God-like overhead. He passed his handset to the forward air controller, Vick, who had returned to Jock's position and then read out in a staccato delivery a series of grid coordinates as close air support targets.

'Thanks, bud,' he said to Jock.

Two single-seater F/A-18C Hornets swooped over the Shahi Kot, strafing enemy positions with their 20mm cannons at what is known as 'danger-close' range to the coalition forces on the ground. Despite the danger, the soldiers' spirits lifted instantly.

'*Hoo-ah!*' came the roar of approval from the bowl.

The fast movers each made three passes over the valley,

delivering a total of 400 rounds from their guns. As they sped off, Jock looked at what had been active mortar positions and saw bodies hanging over the rocks.

Thank you, fast movers, he thought.

The strafing run slowed things down for a moment.

The young wounded bloke that Jock had dragged to safety six hours earlier was ensconced in Jock's pit. Jock had been looking after him throughout the day, giving him a cigarette when he asked for one and making sure he was kept warm and out of harm's way. He had shrapnel wounds and a gash around his eye. One centimetre lower and it would have taken out the eye or, worse, killed him. Jock had positioned the kid beneath him for protection, but they were facing each other, looking over each other's shoulders, watching out for encroaching enemy fighters, ready to snipe them if they rose into the line of fire. Waiting. Waiting.

As the last light faded, the blood-spattered kid looked at Jock. 'Hey, bud, we gonna be alright?' he said in a strong American accent that Jock couldn't precisely locate.

Jock's honest-to-God feeling was that they were both going to be shot in the back of the head by al Qaeda running over the top of one of the surrounding slopes of Hell's Halfpipe. But he couldn't bring himself to crush the young kid.

The kid was terrified, shitting himself, and Jock was too, but the young GI was looking for reassurance and Jock wasn't going to let him down.

'She'll be right, digger,' he said. 'Hang in there, mate. We'll take care of it.'

The soldier sat there for a couple of seconds and looked at Jock, the look on his face changing as he realised what he had to do.

'Good luck,' the young infantryman said, getting up on one knee, cocking his rifle, ready to move out.

Jock was stunned. *The kid's got balls.*

'I have gotta go do my job, *hoo-ah*,' he said, running off to join his section further up the bowl as bullets pinged all around.

'He knew he wasn't wounded enough to lie there and do nothing,' says Jock now, full of admiration for the young grunt's courage. 'He knew, despite the fact that he was wounded, he was still capable of fighting and this was his time. Despite the fact that he obviously was shitting himself to death, he rose on his own accord, without prompting, to get up and go and fight with his mates, the people he had come into battle with. And he wasn't going to lie down there and take the arvo off because he had a headache.

'*Sorry, mate, the Panadols didn't arrive.* I had respect and pity all at once for him. Respect in that he had made the choice to make a better choice and not just cop what was coming, and then he had the balls to follow it through. He not only had the heart to come up with the right decision but the balls to carry it out.'

Command Sergeant Major Frank Grippe is proud of his young GIs and the courage they displayed under fire.

'Throughout history, infantry forces have always been younger soldiers,' Grippe says. 'You have got to have younger soldiers ready to carry the load. Their testosterone level makes them a little bit more focused to charge instead of duck.'

The casualties kept coming. Most of the soldiers' initial injuries were frag and shrapnel wounds, but towards the afternoon and last-light attacks, troops were getting hit by sniper and rifle fire as the enemy crept closer. By 6pm, there were more than twenty wounded in the bowl.

'This is fucked up. Mogadishu ain't got nothing on this,' yelled an older soldier who had been involved in the Black Hawk Down incident. Surviving that had been hard work and getting all their soldiers home – some of them dead – was a badge of honour he wore proudly.

Sergeant Robert Healy had been shot up by shrapnel earlier in the day. Like Grippe, who was carrying about eight pieces of shrapnel in his leg courtesy of al Qaeda, Healy had stayed in the fight and was leading the charge. After a long day in the halfpipe, Healy was looking forward to the coming night.

He had worked with the AC-130 aircraft, the Spectres, and had no doubt they would help carry the night. 'Hey, don't worry about it,' he told the troops near him. 'Papa Spectre's coming. He'll take care of it.

'We own the night. We can see them. They can't see us.'

Looking back, Healy says of the Spectre crew, 'I have the utmost confidence and respect for those guys.'

Grippe echoed his sentiment. The creeping night was a blessing because the soldiers could pinpoint the exact location of enemy positions by the flashes from their gun muzzles.

'It's a lonely place being in a valley in the middle of Afghanistan,' Grippe says now. 'You know, 82 guys are surrounded – but I know with our air power, and especially at night, we are able to go out into the field and get our rucksacks off the field and get our night-observation devices back on.

'And to tell you the truth, I was looking forward to the dark so that we could actually attack up in the hills and smoke these sons of bitches, kill them, engage them, tactically manoeuvre our angles.

'At first dark we really took a heavy pounding of fire ... we were, more or less, almost 360 degrees surrounded and taking fire from 360 degrees. I remember Wallace being off to the right and he had a group of wounded down there and he had his radio set up. And I remember being out in the open and taking and engaging this one guy about 400 metres away, and we are just putting fire back and forth on each other.

'He [the enemy fighter] would spray automatic weapons fire and tracer would just whiz by me. But it doesn't even dawn on me that there's five bullets between each of those tracers. And it went by my face and you just keep a steady aim and I'm watching my tracer hit right where his muzzle flash was.'

Nevertheless, any hope that Jock might have had earlier that he was going to get out of the valley alive were gone – washed away by the rain of bullets. He truly thought he was going to die. But he couldn't worry about that. He accepted it, the way all good soldiers do and he wasn't going to go down without a fight. He would not dishonour himself or his uniform, no matter what he thought of the situation. Not that Jock had a death wish, but despite the continued close air support that had had a devastating effect on the enemy, al Qaeda just kept coming. *Like the Energiser bunny*, he thought. It was as simple as that.

Jock was shitting himself, no doubt about it. But his greatest fear was not a full frontal meeting with the enemy, head-to-head, nose-to-nose, or taking a bullet or dying on blood-soaked foreign soil. This was war; soldiers die.

His greatest fear was the unknown and there were plenty of unknowns. He could only look in one direction, southeast down the valley, and couldn't see if al Qaeda or Taliban fighters were sneaking in behind him from the north, or on the west, or from their cave hideouts on the eastern ridge, ready to place a well-aimed bullet in his head.

Jock had packed three hand grenades in his webbing and rummaged around to drag one out. He pulled the pin that locked the safety bail on the small explosive and carefully tucked the pin in his ammo pouch. Gently, he shifted his torso and placed the grenade under his chest. The weight of his body kept the safety bail down, preventing the fuse in the grenade from being lit and detonating under him.

If he got shot now, Jock would have the last say. He had, effectively, booby-trapped his body. If the al Qaeda terrorists shot him and turned his body over to claim his weapons as a trophy – then, eight seconds later, *boom*. They'd be toast.

Goodnight Irene.

It was a dangerous tactic, but if worst came to worst, Jock thought, it had a certain ironic beauty about it.

'I really thought they were coming over the top and I was anticipating they were coming over from the western side, or from the north, and that wasn't comfortable for me because I had to watch to the southeast,' Jock says. 'I would have just got one in the back of the head. That's why I lay on my grenade – because I thought, if they start coming in and nicking my equipment, then they're going to get a surprise.

'*Stuff them!*'

CHAPTER 21

*'I had two guys who were out with an American unit
that was in serious trouble. There was a clear belief that
they may not survive it in their current situation and
particularly if they remained there all night.'*

LIEUTENANT COLONEL ROWAN TINK, THE COMMANDER OF THE
AUSTRALIAN SAS REGIMENT IN OPERATION ANACONDA

'One Oscar, this is Niner Charlie, over.'

Jock was lying on the ground talking into his handset,
radioing back to the Australian SAS communications tent
at Bagram.

'Roger, this is One Oscar. Wait,' came the reply from the chook
on duty.

The tent was chockers and several soldiers stood around with
worried looks etched on their faces. Jock's previous
communications had not painted a pretty picture and they could
hear, loud and clear, the battle raging in the Shahi Kot Valley and
it was nothing like the soundtrack of *Apocalypse Now* or *Full
Metal Jacket*. It was much worse.

Jock was on the radio, this time asking for the regimental
commanding officer, Lieutenant Colonel Tink, on behalf of Clint,
the SAS's liaison officer with the 10th Mountain Division.

The two Aussies had spent the past ten minutes nutting out
their strategy because it didn't look like one was forthcoming
from Bagram. They had no idea if they were going to get out of
the valley alive.

Jock and Clint discussed an escape and evasion plan in case the al Qaeda and Taliban fighters outsmarted the CAS and outflanked the company in Hell's Halfpipe. As it was, they were completely surrounded. If Jock and Clint had to execute their E&E, they had to head south.

'We weren't going to leave them [the US troops], but in the event that we were overrun, or there was a sprint foot-race scenario, then we were going to lead the fight south and try and link up with the Australians,' Jock says now.

Jock's mate Johnny and his SAS patrol had relocated to a new observation point in the south but were just a couple of kilometres away. They listened to the gunfight as planes roared in overhead, delivering death to the enemy and sending clouds of smoke and fire into the sky. An American forward air controller had been placed with the team and they could hear the CAS being called in over the Yanks' nets. Nine other Aussie patrols were in the AO, ready to take out any fleeing al Qaeda or Taliban fighters. But the enemy had stayed in the valley and were closing in on Jock's position, fighting to the death in their jihad.

'There was no doubt that we knew we would be dead if we stayed there overnight,' Jock says. 'We had taken that many casualties that there weren't enough men to carry the casualties out – you need two men per casualty. Then, as a result of that, there was no one providing protection and we were in very dire circumstances.'

Clint needed to talk to the brass. *Now*. He was about to let Rowan Tink know just how precarious it was and Jock was only too happy to oblige his mate.

The lieutenant colonel was in the chow line at the back of the main hangar, about to grab his first bite to eat for the day, when he was interrupted by the SAS operations officer, Gavin. The OpsO told Tink that he was needed back in the comms tent. Clint had a sitrep and things were getting worse. Until now, most of the communications from Clint and Jock had been passed through staff to the CO, who was based in the TOC with the American command. As soon as Tink walked into the tent, he clocked the worried faces and realised just how bad things had become after the last-light attack.

Tink took the radio.

Jock recalls: 'Clint was attempting to look after other people's welfare, just basically having a positive input on the battle. He was fucked off and infuriated at the situation and he was telling Tink, the colonel, "Listen, you have to make a decision."'

'And Tink is going, "You are to remain where you are."'

'[Clint said] "And you don't know what we're doing here, do you, mate? What have we been doing for the last fourteen hours? Fourteen hours we've been fighting tooth and nail for our bloody lives and haven't moved a friggin' inch up the valley."'

'"You will stand your ground."'

Tink told Clint to keep digging in.

Clint replied that unless someone came up with a plan to extract the troops fast, he and Jock would be coming back from the Shahi Kot Valley on 'a fucking medevac helo', dead or wounded.

'He's not just saying, "I'm going to grab a free ride", he's trying to get a point across,' Jock says now.

The point being that they were surrounded and the enemy was moving in, gaining ground. If the soldiers weren't extracted from the valley soon, they'd be dead.

Clint's 'ground truthing' was powerfully confronting; a heat-of-the-battle eyewitness account loaded with danger, anger and a desperate and frustrated sense of impotency because they had been ambushed. The wounded kept coming, some had been there for more than ten hours; ammo was running low – the 7.62 machine-gun ammo had been exhausted in the early hours of the day. As well, their shell scrapes were full of wounded and the two SAS soldiers were surface dwellers with nowhere else to dig.

Clint and Jock felt stranded.

Tink didn't doubt the gravity of the situation Clint was outlining in his bull-headed way. The CO turned off the speakers that had been broadcasting the conversation.

'There was a concern [in Clint's voice] that you could only attribute to someone believing that they may not get out of this alive,' Tink says now at HMAS *Kuttabul* at Garden Island, on Sydney Harbour. 'He believed that there was a good chance that they may well die out there in that location ... this was not the sort of information that I wanted everyone to hear.'

'In that report Clint referred to the sequence of events that had occurred throughout the day. He referred to the fact that they had been attacked on three sides. He referred to the number of injuries that the Americans had suffered up to that particular stage.

'Clint's assessment, at the end of the day, was that he believed the enemy would have a decided tactical advantage come night time, in that they would be able to get in much closer to them. Whereas, at the moment, they were able to hold these guys off at a distance.'

Clint's forceful tirade was accompanied by the symphony of war. Ordnance was being dropped, machine-gun fire was going off, orders were being barked out, and the wounded were moaning and begging for morphine. Soldiers were shouting pumped-up war cries as they aimed and fired. It was war.

Hoo-ah, motherfuckers.

Jock could hear Clint getting more and more pissed off because he wasn't getting the answers that he wanted.

'Just trying to relay shit under that noise was difficult,' Jock says.

'Clint was fully aware that he had my life as well as his own to look after, and that we were with a coalition force,' Jock says. 'We had been on the ground all day ... we'd had casualties for over eight hours when this was occurring, and Clint had had enough. He just said this is bullshit and he told them in no uncertain terms.

'Clint said that we are not in a very good position at all, tactically. We haven't moved all day. Are there plans to get us out of here and if not, are we allowed to E&E ourselves, basically escape and evade ourselves?'

Clint was a senior warrant officer telling his CO that he'd been stitched up and would like the opportunity to fight his own way out of there; would like permission to fight for his own life in a manner that he considered appropriate. To Jock, Clint was a hero and the brass cocooned inside the safe HQ were a bunch of REMFs who had no idea what it was like under fire in the halfpipe.

When Clint told Jock that one of the orders was to continue digging in, Jock pissed himself laughing, a mix of dark humour and disgust.

'Bloody handy hints from the supercoach. What do they think we've been doing all day?' Jock said.

The SAS patrols in the valley could hear the discussion between Clint and Tink over the Australian radio network. Jock's network wasn't working as well as it should have been. His antenna, which the guys jokingly dubbed the 'death ray', had been repeatedly knocked down as the injured soldiers manoeuvred to safety, causing brief, occasional dropouts.

'Once the wounded were piled up in there, [other] people were standing over them and tripping over the antenna. It was a bit of a battle round dark just to keep the comms up, because the antenna was getting knocked arse over head the whole time,' he says now. 'You can't blame anyone. There were wounded people lying everywhere and other people trying to do their jobs and you've got very little space to do it and so you adjust. You realise that when you've been flapping your gums for a minute or so and no one has answered you, it's probably because the antenna is down.'

Despite Tink's response to Clint, the report made an impact on the CO, who understood that the two men he had assigned to the 10th Mountain Division were in perilous circumstances. Lieutenant Colonel Tink was responsible for his men and, after the tragic death of SAS trooper Sergeant Andrew Russell two weeks previously, he did not want another fatality in his unit. One was too many, and Russell's death had been keenly felt among the troops and by the CO. It was another reason why Tink had been such a hard-arse with the American command on the issue of deconfliction.

Earlier that afternoon, Tink had begun to suspect that Major General Hagenbeck's statement about the valley being in a stalemate situation was off the mark. The information Tink's staff had pieced together indicated the opposite. Now that he had spoken directly with Clint, the CO was 100 per cent sure of it. Over the next couple of hours, more conversations were had with Clint, resulting in a passage of information via Tink back to Hagenbeck in the TOC and his deputy general and chief of staff.

Based in the Tactical Operations Center, Tink had a wider view of the entire battle. Unlike Clint, Tink didn't believe the situation would deteriorate at night because the Americans and Australians had the technological advantage of night vision devices. But there was another critical issue. He knew that a quarter of the company were wounded, which meant the blocking force had been neutralised and had to be reinforced or withdrawn by dawn. After first light when the sun rose over the Shahi Kot Valley, the advantage would revert to the enemy on the high ground. Hagenbeck already had decided that the medical evacuation would go in after last light, but no decision had been made about the option to reinforce the troops or withdraw them.

'Indeed, Hagenbeck had advised earlier that he would not make that decision until first light the next morning,' Tink says now.

Referring to the discussion about whether the two Aussies in the bowl should have an E&E if things turned really bad, Tink explains, 'This is typical military planning, particularly on our part. If this really turned bad overnight, how would we get them out?

'And at this particular stage my response to Clint was that the survival of that group was dependent on all remaining in location, sticking together and awaiting extraction, which I indicated to him I would report to Hagenbeck and recommend in the absence of other information.'

Tink had also asked where Lieutenant Colonel LaCamera was. Clint reported that he was at the other end of the bowl and that because of the nature of the enemy fire it was too dangerous to get him.

It was clear to Lieutenant Colonel Tink that Clint was seriously disquieted about the mortars and firepower of the enemy.

'My direction to him was to continue to dig in as best he could because, statistically – this is a dreadful thing to have to say to someone, but it's a fact – statistically if he was below ground the chances of survival were good,' Tink says. 'Now I think they had already done a fair bit of digging.

'I had two guys who were out with an American unit that was in serious trouble. There was a clear belief that they may not survive it in their current circumstances and particularly if they remained there all night. I was steadfast in the fact that they would remain with this unit.'

Tink did not take the decision lightly, because he knew the possible implications of his order. It was one of the hardest decisions he'd ever had to make. 'You may well be committing these guys to their death,' Tink says. 'I'm not trying to dramatise it.

'To a large extent [a man's] survival may well depend on what you do or don't do, or what you tell him to do,' Tink says. 'But at the end of the day he is putting over what he is seeing and he is waiting to hear what I direct him to do.'

Tink knew the best he could offer Jock and Clint at that point was the direction to dig in. He ordered the SAS staff to remain in regular contact with their colleagues. Tink wanted to ensure that the two troopers out in Hell's Halfpipe were kept abreast of the evolving battle plan and reassured they had not been abandoned in their darkest hour.

'The last thing you wanted to do was have your arse in a sling and have no one talking to you,' Tink says. 'It can be very lonely out there when you're having your arse shot off and no one is on the end of the radio.'

Once again Jock's radio was the umbilical to the HQ. The US airmen operating as forward air controllers on the ground could call in CAS to the Bossman flying overhead in the AWACS, but Jock was passing information that was crucial to the strategy planning in the Tactical Operations Center.

'That's why they were saying my radio was essential, because Hagenbeck was the decision maker but Hagenbeck wasn't getting fed by LaCamera,' Jock says.

Six months later, Hagenbeck would tell *Field Artillery* magazine that he had challenges communicating with his brigade and battalion commanders on the ground in the Shahi Kot Valley.

'Operation Anaconda quickly became a platoon fight led by platoon leaders. From that perspective, it was very decentralised. This was not a "push-to-talk" war.'

Over the next hour, from 6.39pm, Tink and Clint spoke three times. Armed with Clint's first sitrep, Tink and his OpsO strode into the Tactical Operations Center where they met with Hagenbeck and his two deputy commanders: Brigadier General Gary Harrell, a one-star general and the top dog of the intelligence cell located at Gardez; and Brigadier General Mike Jones, a Special Forces soldier who was the military's liaison to the CIA. Harrell's legend was cemented in 1993 when he was the US Special Forces commander who hunted down the Somali warlord Mohammed Farah Aidid after the Black Hawk Down crash in Mogadishu. Also present at the TOC meeting was Hagenbeck's chief of staff, Colonel Joe Smith.

Tink began relaying what Clint had told him.

'Between the wounded, the attacks that had happened on the ground during the day and what they expect to occur tonight, if they remain in that area, they are going to be in a worse tactical position than they have been today,' Tink recalls telling the meeting.

'From where my guys stand, this is what they see and this is what they are reporting to me.'

Tink looked directly at Hagenbeck. 'Sir, this is not what I would describe as a stalemate.'

'Goddamn,' Harrell declared.

'They did not have that sort of information; they were surprised when I went over and gave it to them,' Tink says now, adding that he was not surprised at Harrell's response – it was typical of the big bloke.

'I did not come up and say, "You have to withdraw them,"' Tink says now.

He didn't have to.

Hagenbeck asked if he could see the transcript of the conversation between Clint and Tink.

'No worries,' said Tink, believing that this would further improve Hagenbeck's 'situational awareness'.

Tink had deployed the highly skilled Australian SAS patrols at various OPs in the valley and they had updated their sitreps throughout the day. The Aussies were, as Hagenbeck says, his eyes and ears.

The information was critical and Hagenbeck and his top aides consulted on a course of action. The general had decided to send in casualty evacuation choppers and with Tink's information added to other intelligence that was coming in, they decided to withdraw the remaining forces later that night. He further planned to reinforce the northern blocking points that had been secured by the Rakkasans and other Charlie Company troops and fly in more troops as reinforcements for the south the next morning.

Over the next hour, Tink received two more sitreps from Jock and Clint.

They confirmed the 'gravity of the situation in their location', he wrote in his war diary.

Tink was busy coordinating between the Australian Regimental HQ and the TOC, delivering the sitreps to Hagenbeck and company.

'That particular hour [from 1409 to 1507 zulu] was quite important to me because (a) I had become aware of the perilous situation both men were in and (b) because I had become closely engaged myself, whereas I hadn't up to that particular stage – I had depended on my staff. I am over in the main tent the whole time, and they are passing information forward to me and I'm briefing and being briefed about every hour or two. But it became quite obvious to me that we have got a problem over here and it was not as Hagenbeck believed.'

The small village of Marzak had sprung to life again after the mid-afternoon B-52 blitz. Al Qaeda and Taliban fighters had begun to emerge from hiding-holes like woodworms in summer, snaking south toward the ambushed soldiers. The 10th Mountain had a platoon and hunter-sniper scouts on interdiction missions in the hills overlooking Marzak, and a ground forward air controller radioed in for CAS.

Fucking Smufti and Snegat, Jock thought when he heard the call. The enemy didn't get far.

At precisely 6.28pm, a B-52 responded to the call. The long-range heavy bomber, which had launched from mainland USA six hours previously, located its target near the crop of small adobe houses on the hillside. Jock, tuned into the radio, heard the crew of the B-52 prepare to drop their bombs and eavesdropped on the chatter between the TOC at Bagram and the FACs on the ground.

'They're gonna wipe it off the map,' a voice said confidently.

Jock waited for the ominous telltale sound of the JDAMs dropping through the pitch-black sky, then *whoooshka*, the darkness exploded as massive orange-red fireballs shot into the air.

'It was a helluva strike,' Jock says now. 'You wouldn't drop that sort of shit during training and, as a result, every man was thinking, "I hope they are on target," because if they are not, we were well stuffed.'

Hoo-ah!

Frank Grippe and his men welcomed the plume of fire and smoke that broadcast the end of Marzak.

'We made it disappear. Killed a lot of people in that air strike,' Grippe says now. 'There were no civilians up there, there were no farmers or families [just enemy].'

There was more to come.

The US military had again dispatched the AC-130 gunship. During the Vietnam War era it was dubbed 'Puff the Magic Dragon', but now it went by its more threatening nickname of 'Spooky'.

Night had fallen and the Americans were about to reclaim the dark from al Qaeda.

CHAPTER 22

*The distant drone of the Spooky had risen to a roar
as the aircraft swooped over the valley floor, drowning
out everything for a couple of kilometres and sending a
tsunami of sound down the valley behind it like
a shockwave after a blast.*

Jock Wallace was lying on his hand grenade listening to the traffic over the radio and looking down the valley through his night-vision goggles when he heard the Bossman give the Spooky call sign.

'You are one five mikes from your loc,' the Bossman told the pilot.

Jock instantly recognised the arcane language of signallers. It meant the AC-130 gunship was fifteen minutes from the Shahi Kot Valley, or as it would look on the Bossman's logbook, 1–5 M away.

You bloody beauty, Jock thought, remembering the earlier thunderous run that afternoon.

US soldiers like firepower; the bigger the better. They like vehicles that have been cut down and armed to the teeth with 50-calibre machine guns and high-tech infrared equipment and long-range sophisticated communications equipment. They like a sniper rifle that can shoot 1600 metres and they like the sniper who can shoot it further even better. They like their Special Operations task force teams and gunships to have names that strike fear into people's hearts: names like Dagger,

Cobra, Sword, Mako and Apache. And they really like their air support to be awesome. Spooky was just that.

Jock decided to be the bearer of good news. He was lying, literally, on top of a bloody carpet of wounded and those that were still conscious could do with an injection of confidence, although he wouldn't mention the hand grenade.

He told the blokes nearest to him that a gunship was coming in and everyone lifted.

'You could see everyone rise up a centimetre on the ground,' Jock says now. 'And word passed around that the Spooky was coming and everyone was like, "Yeah, fucking great, about time."

'Everyone knows what an AC-130 can do. They are the top shit – you wouldn't move on the ground with one of those chasing you and, if you did, you wouldn't be there for long.'

Jock had some unfinished business. Immediately after spreading the word, he reached down under his chest where he had nestled the grenade ten minutes earlier after taking care of the RPK machine gunner and several al Qaeda and Taliban swarming out of their caves. He felt like a chook sitting on an egg, only this one was infinitely more lethal than the ones he had watched over as a child at home in Tamworth. With the Spooky inbound, Jock had no need for the grenade.

Jock was careful to wrap his right palm entirely over the grenade's safety bail, keeping the pressure firm and constant. With his left hand, he reached into his ammo pouch where he'd slid the grenade pin. He peered down and gingerly reinserted the pin into the grenade, making it safe. Jock arched his body to one side and pushed the grenade into his webbing, nestling the explosive next to the other two grenades. He wouldn't leave it, he might need it later. Shit happens.

Satisfied, Jock breathed a sigh of relief. *We might just get out of this yet*, he thought to himself.

Jock had mentally ticked off more than ten minutes when his ears picked up the distant drone of the Spooky. It was unmistakable. The fast movers operate at enormous speeds and disappear from sight before their bombs reach their target. The Spooky gunship, by contrast, is a slow-moving fire platform that operates at a low altitude. And its four Rolls Royce turboprops have a signature whine.

A converted C-130 Hercules transport plane, the gunship has been turned into a heavily armed fighting machine that is highly effective in providing surgical CAS and more than able in performing reconnaissance missions, escort roles, and combat search and rescue (CSAR).

The gunship's infrared thermal imaging gives it an unbeatable advantage in poor weather and at night, and because it is a slow mover, it can remain over station longer, effectively giving it another crack at the enemy with its sophisticated side-firing weapons system. The firepower includes a 25mm Gatling gun toward the front of the aircraft and a 40mm rapid-fire Bofors cannon and a 105mm howitzer toward the rear. The Gatling gun fires 1800 rounds per minute, more than enough to inspire confidence among the men under ambush on the ground below, including Jock Wallace.

Another bonus is that the sophisticated weapons system provide dual-attack capabilities, using two guns simultaneously and attacking targets up to a kilometre apart. To Jock, that meant that the Spooky could take care of both the enemy trying to kill him and the al Qaeda forces coming out of Marzak, or other fighters filtering into the valley.

As Jock proudly says: 'It can carry shit-loads of ammo.' Perfect for taking out hardcore al Qaeda loitering in the hills.

The Spooky also has a spectacular array of electronic countermeasure flares and chaff that can thwart potential attacks from al Qaeda's anti-aircraft weapons of choice, the SAM and the RPG. When engaged, it looks like a meteorite shower cascading from the tail of the aircraft, almost like a rain of fireworks tumbling from the Sydney Harbour Bridge on New Year's Eve.

Jock was doing his magic, searching for the Bossman on a clear channel and handing the radio handset to the forward air controllers, Vick and Achey, who spoke directly to the Spooky's battle management centre located in the bowels of the aircraft.

The distant drone of the Spooky had risen to a roar as the aircraft swooped over the valley floor, drowning out everything for a couple of kilometres and sending a tsunami of sound down the valley behind it like a shockwave after a blast.

The electronic-warfare officer on board the AC-130 made sure the aircraft was protected from potential enemy fire and the gunship's fire-control officer engaged the targets and let rip, spraying the jagged terrain with deadly bursts from the Bofors and the howitzer.

Phoop, phoop, phoop, phoop, phoop, phoop. Phoop, phoop, phoop, phoop, phoop, phoop. Phoop, phoop, phoop, phoop, phoop, phoop.

The aircraft flew repeated pylon turns over the Shahi Kot Valley, opening up on the eastern ridge then cleaning up in the north, near Marzak, and coming back for an assault on the western side.

'The AC-130 saved our lives. He came droning in over the top of the mountains,' Jock recalls. 'And the next minute, his guns arced up . . . They just kept doing circles and shooting the shit out of anything that moved. He really changed the situation of the battle. The enemy then couldn't move because he had thermal imaging, and if they moved at all, or were out in the open, then the AC-130 gave them a pasting. And he pasted quite a few of them. Prior to that it was just non-stop battle.'

The Spooky stopped the northern ground assault dead in its tracks and laid down effective suppressive fire on both ridges. When the enemy heard the plane overhead, they took cover in their caves.

Al Qaeda and Taliban fighters had slowed their attack, hampered by the night. While dogged and ferocious combatants, they were not as well equipped as the Yanks. Few had access to high-tech night-observation devices (NODs) or night-vision goggles, and couldn't see the enemy down below them with the naked eye. There was little ambient light as a blanket of cloud had obscured the moon. But the disadvantage of darkness hadn't brought a complete stop to the battle, and the enemy were not about to shut up shop for the night and grab a bit of shut-eye.

They were in a fight to the death and still had their mortars, which were pre-registered and still exploding in the halfpipe. But in using them they exposed themselves to the Americans' superior technology, which had come into its own with nightfall.

'We were all excited when night came,' Sergeant Major Grippe says. 'After that last gunfight, things settled down and we brought in more B-52s, more JDAMs, and killed a whole bunch of arseholes. Then our AC-130 flew overhead and started engaging enemy targets because they could see with thermal devices and forward-looking infrared. They started really hammering some positions that we really couldn't see, and [they were] giving us some guidance and some situational awareness of where the enemy locations were.'

Some of the men from Charlie Company had worn their NODs instead of packing them in the rucksacks they abandoned when they first came under fire that morning. Each time al Qaeda fighters edged out of their caves and launched a mortar, the soldiers fixed their location and fired, which brought return fire from the machine-gunners, effectively confirming the enemy positions.

They recorded the grid coordinates for the FAC on the ground, who called in CAS to the gunship. The soldiers also used the laser sights on their rifles to identify an enemy mortar position, effectively guiding the Spooky to its target. The laser was invisible to the naked eye but clearly visible to the high-tech sensors on the gunship. The soldiers on the ground would paint the target with an infrared bead and the AC-130 would point and shoot.

The realist in Jock Wallace had been disinclined to let the presence of the Spooky seduce him into thinking everything was on the up-and-up, but the warplane had put on a sensational show and handed the men in his slice of the Shahi Kot Valley what now felt like a bona fide get-out-of-jail-free card. To Jock it spelt relief and his fear that they might not make it back to Bagram alive was starting to subside again, if only fractionally. And the troops sardined into the bottom of Hell's Halfpipe had risen to the challenge and once again refused to say die.

Jock allowed himself a quick thought about his mum, Margaret – or Stix, as he affectionately called her – at home on the south coast of New South Wales. He knew she'd be worrying about her youngest son, as she always did when he was away on operations, but she never showed it, out of deference to him. She respected his tenacity and didn't doubt for an instant his capabilities, but she was a mother, and mothers worried. It was all part of the job description.

Jock had tried to put her mind at ease and wrote frequent letters from the frontline in an upbeat tone, filling them with information about life on base.

22 February 2002

Dear Stix,

We are in good spirits and making best use of the time, preparing our equipment and studying our area of operations. You should see our cars, they look so awesome and brimming to the teeth with weaponry, everywhere we go people look at them in awe.

Jock even sent back the tiny bottles of Tabasco sauce from the MREs for his brother James's partner, who liked the spicy sauce, and souvenirs from Afghanistan for James so James could get a feel for what his younger brother was up to on the other side of the world, fighting the war on terrorism.

Just before Anaconda began, Jock wrote to his mum.

Dear Stix,

The show is about to start for us, so will be a bit busy for a while. Hope everything is okay with you. Try not to worry – I get into more trouble on an average day in Australia. Will write again soon.

Love,

Martin.

P.S. When we beat the Poms at soccer the whole mess just pissed themselves laughing. Nice. Poms didn't think it was so funny.

But Jock had never been in this much trouble ever – not on an average day in Australia or an extraordinary day anywhere else.

He had no idea how he'd tell his mum about the past twelve hours. In fact, he reckoned it was probably better not to.

CHAPTER 23

*The enemy couldn't guarantee a direct hit so they opted
for the airburst to maximise the chances of knocking the
medevac chopper out of the sky. For the pilot it would
have been like flying through a deadly hailstorm.*

Jock Wallace was in the pitch black of Hell's Halfpipe with his
night-observation monocular slung over his right eye, tuning
into the radio. Lieutenant Colonel Tink had passed information
to the HQ from Major General Hagenbeck, and the news, as
welcome as news ever could be in a war zone, was subsequently
forwarded via the radio to Jock.

Hagenbeck had finally dispatched two modified Black Hawk
choppers to medevac the wounded. Once the most seriously
wounded of the 28 injured US soldiers were safely en route back
to their base at Bagram, the plan was to send a second lift to
extract the isolated company. Both lifts would be escorted by
Apache gunships with the Spooky prowling overhead. The
medevacs were on the way, but no time had presently been
scheduled for the final extraction.

'Roger, that. Out,' Jock said, passing the word to soldiers nearby.

Sergeant Robert Healy had been right. Papa Spooky had come
in and fixed the problem. The AC-130's recent pasting of enemy
positions had had the desired effect and the battle had slowed to
an intermittent gunfight with sporadic small-arms and machine-
gun fire coming from the surrounding ridges. Spooky had
eradicated the threat from the north and the B-52s had taken out

259

the staging base at Marzak; and the soldiers in the halfpipe breathed a sigh of real relief.

Jock had turned from rifleman and radio operator to ersatz medic.

The sub-zero conditions that came with nightfall began to cause new problems for the injured men, most of whom were jammed solid in Jock's part of the halfpipe. Apart from their original injuries, many were at risk of hypothermia. Hagenbeck had delayed Operation Anaconda twice previously, once because of a lack of aviation fuel and secondly because of the appalling weather conditions when excoriating sleet had made it impossible to air-assault the troops in. There was no danger of rain now, but the temperature wasn't doing anyone any favours.

'You have got to stop these guys going into shock, so you have to keep them warm,' Jock says. 'I had my pack right in there amongst the wounded and there's no point in my cold-weather gear just sitting on top of my pack when these guys actually need it.'

Jock had no hesitation in pulling it out and giving it to the wounded. 'It sort of goes two ways with me. It was all my free shit from the Americans. I wasn't happy about that, but in the same boat it was their shit and their soldiers, so I figured, *righto, bang.* I was just carrying it.'

The casualty collection point was a bloody bog. The melting snow had turned parts of the ground into muddy puddles and the blood from the soldiers' wounds had turned it into a slimy mess. Torn uniforms and discarded bandages were strewn everywhere.

The most seriously injured soldier, Sergeant Andrew Black, had lost around a litre and a half of blood but so far Doc Byrne and the well-trained medics from the 10th Mountain Division had managed to save his leg. Black was heavily sedated, but other soldiers with lesser wounds weren't and had been lying in the bowl suffering, some for nearly twelve hours.

Jock kept an eye on the soldiers closest to him, making sure they had their bandages changed when needed, wrapping them in cold-weather gear and passing equipment to the medics when required.

He made idle chit-chat with some of the young soldiers to quietly check that they weren't about to slip into unconsciousness while the doc and the medics concentrated on keeping the Priority Ones alive.

'How ya goin', mate?' Jock would ask, his Australian accent cutting through the silence.

Among the Americans, it stood out and never failed to get a positive response that usually involved some mention of the crocodile hunter Steve Irwin, whom the soldiers had watched repeatedly on the telly at home and variably described as 'that crazy mofo' or 'awesome dude'.

'Not bad, bud. When we gonna be medevaced out?'

'Real soon, mate, real soon. The birds are on their way now.'

'We gonna make it?'

'Bloody oath, mate, we haven't come this far not to make it.'

Jock monitored the radio out of Bagram and beyond, and cracked jokes in a hushed whisper with the soldiers who just wanted to talk to make sure they were still alive.

Jock considered the range of reactions from the wounded soldiers. Some, like the sar-major, were oblivious to danger and had kept right on going. Sergeant Healy ignored the pain from the shrapnel lodged in his body and soldiered on. In any other circumstance, the two non-coms wouldn't be able to walk, but adrenaline, leadership and a courage they would never admit to had pushed them on. They were hard at it.

Healy was organising his soldiers and making a manifest for the Black Hawks with Doc Byrne, working out the logistics of which soldiers needed to go first. Black was priority number one. By rights, Healy should have been on one of the choppers too, but he, like Grippe, was having none of it. Healy planned to stay until every last man from Charlie Company was on the extraction choppers. The 34-year-old soldier and father of three didn't care how long it took; he was not leaving his men behind.

'Without that leadership and direction and experience on the ground we would have been history,' Jock says. 'And [Grippe,

Healy and Peterson] really came to the party, and earned every dollar they ever made. They can definitely rest easy at night knowing they did their bit and more.'

Some soldiers who had sustained frag wounds showed amazing courage and didn't report their injuries to Doc Byrne in the bowl. Instead, they turned up at the Spanish Hospital at Bagram the next day to make sure their wounds had not been infected before getting back on a chopper and heading out to finish Operation Anaconda.

But not all the soldiers acted honourably and Jock remembers the odd one or two who disgraced themselves in the eyes of their fellow soldiers.

'I remember nearly shooting one of the whingeing wounded, this little prick who had nothing wrong with him compared to the injuries around him. He was just moaning like a dog,' Jock says. 'I just felt like slapping him. Obviously you have to have a bit of compassion but even the medics thought it was a bit inappropriate at times. I remember one of them telling him to shut up and telling the other one to juice him up with some morphine just to shut him up.'

If Jock had got hold of Healy's medevac manifest he would have put the whinger at the top of the list, just to get him away from everyone else. They were in enough trouble as it was; the soldiers in the bowl didn't need an oxygen thief to bring them down with his whingeing and whining.

They could see the light at the end of the tunnel and, even though it might have been nothing more than a tiny flicker, it was a light nonetheless.

The medevac birds were on the way.

Robert Healy was the operations sergeant major of the 1-87, a key member of the 'think tank' that planned the missions and security. He ordered around everyone below him in the chain of command and called himself 'the grumpy sergeant', but the description did him a disservice. He wasn't grumpy at all, he just had to answer to his bosses, including Sergeant Major Grippe, who simply called him 'Ops'.

'You make it happen, Ops, I won't ask you how,' Grippe barked at his right-hand man.

Healy did make things happen. Nothing was different out in Hell's Halfpipe, even with a bullet lodged deep in his calf next to his shinbone and shrapnel behind his ear and a few pieces dug into subcutaneous tissue elsewhere. Together with Lieutenant Colonel LaCamera, Grippe and the battalion's surgeon Major Byrne, Healy planned every element of the medevac with strategic precision once they got word the evacuation was en route. The small group had honed their skills, drills, tactics and techniques through years of active service and they would put them to best use now. The lives of their injured brothers depended on it.

The leaders tasked their sergeants who then instructed the young privates in their platoons. The chain of command was sacrosanct.

Soldiers who had not been wounded were divided into security squads and evacuation teams. Not all of the 28 wounded would be evacuated. The Priority One casualties would be the first on the chopper, and those able to walk would be assisted by two soldiers each who would then return to the fight, waiting for the full-scale extraction later that night. Those with non-life-threatening injuries would be on the second chopper and the least seriously wounded who were physically able to would remain behind and man their weapon systems until the extraction.

The soldiers were physically and mentally exhausted but they nodded that they understood their missions. Their sergeants, like Peterson, knew they would perform. Except for the couple who had failed during the day to live up to the 10th Mountain's creed of 'To the Top', the rest of the men in Hell's Halfpipe had done themselves proud.

Things were looking good. Al Qaeda had been relatively quiet since Spooky did his gun run earlier in the night. *Said their prayers and gone to sleep*, Healy hoped.

WO2 Clint was back and forth between the 10th Mountain's

command-and-control element and Jock, who was listening to his radio for the alert that the CSAR choppers were inbound. Some of the American nets were down, and Jock would pass the word. The rest of the soldiers in the bowl were listening, concentrating on their roles for the medevac and their missions immediately post-evacuation.

Thwomp, thwomp, thwomp. The telltale noise of the choppers' rotors came like a slow rolling thunder over the bombed-out hostile village of Marzak to the north, growing louder as the Black Hawks came closer.

Halle-fucking-lujah, Jock thought.

The CSAR choppers belonged to the US Air Force and were actually HH–60 Pave Hawks, a highly modified version of the US Army's Black Hawk. Despite the modifications, the soldiers still referred to the choppers as Black Hawks. The call signs for the choppers were Gecko One One and Gecko One Two. They were crewed by highly trained para-rescuemen whose job was rescuing soldiers injured in the line of fire. They operated in NVG lighting so the enemy on the ground would not see the incoming birds.

Spooky was still on station, higher in the sky, loitering in case he was needed, his drone a soothing presence.

Soldiers from Charlie Company raced out from Hell's Halfpipe and set up a landing zone about 200 metres southwest of Jock's location, marking it with infrared strobe lights visible to the high-tech sensors on the aircraft but not to the naked eyes of the al Qaeda and Taliban forces. The Apache swept in first to ensure the LZ was safe. The Black Hawks were just seconds behind, flying slightly to the east of the bowl ready to make a J-turn to the designated pickup spot.

The casualty collection point was crowded with tightly coiled soldiers who had taken their places, ready to bolt out with the wounded as soon as the choppers touched down, not waiting for the dirt and dust to settle. There was no time for such luxuries even if it meant that the wounded would be covered in yet another layer of Afghan earth.

'Everything had been quiet from when we engaged [the machine-gun position in the southeast] up until the CSAR Black Hawks came in,' Jock says now.

As the first chopper banked around the southern end of the bowl, the flash of an RPG burst from the position where Jock had earlier taken out the RPK machine gunner and several other al Qaeda enemy.

Holy shit, he thought.

The rocket had been set to air burst and roared by, exploding in a brilliant red flash about 50 metres behind the Black Hawk, sending a high velocity spray of shrapnel into the air. The enemy couldn't guarantee a direct hit so they opted for the air burst to maximise the chances of knocking the medevac chopper out of the sky. For the pilot it would have been like flying through a deadly hailstorm. The RPG missed, and the pilot skilfully put the bird down on the LZ.

'Oh God, here we go again,' Healy said out loud to anyone in earshot.

As the second chopper swooped around preparing to land, another rocket exploded from the same location. *Schwwoooooooooo.* A red streak sped by the helicopter, missing it by centimetres. It smacked into the valley hundreds of metres away. Suddenly, the hills erupted with machine-gun fire as the surviving al Qaeda and Taliban fighters popped out of their caves and opened up their long-silenced weapons.

'Go, go, go,' yelled Healy.

The soldiers in the halfpipe returned fire with their machine guns and small arms and, within seconds, the 10th Mountain troops tasked with getting the wounded to the choppers had swung into action, running into the line of fire.

Ttttt ttttt ttttt ttttt ttttt. Al Qaeda and Taliban machine gunners opened up their Dishkas, spraying a torrent of ammo in the direction of the vulnerable choppers. Doc Byrne was with Sergeant Black, who was lying prone on a stretcher being carried by four GIs about to be met by the para-rescuemen from the chopper. The walking wounded limped as fast as they could out of the bowl, searching for the choppers amid the dust and dirt being tossed up by the rounds and the downdraft of the turning rotors.

'We thought, "Holy shit, the enemy's at it again." And the AC-130 came down and belted them,' says Jock.

Jock could hear the AC-130 droning overhead; its signature *vvvvvrrrr* monotone rising in pitch until it sounded like the Spooky was in a dive, screaming down into the valley with guns blasting.

'We are trying to run wounded towards the helicopter and those rounds are dropping all around the helicopters and that's when the AC-130 put paid to them as well,' Jock recalls. 'He came out of his loiter position and started smashing them. It was almost like he put this plane into a dive and came in doing a gun run, but at the same time the enemy is arcing up with another machine gun just after they've fired the second RPG.'

Soldiers began shooting back, laying down a deadly hail of suppressive fire as the casualty evacuation teams pushed on toward the Black Hawks.

As Black's litter neared the chopper a bullet tore through his knee, the same one that had been blasted to pieces by the mortar hours earlier. Fortunately, the morphine had knocked him out and the soldier, who had been largely unconscious most of the day, felt nothing. Neither did any of the soldiers carrying him. There was so much noise from the gunfire, the chopper engines and *thwomping* rotors that the bullet and the thud that came with it as it slammed into Black's knee were just one more piece of the chaos of war.

In fact, Healy didn't know Black had been shot until a week later, when doctors at the Army hospital in Landstuhl, Germany, removed the Dishka machine-gun bullet during surgery.

When told of the surgical find, Healy was stunned. He thought the brutal mortar round that exploded in Hell's Halfpipe, ripping into himself, Grippe and Major Jay Hall, as well as Black, had been the sole cause of Black's injuries.

The gods of war had clearly shone on the soldiers who had

been performing the medevac. *Skills, drills, tactics and techniques.* None of them were hurt.

'It was amazing, *amazing*, that nobody went out of there in a body bag,' Healy says. 'It was just amazing with that intensity of fire and overwhelming numbers. I'm still amazed.'

It was a fast but completely controlled manoeuvre. The soldiers coming under fire held their ground and completed their mission. Black was rushed onto the first chopper, followed by two more of the most seriously wounded soldiers. The crew gave the thumbs-up sign to the pilot, who immediately lifted the bird off the ground while the helo's aerial gunner kept his finger on the trigger of his mini-gun.

One of the Black Hawk's crewmen noted that Sergeant Black was 'pale and cold; his blood pressure could not be measured'.

The prognosis was bad. Black had lost a lot of blood while lying in the valley for nearly six hours.

Thinking quickly, the para-rescueman pushed in an intravenous line and began giving Black a blood transfusion as the chopper roared towards Bagram, arriving at the base in record time. Black would survive both the mortar round and the accidentally accurate al Qaeda machine-gunners firing blind towards the choppers. He ultimately received a medical discharge from the Army, but only after being presented with the Purple Heart for his actions in Operation Anaconda.

The Black Hawk's gunner would later view the videotape taken of the medevac by the AC-130 crew supporting the mission.

'I watched the video taken from the escort gunship a month after the mission and saw all that was going on,' the Air Force man later told the Pacific Air Forces News Service. 'My mother would probably cry if she saw that video.'

As they had done for the Spooky earlier that night, the men from Charlie Company started pointing their infrared lasers onto the location of the flashpoints from the RPG and Dishka machine guns, again effectively handing the enemy's hideouts to the crew of the AC-130. The Spooky did a run but couldn't engage the positions, so roared over the valley and banked around for a second assault, this time hitting the targets full on.

'The Spectre [Spooky] did his turn and basically blew up that position pretty bad,' Robert Healy says now. 'There were a lot of secondary explosions after that. It sounded like there was a bunch of animals up there where they were shooting from, so he started pumping 40-mm at it and things started blowing up up there.'

The explosions lit up the night sky for several minutes, indicating that the enemy had massive stockpiles of ammunition. The mission report for the Spooky, call sign Grim Three One, stated that the gun run killed two or three enemy fighters.

Within minutes, six more wounded US soldiers were loaded in the second helo as soldiers on the ground scoped the hills, ready to attack if an al Qaeda sniper reared his head. Just before the second Black Hawk lifted off, a young lieutenant who had sustained no injuries during the day ditched his weapon and made a desperate run for the chopper. Whether he was emotionally and psychologically defeated, completely physically exhausted, or just plain cowardly, no one knew and they weren't stopping to find out. A soldier loading the casualties grabbed the man and heaved him off the chopper.

'I don't know who it was but I know he wouldn't have been able to jump on there,' Healy says now, his comments dripping with understatement.

Everyone knew the Black Hawk was for the wounded, not the shit-scared.

Jock held his breath, waiting for another machine gunner to open up at the birds on the valley floor with their Mix Masters, as he called their rotors, turning. Nothing.

The pilot got the thumbs-up and reciprocated. Soldiers moved away from the helo as its rotors *thwomped* into life. The second Black Hawk gained altitude and went at full throttle with its nose pointing towards the ground and tail up above them, gaining speed and catching up to the first bird.

Lucky bastards, Jock thought as they disappeared from view.

But Jock was waiting for the bubble to burst and he didn't want to bet the house on a successful mission just yet in case he jinxed it.

'I wasn't sure that they were getting out of there,' Jock says now. 'I felt relief that the enemy hadn't hit these helicopters yet, and elated that the guys had been able to get the wounded out finally, especially the ones who had been lying around for ten or so hours. But I was still not a hundred per cent confident ... that the helicopters were going to get out of the valley.'

Jock's fears, while appropriate, were thankfully not realised.

The evacuation was a success. The most seriously wounded were roaring back to Bagram under experienced medical attention. The radio crew on the choppers called the hospital at the air base, preparing the emergency teams in the triage centre. They stabilised the soldiers before sending them off for surgery and more intensive treatment at the US Army hospital in Germany.

'The lead pilot, I believe, was awarded the Silver Star for flying in,' Frank Grippe says now. 'And I'm reading this account of the pilot's Silver Star [citation] ... and the pilots flew through flak and mortars, through the Valley of Death. And man, the hair on the back of my neck is standing up. I'm like, "Holy shit, this guy's a hero." And I'm thinking, "I was there *all day*, goddamn." No disrespect to those guys – they had it going on. And it was good to get our wounded out. My men did a really wonderful job. Everyone should have had a Silver Star in that fight.'

Nine wounded men had got out alive while under heavy and direct fire.

Robert Healy took a moment to enjoy the victory, but the night had some hours to go and 73 men were still left in the Shahi Kot Valley. The command-and-control element got stuck into finalising the extraction plans for the soldiers in Hell's Halfpipe.

Jock peered down the bowl nearest to him and it looked half empty with nine of the injured soldiers gone. He radioed in to the chooks in the HQ and confirmed that the evacuation had gone off without a hitch. A quiet wave of jubilation swept through the tent.

Minutes later, the word came back from Bagram.

'Niner Charlie, this is One Oscar. Extraction scheduled for 1900 zulu. Stand by. Out.'

It was still two hours or more away, but at least it was an answer.

CHAPTER 24

*Jock was desperate to go. His heart was beating
at an accelerated pace and felt like it would burst
through his bulletproof vest. 'Get this fuckin'
helicopter off the ground.'*

Time ticks by differently in a war zone and it ticks by differently for each man fighting for his life. To Jock Wallace it seemed like every minute since the Black Hawks left the Shahi Kot Valley had been stretched to infinity and beyond, each one taking longer than the one before. He was increasingly frustrated, and impatient to get the hell out of Hell's Halfpipe, but at the same time he had a deep sense of responsibility and honour and his personal ethics meant he couldn't leave until the job was done. *There's also the small issue of transport*, he thought to himself with a laugh.

The enemy had gone quiet. Jock didn't know if the Spooky had wiped them out, or if the al Qaeda and Taliban fighters had fled the valley through the rat lines into Pakistan or were just playing doggo waiting to pop up at any time. Similarly, they could have retreated into their caves to regroup and come back stronger at first light a few hours away. First-light and last-light attacks were always the most dangerous. Jock didn't care to go through one again.

As the minutes ticked by and without the distraction of gunfire and Smufti and Snegat ducking in and out of their

271

hideouts to unleash an unholy jihad, Jock was beginning to lose that loving feeling.

The waiting was its own kind of torture.

Every ten minutes Jock hunkered down over his radio, crushed his handset to his ear and called in to the chooks back at Regimental Headquarters. The radio calls became his personal metronome, something to mark the time.

'One Oscar, this is Niner Charlie, radio check, over,' Jock whispered into the handset.

The only thing keeping the enemy on the surrounding ridgelines at bay from the troops in the halfpipe was the gunship hundreds of metres above, so Jock whispered to keep the company's position noise to a minimum.

'Roger, over,' replied one of his fellow signallers.

'Roger, out.'

The calls lasted less than five seconds and were a mental safeguard for Jock because they confirmed his radio link was still up and making effective contact after sixteen-odd hours of nonstop use. He had maintained its integrity and hadn't dropped the codes, even when he swapped the batteries. Notice of the extraction would come via his radio and Jock did not want to be inadvertently off the air when it did because he hadn't adhered to his usual checks and counterchecks while sitting in the darkness twiddling his thumbs and getting dirtier on the Ruperts responsible for putting the 82 soldiers into a hornet's nest.

He'd rather be doing more productive things, like providing the comms network and being the bearer of good tidings to the brave young grunts who had stayed to man their positions despite being fragged. *Jesus, they'd fought their rings off, they deserved nothing less*, he thought.

Two hours and counting.

Command Sergeant Major Frank Grippe and Sergeant First Class Robert Healy were issuing orders. Healy issued an edict for accountability – meaning he wanted all personnel accounted for, with their gear squared away, ready to board the CH-47 helicopters as soon as the Chinooks appeared. Helo LZs were dangerous places, as they had found out twice already that day. There was no time to dick around.

Grippe ordered the GIs to retrieve their abandoned rucksacks – particularly the ones that were still intact and had not been used for target practice by al Qaeda. They were loaded with machine-gun ammunition, radios, GPSs, NVGs, cold-weather gear and rations – all of which would come in handy for any lingering enemy fighters. Anything in a salvageable condition that could be collected would be collected.

'Grippe was determined that those bastards wouldn't get it, one, to use it themselves, or two, to compromise radios,' Jock says now. 'So Grippe is out there trying to square the battlefield away.'

Technology helped. The Spooky shone its infrared search beam the size of two football fields down into the valley, turning the blackness of the Afghan night into a green-coloured daylight for the soldiers wearing NVGs. The infrared beam looked like a lighthouse searchlight as it swept back and forth over the soldiers on the strategic scavenger hunt. To identify themselves as 'friendlies', the troops wore around their necks infrared strobe lights detectable by the two sensor operators on the AC-130 who controlled the aircraft's infrared detection set (IDS) and its all-light-levels television system.

If the crew screwed up and misidentified the troops as enemy fighters, they ran the risk of sending a lethal burst of cannon fire their way.

'You just get this really eerie feeling when that light passes over you – "I hope he is identifying us as friendly",' Jock says now. 'The AC-130 is infinitely more dangerous to us and infinitely more deadly than the enemy. The AC-130 attacking the wrong coordinates is a very, very big danger and to combat that we openly wore infrared strobes.'

Jock was able to find some humour in the situation. Instead of seeing a battalion out in a kill zone collecting their discarded rucksacks, he saw a battlefield lit up like a Christmas tree.

'Had the enemy had any good kind of night vision devices he would have seen what I saw, twinkling lights all over the hill, and there's your target,' Jock says wryly.

Grippe was keen to recover valuable strategic equipment including Sergeant Pete's 120mm mortar tube and base plate, and the lanky soldier was more than happy to comply.

Sergeant Pete felt responsible for bringing the 120 into battle and called his decision to do so his 'snafu' – situation normal, all fucked up. He didn't want to leave the tube for al Qaeda to use against other Americans arriving to reinforce the valley over the coming days, including his own mortar platoon. It was not going to be left as a potentially fatal souvenir.

'It got hit [by mortars] a couple of times but never broke,' Peterson says now. 'They blew up our sight box and when we got back we were pulling shrapnel out of our stuff. It got all my gun equipment. One mortar landed right next to it – dinged it up a little bit.'

The retrieval mission was a success and brought an unexpected small victory for Sergeant Pete that might seem trivial to anyone but a combat veteran.

While dragging the mortar tube closer to the designated LZ, he found an al Qaeda mortar. *Yeah, payback time.*

'I took one of their mortars, it's in the 10th Mountain museum,' Peterson says now, unselfconsciously proud. 'We got the tube, brought it back, and in the museum it says, "Captured by 1-87 Mortars". I drove that thing around for ten days because I was so mad at those guys. I stole their mortar, I was like, "You'll never get this back." So their instrument of my pain – I got it and brought it back. They have none of mine. I definitely one-upped them.'

Healy instructed the 1-87 soldiers that items that were regarded as beyond retrieval should be clearly marked for the Spooky's IDS. The gunship would stay in its loiter position after the extraction, ready for a final gun run, during which time it would blast the ruins of war to pieces.

If the enemy thought it was going to get its hands on US Army equipment, it was sorely mistaken.

274

Signalman Jock Wallace received confirmation that two CH-47 Chinooks were inbound just before midnight on 2 March. The extraction was on. Grippe's men marked out a landing zone about 200 metres from Hell's Halfpipe and not far from where the medevac choppers had arrived a couple of hours earlier, and the troops began moving into position.

Jock remained in the bowl. He had to keep his radio transmission up until the very last minute.

'I'm not taking that thing off line till I start physically moving to the helicopter, so I've got everything else squared away. You have to stay up, so you are one of the last ones to leave position, one of the last ones still working, so to speak,' Jock says now. 'That's why they pick sigs of a certain breed. Sigs have got to do their own stuff regardless of what everyone else is doing a lot of the time, so you have to be resourceful and independent and have a certain manner. You know your job and you know that the other people don't give a shit about your job. When it comes down to it, if you are going to do your job properly staying behind is one of the risks that you take.'

Clint stayed in the bowl with Jock – they'd come this far together, they were going out together. Clint was stubborn but, moreover, he was loyal and this was mateship Australian Army style.

About ten grunts crawled up the eastern slope of the bowl, pulling security for the men on the LZ. Jock checked his immediate surrounds to make sure he hadn't left anything. Good to go. He checked his pack, making sure its contents were secure, and deliberately left the top open.

Spooky droned overhead.

Nice one.

The thwack and thwomp of the Chinook's blades grew louder in the dark, as the helos drew near. The first Chinook flew in, found the landing zone and touched down blasting dust and dirt into the air and browning out the vicinity. A sprawl of soldiers immediately charged up the rear tail ramp dragging the remaining wounded with them and crammed into the chopper's belly as the second Chinook touched down about 50 metres away. There was no time to waste.

Clint looked at Jock.

'You wanna catch that one?' he yelled under the din of the rotors and shouting soldiers. It was a rhetorical question. Clint didn't need an answer.

Jock radioed the SAS HQ.

'One Oscar, this is Niner Charlie. Extraction is here. Closing down now. Out.'

Jock didn't wait for a reply. He quickly packed up and slammed his antenna into his open pack and slung it over his shoulders and with his free firing hand picked up his M4 and started legging it out of Hell's Halfpipe.

'There was shit hanging out the top of my pack, but I got everything. Had all my equipment, it just didn't look too neat. There was stuff bulging out the side, but that's because of the way I left the position. I kept my means up for everyone's benefit and suddenly found I'm packing my antenna up and 30 people are running past me for the choppers.'

Jock lost sight of Clint when one of the helos lifted momentarily after its first approach and looked like it was going to make an attempt to land where they were. He skidded to a halt, spitting up gravel underfoot, tacked and ran back, then turned looking for Clint, his chest screaming in pain as his lungs tried to suck in the thin, cold air. But no Clint.

Shit, he thought.

Jock could hardly breathe and seriously considered ditching his pack and the radio equipment but thought better of it.

'The tight-arse Australian Government would have made me pay for it,' he says now, with a laugh. And besides, to leave it behind would be against the very principle of being a highly skilled signaller.

Jock took one last look around for Clint but couldn't see him. Most of the soldiers had already boarded the Chinooks. *Must be on the other chopper*, he thought, and kept running towards the CH-47.

The last 50 metres were the toughest. Jock fought off fears that the ninja al Qaeda fighters would pop out of their caves one more time and deliver an RPG or mortar round into the waiting Chinooks as they'd almost done when the medevac choppers landed.

Sergeant Robert Healy had exactly the same thought.

'I'm going, "When are they going to start shooting at us again?"' he says.

Lieutenant Colonel Rowan Tink was in the TOC with Major General Hagenbeck and various colonels, captains and commanders watching the Predator vision on the video screen at the front of the tent. The CIA were hoping to capture Osama bin Laden or his most senior lieutenants and had their UAV focused on the valley, directly over the extraction site. Hagenbeck also had the Army's drone dedicated to the area for the extraction mission.

The Predator vision distorted the action and made the rotor blades look as if they were turning in slow motion, but the troops on the ground were moving in double time.

Jock raced up the rear tail ramp into the blacked-out Chinook and peered through his night vision monocular. A sea of exhausted green-tinged faces looked up at him, packed in like cattle. He collapsed on the floor with his back to the right side of the bird, shoulder to shoulder with the nearest soldier, facing east and looking out the ramp and back into the valley. He looked straight to where the last RPG was fired from, the same spot at which the RPK machine gunner had been earlier before Jock whacked a round from his M4 into him.

Jock was desperate to go. His heart was beating at an accelerated pace and felt like it would burst through his bulletproof vest.

'Get this fuckin' helicopter off the ground,' he yelled at the Chinook crewie to no avail.

The seconds stretched on forever. Jock thought he was dead.

How long are we just going to sit here?

'I didn't come all this way to sit here while you fuck around for ten minutes and get an RPG through the side of the helo,' he roared.

He sat there for what seemed like an eternity, like a lifetime, waiting for that stinking helicopter to lift off.

'I was sitting on that helicopter just waiting for the side to rip open, just waiting to see an explosion. That's one of the worst feelings I've ever had, because you are just so close to getting out of there, you are nearly there. You are actually on that bloody bird and the bird's sitting on the ground, and why is the bird sitting on the ground? Because they haven't brought the rest of the fucking wounded – there are still guys limping towards us ...'

Jock was looking out the back and saw two soldiers about 50 metres away, limping toward the back of the helicopter. Two of the walking wounded. They'd been left to their own devices and had packs over their shoulders and equipment in their hands.

Unfuckingbelievable.

Jock dropped his pack, launched himself from the floor of the crowded chopper and bolted down the back ramp toward the incoming soldiers. Another young grunt took his lead and followed. They grabbed the equipment of the young privates and helped them onto the Chinook.

'It was just like every man for himself getting to that helicopter, that's the way it seemed to me,' Jock says now.

It was a similar story for Sergeant Healy and his radio operator who were heading toward the other chopper, loaded like packhorses with their own equipment as well as the radio gear left behind when Sergeant Andrew Black had been medevaced earlier in the evening. Healy was covered in a mix of his own and Black's blood. The Doc had cut one leg of Healy's battle fatigues open, and he was limping and dragging his wounded but bandaged leg through the dirt.

'Everybody got on the aircraft and I'm like, "Oh shit, they're gonna take off without me." So we dragged up there and got on, and everybody's on there, and I'm, "Okay let's go, let's go",' Healy recalls.

'When we took off you held your breath for a few minutes to see if you weren't going to get shot down. I was just expecting to start seeing bullet holes in the side of the aircraft, but I guess Taliban went to sleep for the night. They just didn't want any more Spectre, the AC-130.'

The boarding had been chaotic and according to Sergeant Pete 'probably the worst part of the fight'. The soldiers had gathered in one spot before charging up the back ramp and, to Sergeant Pete, that represented a huge and attractive target for al Qaeda.

Like Jock, neither Peterson nor Healy had discounted al Qaeda or shown any hubris by underestimating AQ's threat to fight to the death.

Sergeant Pete was manoeuvring towards the chopper and saw the injured Major Hall and a couple of other sergeants loading up with Charlie Company's rucksacks and ran over to help.

'Everyone had just made a beeline for the birds and these guys were stuck out there, loading rucksacks by themselves,' Peterson says. 'And so we were sitting on the LZ all that time, and I just think some people probably need to be smacked a little bit ... Some of them, self-preservation was their priority.'

With almost all the troops crammed into the choppers, the soldiers bringing up the rear did a quick scan of the bowl to ensure no one was left behind. There was nothing but an empty battlefield. It was the closest thing to a head count, but with the choppers firing up and ready to roar less than a hundred metres away, there was not a chance in hell that any soldier worth his salt was staying in the halfpipe. No one was going to be left behind. Confident of their scan, the men didn't linger and moved up the ramps into the Chinooks, taking their place at the very back, exhausted and relieved.

The Tactical Operations Center at Bagram was tense with expectation. The Predators showed the two Chinooks lifting off and turning to fly back to base. Every metre higher brought the soldiers closer to safety, but they had to get past the hostile eastern ridgeline.

As soon as they cleared the valley floor the pilots radioed in with a mission success report. Seventy-three soldiers, including two Australians with the elite SAS Regiment, were on board the two birds and coming home. And they were all alive. The extraction was complete. The excitement in the TOC was palpable but, within minutes, the atmosphere went from one of utter jubilation to disbelief.

'Hey, have a look at this,' an American officer yelled back in the TOC.

'Holy shit!'

At least a dozen armed men were swarming over the landing zone where the Chinooks had just been and were picking through Charlie Company's discarded booty, the equipment that posed no security risk.

'That's al Qaeda!'

Rowan Tink couldn't believe it. 'Within a matter of minutes of the helo extraction taking off, a bunch of people appeared right on the location,' he says. 'It was only a matter of minutes, so they were close – that's the point. The helos came in and took off, and the next thing, you have enemy wandering on.'

But the Spooky was on station, loitering overhead and doing pylon turns around the snowy mountain peaks, ready to rock if needed.

Sergeant Healy's earlier instruction to mark the non-retrievable items with infrared sensors was about to pay off. The gunship's battle management centre was a hive of activity, processing coordinates, prepping the fire team and briefing the pilots who flew the AC-130 into the valley. As it swept in, the gunners let rip with the 105mm howitzer and the 40mm Bofors cannon.

Boom!

The enemy were taken care of. The Predator vision showed them laid to waste.

For Jock, the Spooky's final delivery was the best possible kind of salvation, although he didn't hear about that until later.

'They just started moving in and trying to rip shit off, looking for things like coded radios and any sort of weapons and information,' Jock says now. 'They would have been loving that, any sort of equipment that they could have captured, especially a radio with a code. I'm not sure what sort of procedures Osama has in place for his operatives but I'm sure he would like to get his hands on something like that.'

With the enemy killed it is impossible to know why al Qaeda and Taliban fighters did not attack the extraction choppers and the surviving men from the 10th Mountain as they previously tried to destroy the medevac helos. No doubt, they would have heard the Spooky droning overhead and knew they were up against overwhelming firepower, and that to expose themselves would have meant certain death. Alternatively, they might have been out of ammunition, or perhaps, contrary to what the commander of the 5th Special Forces Group had said earlier, this lot were not, at this point, in a fight-to-the-death scenario but wanted to live to fight another day.

Whatever the motive, that certainly wasn't going to happen now.

Jock was spent, physically and emotionally. He felt a ripple of relief but a knot of anxiety stopped him from relaxing. He still fully expected to be hit by a rogue RPG from a dirty AQ man hiding along the Takur Ghar ridgelines or in one of the adobe houses in the villages on the valley floor.

There'd be one lucky bastard who'd survived the day, he thought.

Jock looked around at the crush of humanity and the hollow looks staring out from the young faces that had been so eager to charge into battle eighteen hours ago. They were not so sanguine now. Their uniforms were stained with blood and covered with mud from the Shahi Kot Valley. Their hands were like Jock's – red raw and bloody with white knuckles pushing through ragged skin. Some were wrapped in bandages. Their eyes told a tale of exhaustion, elation, fear and frustration.

Holy fuck, he thought. *How the hell did we get out of that alive?*

'I cannot explain why we didn't have any deaths on the day,' Jock says. 'I don't know why the al Qaeda didn't keep smashing us with their mortars. They seemed to drop a few mortars eventually into the halfpipe but they could have been dropping them in there all day and basically just smashed us by morning tea.

'They really wanted us badly, they were out there to take some names and they did a reasonable effort with the resources that they had at their disposal.

'For the life of me I can't explain why they didn't persist with the mortars and drop them into the halfpipe earlier in the day.'

On board the helo Jock let out a sigh of relief. Some of the soldiers around him fell into a deep sleep. Kids began snoring like old men, exhausted from a day of fighting for their lives. Extreme situations provide their own solace and silence.

Sergeant Pete was exhausted. He leant on a young private and dropped into a sleep of the dead, half smothering the poor soldier. The GI was probably too afraid to wake the non-com who had just led him through the most frightening and exhilarating day of his life.

'I woke up and I was back in Bagram. I was physically drained, and you are beat up and you are all bloody from beating yourself around,' Peterson says now. 'You are exhilarated and then all of a sudden, *boom*, you snap out of it and you're like, "Oh man, I just survived something that only holy shit knows."'

En route to Bagram, Jock was hoping like hell that that bull-headed bastard Clint had managed to get on the second chopper. It was a baseless fear because he knew the 10th Mountain would never leave a man behind, but even so, Jock would have felt a thousand times more comfortable if his mate was sitting cheek by jowl with him now.

He couldn't sleep, wouldn't sleep, on the aircraft.

'I was completely exhausted but I refused to go to sleep on that friggin' helicopter just in case it got shot down on the way home,' Jock says now. 'I don't know what difference it makes dying while you're awake or dying when you're asleep, but I didn't want to die asleep. If this was going to be my last hour I was going to be awake for all of it ... I was going to die with my eyes open if I was going to die.'

It was 1955 zulu, 25 minutes past midnight on 3 March, when the Chinooks roared out of the Shahi Kot Valley.

Signalman Jock Wallace and Warrant Officer Class 2 Clint from the SAS Regiment in Perth and most of the 80 soldiers from the 10th Mountain Division had been in the bowl of death for eighteen hours.

Eighteen long, brutal hours, and every single one of the men had survived.

The first thing Jock Wallace did when he walked off the tail ramp of the CH-47 chopper was look at the snowcapped mountains surrounding Bagram Air Base and search the skies for the second Chinook. He was filthy, hungry, bloodied, and his wind- and sun-burnt face was gaunt and ghostly; a ravaged mix of exhaustion, relief and shock. He looked exactly how one imagines a man coming back from battle would look and he felt he'd aged at least a dozen years during those eighteen gruelling hours. Jock was wrecked, but adrenaline was still keeping him going. It was at once the best and worst moment of his life.

Sergeant Pete sent some of his men to the dispensary for treatment and led the rest back to the mortar platoon's tent off to the side of the 10th Mountain Division's hangar. The blokes who had been left at Bagram waiting for the second airlift into the Shahi Kot Valley welcomed them like heroes. Sergeant Pete lit up a smoke, the first one he'd had in years.

'No one is playing "Danger Zone",' he ordered. 'If you turn that song on, I will kick your arse. No one plays "Danger Zone".'

Even now, four years after returning from the Shahi Kot Valley, Peterson is affected by the Kenny Loggins tune. 'To this day, if I hear that song I am like, oh my God, when am I going to start getting shot at?' he says.

A few of the Aussie brass had come to the apron on the side of the runway to welcome Jock and Clint, but Jock didn't give a shit about them.

Where the fuck is Clint? he wondered.

The second chopper arrived a couple of minutes later and Jock fought his way through the crowd of disembarking bone-tired but jubilant Americans to look for his mate, the one other Australian who knew what it was like to be ambushed in Hell's Halfpipe for eighteen hours. Clint was the only bastard Jock wanted to see.

Finally Clint staggered down the ramp, the weight of his gear pressing on his nuggety frame. Jock grabbed him in a bear hug, while someone else ripped the pack off Clint's back.

'Bloody great to see you, mate. Where the fuck did you get to?' Jock said before releasing him.

Clint and Jock had defied death that day. Nothing more needed to be said.

They hitched a ride back to their tent about a kilometre away at the other end of the base for a chat, a feed and something akin to shut-eye.

'When I got off the helicopter that's actually when I felt relief, because ... I *have* made it out alive,' Jock says.

'Once I got off the helicopter and cleared the rotor blades and looked back at the bastard, then I knew the was mission was over. That job was over. That's when it dawned on me that I had made it out of there. And if I died now, it wasn't as a result of anything on al Qaeda's behalf. They wouldn't get the satisfaction.

'We all nearly went to hell.'

Jock pauses, taking a minute to reflect on how close he had come to death. 'That's what it was like – walking through the gates of hell and back.'

CHAPTER 25

*'It was the largest scale battle fought since Vietnam.
It was the largest close air support fight, the largest
ground fight, and it was won handily.'*

GENERAL FRANKLIN 'BUSTER' HAGENBECK,
THE US COMMANDER OF OPERATION ANACONDA

'At the end of Day One we had suffered a setback,' Lieutenant Colonel Rowan Tink noted in his war diary later that night.

'If Major General Hagenbeck does not carry the day tomorrow it is difficult to imagine the second iteration of this battle will conclude before mid to late March. At the moment, he does not favour withdrawal and is staking a lot on the ability of the USAF to bomb their way to victory.'

'And that's essentially what happened; they bombed their way to victory,' Tink says now.

Early the next morning in the TOC, Hagenbeck's chief of staff, Colonel Smith, gathered the commanders together for a briefing.

'We've found them, we are gonna fix 'em and we are gonna kill 'em,' he said.

Smith was referring to al Qaeda and Taliban fighters in the Shahi Kot Valley and his words echoed the OpOrd set down by Hagenbeck less than two weeks earlier, only much more graphically and colourfully.

Operation Anaconda would last another fifteen days before the generals on the ground in Afghanistan and back at CentCom in Florida, together with the Secretary of Defense Donald Rumsfeld, declared mission accomplished.

What began as a 72-hour operation had turned into a pitched battle involving more than 1400 American soldiers, a thousand-strong Afghan force, plus special operators from the US and six other nations: Australia, Canada, Denmark, France, Germany and Norway.

Several patrols from the Australian SAS Regiment would remain in and around the Shahi Kot Valley the entire time performing vital and, at times, life-saving work, for which they would ultimately be recognised and highly praised by the American commanders.

After returning from the battlefield, Jock and Clint were greeted as conquering soldiers but Jock didn't buy into it, thinking it was a load of bullshit.

'We weren't heroes, we were just doing our job basically,' he says. 'We were in a survival situation fighting for our lives, there was no glory there. We were unfortunate victims of bad planning. That really pissed me off.'

The planning and execution of Operation Anaconda have been a subject of heated conjecture since the end of the mission and those in the US defence forces have argued about the problems and their causes.

The US Army, Air Force, Navy and Marines all conducted after-action reviews of the battle plan and its execution to ensure the combined forces would learn from any real or perceived mistakes and avoid them in future operations.

One of the more significant issues to emerge was that of intelligence. No one doubted that the intelligence significantly underestimated the enemy strength and led to the chaos in Hell's Halfpipe. The initial estimate of 100 to 250 enemy fighters in the villages of Babukhel, Sherkhankhel and Marzak and surrounding ridges of the Takur Ghar was almost doubled immediately before the operation began. It has since been estimated that on D-Day there were anywhere from 400 enemy fighters – at the minimum – up to 1000-plus.

'Probably the correct figure was 1000,' writes Norman

Friedman in his book *Terrorism, Afghanistan and America's New Way of War*.

Hagenbeck, who has since been promoted to a three-star Lieutenant General, says the more accurate number was 400; while the men fighting have guesstimated the number to be anywhere between 800 and as many as 1400.

Before the first week of Operation Anaconda was over, the US Secretary of Defense, Donald Rumsfeld, conceded that accurate predictions going into the battle were impossible to achieve.

'We've been looking at that area for weeks and have a great deal of intelligence information, but it is not possible to have a good count,' Rumsfeld said at a press conference in Washington while soldiers were still fighting in the Shahi Kot Valley and searching for Osama bin Laden.

According to the 2005 report by the US Air Force on Operation Anaconda, the planning 'underestimated two things: first, the enemy situation and its tenacity; and second, the difficulty of combining conventional and Special Forces operations in the terrain of the Shahi Kot Valley.

'Inaccurate estimate of the enemy situation – numbers present, reinforcements nearby, and intentions – was perhaps the single major shortfall and it coloured the entire operation,' the report concludes.

'But the fact remains that commanders in every war generally have to make the decision to execute without perfect intelligence. As General Franks said later, "We'll never have the precise picture of any particular place where we're conducting an operation."'

During the operation, General Franks also told the American ABC television program *This Week* that 'we will almost never have perfect intelligence information'. Two years after the battle was over, a now-retired Franks published his autobiography in which he wrote that the 'carefully balanced details of the plan did not survive first attack with the enemy. Anaconda was turning into a hell of a fight.'

Another serious issue that has been raised was the cooperation between the US Army and US Air Force, and each service's concept and understanding of the battle strategy.

Air Force commanders pointed the finger at Hagenbeck, the then Army two-star who had overall command of Coalition Joint Task Force Mountain, and therefore Operation Anaconda. USAF brass said Hagenbeck did not involve the Air Force in planning early enough and that that, effectively, had an impact on the fight.

'Ambiguous command structures established on an ad hoc basis and approved by US Central Command created conditions that inadvertently excluded the Air Force from the planning of Anaconda,' writes US Army Major Mark Davis in his Master's thesis – cited by Elaine Grossman in the online publication *Inside the Pentagon*.

'In the rush to conduct combat operations in Afghanistan, CentCom lost sight of two age-old principles of war: unity of command and unity of effort.'

General Hagenbeck, in published interviews, countered that the close air support was unreliable at times and air power could take anywhere between 26 minutes to an hour to respond to a call for CAS from the valley floor.

Other contentious issues that have been put under the microscope include whether the crucial pre-H-Hour bombing raid on selected al Qaeda and Taliban targets was extensive enough and whether the ambushed troops received adequate CAS during the crucial first day. Similarly, questions have been raised about the decision to omit artillery from the battle on that Saturday, although it was introduced later in the operation; as well as the efficacy of segregated command posts for various services in Bagram, Kuwait, Saudi Arabia and Tampa, Florida, and the complex chain of command that did not always answer directly to Hagenbeck.

On top of that, a cascade of accusations were traded within the US military and between the US and Afghan forces about the reliance on the Afghan Army as the main thrust in Anaconda. Ultimately, that reliance was misplaced on D-Day when Zia's Afghan Forces withdrew in the opening hours of the operation.

Even so, most of the soldiers who fought nose-to-nose against al Qaeda and the radical Taliban militia have no doubt D-Day was a success. Some put it down to sheer good luck, others to prayers and yet others to pure skill, exceptional training and good soldiering. And there are some troopers who would say it was a combination of all of the above.

Any which way, Operation Anaconda can be hailed a success insofar as 82 soldiers air-assaulted into the base of an al Qaeda stronghold on D-Day came out alive. Even though they had failed to secure the southern blocking point, reinforcements would subsequently complete the mission and rout the al Qaeda and Taliban fighters from the region. It just took longer than anticipated.

Command Sergeant Major Frank Grippe believes D-Day was a success, but has in the past said the intelligence had flaws. Instead of looking at the negatives, though, Grippe prefers to focus on the positives, and contrasts it with his second tour of duty in Afghanistan during which seventeen of his men were killed in action. That, he says, puts D-Day of Anaconda into perspective.

'It was quite a significant battle and how we didn't lose anybody still amazes me,' Grippe says of D-Day now. 'We were blessed and there was a lot of skill involved. We were pretty much a well-trained unit, there is no doubt about that – our equipment, our marksmanship, our tactics, just our steadfastness – but we were lucky that we had no KIA that day.

'It was a great feeling watching the boys fight – their braveries and their skill.'

Grippe also sees the victory of D-Day and the overall operation on a broader canvas and sweeps it with the brush of history.

'Al Qaeda thought they were safe up in the mountains, and we historically fought at the highest altitude the US Army has ever fought at,' he says. 'The floor of the valley was 8500 feet [2600 metres], the surrounding mountains, some of them, were over 11 000 feet [3350 metres], and we showed al Qaeda that they weren't safe anywhere. Brought the fight right to their doorstep, literally. Killed hundreds and really disrupted their supply system.

And you know, psychologically, they could talk the talk but they all ran to Pakistan. The little bastards all talk how bad they are . . .' he says, trailing off.

'We went into a valley where the Russians had just gotten their arses whipped twice in a row, and they went into the valley with artillery and tanks and everything else. And we were just in the valley by ourselves – they went into the valley with hundreds upon hundreds – and the first day in the valley there was just 250 conventional American forces and some small teams here and there doing reconnaissance.

'It wasn't like a huge, overwhelming force. Definitely didn't have the three-to-one ratio as per doctrine, but you know, we didn't need that. We kept the small footprint that we needed inside of Afghanistan to show the Afghans that we weren't there to occupy. We were just there in a blood feud, hunting al Qaeda, and the warlords really respected that.

'[We said:] "We're here to hunt al Qaeda, we're not here to disrupt your lifestyle and impose our will on you." And they really accepted that.'

Sitting in the Pentagon, General Hagenbeck says the operation was a victory, particularly on D-Day when all but one of seven blocking positions were secured under heavy fighting.

'This was extraordinary, when it all comes down to it. It was the largest scale battle fought since Vietnam. It was the largest close air support fight, the largest ground fight, and it was won handily,' Hagenbeck says. 'That doesn't mean that there weren't some times when we were holding our breath, but it really was [a huge victory].'

Asked about the criticism that a lot of things went wrong on the opening day of what was originally conceived of as a 72-hour operation, Hagenbeck defends the plan.

'I think a lot of things went right,' he says. 'The plan is always described as only good until the first shot is fired.

'There is, I think, a mischaracterisation that we flew, initially, a smaller number of troops to the fight and there were a thousand al Qaeda waiting for us in the valley. That's not true. There were about 400 on the first day and over the next three days they continued to reinforce and, yes, they did reach in excess of a thousand people in the valley, they sure did. But it's not like we flew everybody into the teeth of a thousand al Qaeda waiting for us. It was about 400 that were there.

'Now, granted, on that first lift we only put in about 250 or 260 infantry against 400 and then they started reinforcing and we didn't get another 250 in, actually less than that, a little over 200, 225, [until] the second lift [the next day].'

According to General Hagenbeck, some enemy escaped but not in the large numbers that were originally reported in the media in March 2002. However, the high-value targets Osama bin Laden and the Taliban's leader, the one-eyed Mullah Omar, were not captured, nor were their bodies found, and by April 2006 bin Laden was still thought to be alive, sending taped messages to his terrorist fighters.

'Now, did a handful of fighters get out of that valley? Sure they did. But did they escape from Shahi Kot Valley in large numbers? Heck, no. You will never convince me.'

Similarly, the Americans are reluctant to reveal how many enemy fighters were killed during Operation Anaconda because they do not want to be accused of engaging in a body count as they were after the Vietnam War. Early reports variably estimated that 400- or 500-plus enemy fighters had been killed in the first six days of ground fighting, but other reports have put the total figure as high as 1000 – a number that some commanders will privately confirm but publicly deny knowledge of.

Still, only about 100 bodies were found, with commanders saying that they had either been incinerated by bombs, buried in collapsed caves, or dragged away by the al Qaeda and Taliban fighters as part of the guerrilla warfare tactics to deny the enemy a benchmark by which to measure success.

On 8 March 2002 in Australia, the commander of Australian Special Forces, Brigadier Duncan Lewis, told a press conference that the SAS Regiment had been pivotal in eliminating enemy forces.

'US battle-damage assessments indicate that a high proportion of those killed is attributed to the actions and professionalism of the Australian Special Forces,' Brigadier Lewis said.

Toward the end of Operation Anaconda, Hagenbeck gave a press conference at Bagram Air Base in which he was quoted saying that the lack of bodies in the Shahi Kot Valley could be attributed to the devastating intensity of the bombs dropped on the villages and the extensive cave system in the surrounding mountains. According to the USAF's 2005 report, 231 bombs were dropped on D-Day.

'We've rid the world of hundreds of trained killers who will now not slaughter innocent men, women and children,' Hagenbeck told reporters in Bagram on 14 March 2002.

US intelligence received credible information that after about 36 to 48 hours into the fight, al Qaeda leaders called for hundreds of wooden coffins to be brought into the valley. On the fourth day of the fight, another call went out to al Qaeda and Taliban fighters to bring in trucks and SUVs to extract their dead.

'The coffins never got in and the SUVs and any vehicles that tried to enter the area never got in,' Hagenbeck said then.

Ultimately, General Hagenbeck is pleased with the outcome of Operation Anaconda, in the course of which eight Americans and three friendly Afghan soldiers were killed and another 80 coalition soldiers wounded.

'When we talk about it being the first big battle of the twenty-first century it has everything to do with the fact that it was a coalition fight; that it was "joint" – meaning that we had the Army, the Air Force and Navy [and] Marine pilots that were involved in it; that we had what we called an integrated battlefield; and that it was fought at great distances and that we used high-tech enablers to assist us in the fight,' Hagenbeck says.

'I think that portends the kind of fight that may be more

common in the 21st century [rather] than the large land battles like the attack to Baghdad.'

Would General Hagenbeck have done anything different?

'I think I would be foolish to say no, but in the end run I am pretty pleased with the outcome of this,' he says.

At the end of the initial phase of Operation Anaconda, the US Army's Major Bryan Hilferty, who was based at Bagram and had the role of issuing daily briefings and conducting press conferences with reporters, said: 'We have destroyed their command and control. We have destroyed their caches [of weapons]. We have killed hundreds of the al Qaeda terrorists who now will not be around to kill innocent men, women and children.'

The war was not over yet, he said, because some al Qaeda and Taliban fighters remained in the valley. 'Do you have every single bit of every place covered? No ... But if I was an al Qaeda guy, I would not be going out for pizza.'

While Hilferty had a dry sense of humour and a matter-of-fact delivery, he began each press conference with a sombre statement, reminding the war correspondents how many days had passed since al Qaeda launched its attack on American soil, killing thousands of people at the start of a beautiful autumn day on September 11. He then read one of several obituaries about an al Qaeda victim that were published daily in *The New York Times*. When done, it was back to business detailing the war effort.

The battle strategy, efficacy of the intelligence gathering and estimates of enemy numbers, and subsequent battle casualties will continue to be debated among the services that participated in Operation Anaconda. But there is one thing on which they agree, and that is the strength and success of the contribution of 150 members of the Australian Special Air Service Regiment involved in Anaconda and the subsequent troops who followed them into Afghanistan on rotation months later.

US Generals Franks and Hagenbeck and non-coms such as Grippe and Healy all have nothing but praise for the Australian soldiers who fought alongside the Americans, particularly Jock and Clint and the SAS troops who would be involved in a rescue mission at a place called Roberts Ridge three days later. Healy says Clint still owes him a couple of cigars.

Sean Naylor in his book *Not a Good Day to Die* writes that 'of all the non-American forces involved in Anaconda, it was the Australians who inspired the most confidence among the US officers'. They were, according to Naylor, 'perhaps the most tightly bonded, least rearranged unit in Anaconda'.

At the end of March, the Australian Defence Minister, Senator Robert Hill, sent the second rotation of about 150 SAS troopers to Afghanistan, offering nothing but complimentary words for the 150 soldiers they were about to relieve.

'All reports that I get are that they've done extraordinarily well on the ground, and they are highly regarded for what they've achieved. In fact, it almost becomes embarrassing, the level of praise we get from our coalition colleagues,' Senator Hill said.

Frank Grippe, who has since completed two tours of duty in Iraq, speaks from direct experience. He spent eighteen hours with Jock Wallace and WO2 Clint in Hell's Halfpipe, and he had seen them in action in the days leading up to Anaconda, preparing their missions and attending briefings.

'Jock, through the day, kept tabs on his sergeant major, kept good communications up, returned fire, and never once was he a flinching type,' Grippe says.

'Passed information back and forth where he would see enemy. He engaged the enemy. Unwavering type of guy. Never had a bad attitude. Not that anyone really had a bad attitude.'

Grippe also understood that the SAS troopers assigned to his infantry division had to adapt to the way a foreign force did business. Not only that, Jock and Clint were special operators and they were attached to a conventional battalion. It's one thing to be among your own special operators with your own language, but it's quite another thing to be attached to a new and different unit under combat. Grippe was impressed with the two Australian SAS soldiers' adaptability and capabilities.

'In our forces, especially my battalion, we pull up everyone under our wing and make them feel comfortable,' Grippe says. 'And I knew they felt like they were a part of the team. And I knew they *were* a part of the team and it was great to have them there.

'When you have two Special Air Service guys with you, you know those are two guys you have no issues with. You know their marksmanship is going to be right on, they are going to be unwavering in the fight, they have the needed medical skills, and they have the extra communications gear that we needed.'

Several days after Operation Anaconda had begun, the commander of Australia's Special Operations, Brigadier Duncan Lewis, commended Jock and Clint's actions at the first press conference in Australia which explored in some detail the SAS patrols' activities.

'Throughout the engagement, the Australian soldiers continued to relay vital information back to headquarters,' Lewis told reporters. 'Their information was key to the subsequent planning of the successful extraction of this force.'

And it was.

But to Jock, the real heroes were the blokes like his mate Johnny who was still out on patrol.

In the coming days, SAS troopers in a hidden observation post high in the mountains, where the temperature had fallen to minus 19 degrees Celsius, would call in devastatingly successful air strikes on enemy positions during a daring rescue mission. The action helped save 36 American Special Forces soldiers under direct enemy fire after a helicopter was shot down on Takur Ghar, an incident in which six US soldiers were killed. SAS soldiers were part of the rescue team that eventually evacuated the trapped soldiers and retrieved their fallen comrades from Roberts Ridge.

SAS men also risked their lives doing surveillance and reconnaissance missions, sometimes using donkeys, reminiscent of Simpson and his donkey in Gallipoli. They engaged the enemy up close. Some troopers like Jock would go on to be honoured for their bravery, including Sergeant Matthew Bouillaut who received the Distinguished Service Cross for outstanding command of a patrol in a later incident in Anaconda. The entire SAS Regiment would ultimately receive a Meritorious Unit Citation for their outstanding contribution in Afghanistan in Operation Slipper. The SAS patrols eventually were withdrawn from the Shahi Kot Valley on 13 March – having outstayed every other Special Forces unit.

Clint and Jock were waiting at the gate when the wild and woolly SAS troopers came in.

'There were two people at that gate when the squadron came home. It was me and Clint. We both knew that we wanted to welcome these guys who had been watching our back, who had been out there before us and came back after us,' Jock says with typical self-deprecation, downplaying his own bravery and achievements.

'And these were *the* guys, they're real SAS. The shit's been sorted from the sugar, and this is the core of the sugar coming in. It's good sugar, fine quality. I've never felt so proud watching them come in.

'That was the best feeling. Elation and relief simultaneously, and pride; you know, mateship to the point of brotherhood.

'These guys, they're men. The guys I'm talking about aren't shirkers, they're the real SAS, real Aussies. Unstoppable – mentally and, obviously, physically. They sit out the lows and they ride the highs and kick arse everywhere else in between.'

Jock hadn't seen Johnny for a while but knew exactly what he'd been up to in the valley. Chooks are communicators. Jock had a camera and began taking happy snaps as soon as the troops came through the gate.

'I remember Johnny coming around the corner and he looked like the rabbit out of *Alice in Wonderland* that was possessed by the devil or something,' Jock says now. 'He had this huge mad grin on his face; beard out here; his hair was like a lion's. He used to have blond tips but they've grown out, so it looks like camouflage. He took his goggles off and had a big white patch over his face and the rest of it was a sea of dust. And he had a big white smile. It was the best photo.

'I, certainly, am under no illusions ... they had the harder part of the task, and mine was simply circumstance and luck that sort of got us through.'

But luck had little to do with Jock Wallace surviving the Shahi Kot Valley. Courage and gallantry under fire did.

As the now retired four-star general Tommy Franks said of the Australians' actions in Operation Anaconda, 'I'm not sure it will ever be fully declassified, [but it] literally brings tears to my eyes. The Aussies brought bravery to a whole new level.'

EPILOGUE

Jock Wallace could hold his head high.
He had left the Shahi Kot Valley with his life and
honour intact. Nothing could beat that.

One year after the first members of the Australian Army's Special Forces Task Group started operations in Afghanistan, Signalman Martin 'Jock' Wallace received the Medal for Gallantry for his actions in Operation Anaconda. The award is one of Australia's highest decorations for bravery in perilous circumstances.

He was the first member of the Royal Australian Corps of Signals to be honoured with the MG since the Vietnam War, and one of a handful of non-Sabre-qualified members of the SAS Regiment to be so recognised for outstanding courage.

The wording of the citation was simple, clear, and devoid of the emotion and danger that had consumed the men in Hell's Halfpipe.

For gallantry in action in hazardous circumstances
while undertaking communications responsibilities in
Afghanistan during Operation Slipper.

The explanation that came with the citation, which was announced in an official press release from Canberra, carried a little more information.

Signalman Wallace displayed gallantry and courage under fire when performing communications responsibilities during Operation Anaconda, as part of Operation Slipper in Afghanistan. He maintained composure under sustained heavy attack from enemy forces while performing his duties as a Signalman, attending to the wounded and providing leadership to those around him. Signalman Wallace's gallantry has brought great credit to himself, the Special Air Service Regiment and the Australian Defence Force.

The Medal for Gallantry is worn on Jock's left breast, positioned to the left of the Australian Active Service Medal with the International Coalition Against Terrorism clasp and, later, the Iraq clasp. Moving to the right of the Active Service Medal, in accordance with official military protocol, Jock's next two medals are campaign medals for active service in Afghanistan during 2001 and 2002, and Iraq in 2003. The next gong to the right is the Australian Service Medal – Minurso and Solomon Island clasps – then the Defence Long Service Medal for more than fifteen years' service in the Australian Defence Force. The DLSM is known colloquially by the troops as the Parramatta medal, because its ribbon is blue and gold, the colours of the Parramatta Eels rugby league team. On the far right, he wears the Minurso Medal United Nations with a number '2' on it for two tours of duty.

On his right breast, Signalman Wallace wears the Meritorious Unit Citation and the Chief of General Staff Commendation for his service in Western Sahara, as well as the Returned from Active Service Badge.

Jock is also entitled to the recently gazetted Australian Defence Medal and the Army Combat Badge.

Jock's Medal for Gallantry also brought enormous pride to the Signals Corps, and in mid 2003 the training sergeant at the School of Signals at the Simpson Barracks in McLeod, Victoria, established the Jock Wallace Award for Communications.

Jock is as proud of the peer-instigated award named in his honour as he is of his Medal for Gallantry.

'It's for the hard chargers; it goes to the radio operator considered to have the good stuff and best prospects of radio in the School of Signals,' Jock says.

'The reason they did it was to give young soldiers something that was real and tangible and something to focus on, and it just adds a modern relevance for these guys.'

Jock's bravery was also noted by General Hagenbeck, who says: 'It was very clear that somebody down there [in the Shahi Kot Valley] was making a difference and that it was coming from the SAS.'

At the time, Hagenbeck didn't know who was making the difference, but in the aftermath of the operation he made inquiries and discovered that the 'somebody' in Hell's Halfpipe was Signalman Jock Wallace.

The Americans were generous with their praise of the Australians, and Hagenbeck wanted to officially acknowledge Jock's contribution to the 10th Mountain Division on D-Day of Anaconda.

'I knew that I could get the Bronze Star to him and so when Tink came to me I said, "Who were your guys that pulled this off?"'

The General says he recommended Jock for the prestigious Bronze Star, the fourth highest award in the US Defense Force that is awarded for combat heroism or meritorious service. Upon Hagenbeck's recommendation, the paperwork was approved by the US Government, and then had to go to the Australian hierarchy for approval.

Hagenbeck also recommended Sergeant First Class Michael Peterson from the mortar platoon for his outstanding leadership on D-Day. Sergeant Pete received the Bronze Star for Valor shortly after Operation Anaconda ended, in a dignified ceremony presided over by General Tommy Franks inside the hangar at Bagram Air Base, along with three other soldiers who fought in Hell's Halfpipe. Sergeant First Class Robert Healy was similarly decorated and also received a Purple Heart; and Command

Sergeant Major Frank Grippe received the Bronze Star for Valor with Heroic Achievement, together with a Purple Heart.

Months later, Hagenbeck would recommend that Lieutenant Colonel Rowan Tink receive the Bronze Star for his planning and leadership in Operation Enduring Freedom.

The Duntroon graduate received the award from Hagenbeck at Bagram Air Base on 16 July 2002 – the night before Tink left Afghanistan after a six-month tour of duty. As with all Bronze Star awards, it had been authorised by the President – George W. Bush.

'The outstanding tactical contributions of Lieutenant Colonel Tink and his Task Force served as a major factor in rendering the enemy a crucial blow to his capability as an effective fighting force,' the recommendation read.

Tink was the first Australian since the Vietnam War to receive the highly regarded American honour. Soon after, Lieutenant Colonel Peter 'Gus' Gilmore also received the Bronze Star for his work in Afghanistan.

That December at Pope Air Force Base in North Carolina, the Secretary of the Air Force, Dr James G. Roche, presented the Silver Star to Senior Airman Stephen M. Achey for his actions on 2 March in the Shahi Kot Valley.

Despite Hagenbeck's recommendation, Jock Wallace, who hung up his royal-blue beret and retired from the SAS Regiment and Australian Army in 2005, is still waiting for his Bronze Star.

The soldier who fought for his life and helped save the lives of 81 other soldiers in the great tradition of the Australian digger isn't worried. That Hagenbeck recommended him is enough; and if the paperwork became stalled in the Australian bureaucracy, well, isn't that the digger's lament?

Jock Wallace could hold his head high. He had left the Shahi Kot Valley with his life and honour intact. Nothing could beat that.

AUTHOR'S NOTE

Unless otherwise stated, opinions expressed in *Do or Die* belong to the author. They do not reflect those of the Australian Government, the Australian Defence Force or Special Operations Command.

The surnames of some serving and retired soldiers from the Special Air Service Regiment have been omitted to ensure that past and ongoing operational, security and tactical matters relating to the regiment are not compromised. Soldiers who have been named in *Do or Die* have given their approval or were cleared by the Australian Army.

SELECT BIBLIOGRAPHY

BOOKS

Anonymous, *Hunting Al Qaeda: A Take-No-Prisoners Account of Terror, Adventure, and Disillusionment*, Zenith Press, 2005

Robert Baer, *See No Evil: The True Story of a Ground Soldier in the CIA's War on Terrorism*, Three Rivers Press, New York, 2002

Mark Bowden, *Black Hawk Down*, Corgi Books, 1999

Steve Coll, *Ghost Wars: The Secret History of the CIA, Afghanistan and bin Laden, from the Soviet Invasion to September 10, 2001*, The Penguin Press, New York, 2004

Anthony H. Cordesman, *The Lessons of Afghanistan: War Fighting, Intelligence, and Force Transformation*, The CSIS Press, Centre for Strategic and International Studies, 2002

Phillip Corwin, *Doomed in Afghanistan: A UN Officer's Memoir of the Fall of Kabul and Najibullah's Failed Escape, 1992*, Rutgers University Press, Pistcataway, NJ, 2003

George Crile, *Charlie Wilson's War: The Extraordinary Story of How the Wildest Man in Congress and a Rogue CIA Agent Changed the History of Our Times*, Grove Press, New York, 2003

Michael DeLong & Noah Lukeman, *Inside CentCom: The Unvarnished Truth About the Wars in Afghanistan and Iraq*, Regnery Publishing Inc., 2004

Yosri Fouda & Nick Fielding, *Masterminds of Terror: The Truth Behind the Most Devastating Terrorist Attack the World Has Ever Seen*, Penguin Books, 2003

Tommy Franks, *American Soldier*, HarperCollins Publishers, New York, 2004

Norman Friedman, *Terrorism, Afghanistan, and America's New Way of War*, Naval Institute Press, 2003

Dave Grossman, *On Killing: The Psychological Cost of Learning to Kill in War and Society*, Back Bay Books, Little, Brown & Company, 1995

Rohan Gunaratna, *Inside al Qaeda: Global Network of Terror*, Scribe Publications Pty Ltd, 2002

Haim Harari, *A View From the Eye of the Storm: Terror and Reason in the Middle East*, Regan Books, 2005

Michael Hirsch, *None Braver: U.S. Air Force Pararescuemen in the War on Terrorism*, New American Library, 2003

David Horner, *SAS, Phantoms of War: A History of the Australian Special Air Service*, Allen & Unwin, 2002 edition

James Kitfield, *War & Destiny: How the Bush Revolution in Foreign and Military Affairs Redefined American Power*, Potomac Books Inc., Washington DC, 2005

Ian McPhedran, *The Amazing SAS: The Inside Story of Australia's Special Forces*, HarperCollins Publishers Australia, Pymble, NSW, 2005.

Eric Micheletti, *Special Forces War on Terrorism in Afghanistan 2001–2003*, Histoire & Collections, Paris, 2003

David Miller, *The Illustrated Directory of Special Forces*, MBI Publishing Company, 2002

Richard Miniter, *Shadow War: The Untold Story of How Bush is Winning the War on Terror*, Regnery Publishing Inc., 2004

Robin Moore, *The Hunt for bin Laden: Task Force Dagger, On*

The Ground with the Special Forces in Afghanistan, Random House, 2003

Timothy Naftali, *Blind Spot: The Secret History of American Counter-terrorism*, Basic Books, 2005

Sean Naylor, *Not A Good Day to Die: The Untold Story of Operation Anaconda*, Berkley Books, New York, 2005

Ahmed Rashid, *Taliban*, Yale University Press, 2001

Linda Robinson, *Masters of Chaos: The Secret History of the Special Forces*, Public Affairs, a member of the Perseus Books Group, 2004

Gary Schroen, *First In: An Insider's Account of How the CIA Spearheaded the War on Terror in Afghanistan*, Ballantine Books, New York, 2005

Mohamed Sifaoui, *Inside al Qaeda: How I Infiltrated the World's Deadliest Terrorist Organisation*, Granta Books, London, 2003

Stephen Tanner, *Afghanistan: A Military History from Alexander the Great to the Fall of the Taliban*, Da Capo Press, 2002

Bob Woodward, *Bush At War*, Simon & Schuster, New York, 2002

Mohammad Yousaf & Mark Adkin, *Afghanistan, the Bear Trap: The Defeat of a Superpower*, Casemate, 1991 & 2001

NEWSPAPER AND MAGAZINE ARTICLES AND WEBSITES

Gay Alcorn & Craig Skehan and agencies, 'Troops Killed as US Enters A Chilling New Phase in Afghan War', *The Sydney Morning Herald*, 6 March 2002

Tom Allard, 'Survivor of Afghanistan's Hell Valley Gets Gallantry Award', *The Sydney Morning Herald*, 28 November 2002

Lance Bacon, 'Secret Weapons: The Airmen Who Are Winning the Ground War', *Air Force Times*, 8 April 2002

Austin Bay, 'Full Report on Operation Anaconda – America's First Battle of the 21st Century. A Complete After Action

Interview with Col Wiercinski', www.strategypage.com, 27 June 2002

Barry Bearak, 'The Bombing, Taliban and War Deliver Double Blow to villagers', *The New York Times*, 11 March 2002

Jason Burke, 'When Uncle Sam Meets 'Stan', *The Observer*, 26 May 2002

Alisha Carr, 'SAS Put on the Squeeze', *Army, The Soldier's Newspaper*, 28 March 2002

Rory Carroll, '$100,000 Bounty on Westerners', *The Observer*, 7 April 2002

Stephen Coates, 'No Stone Unturned as Hunt for the Enemy Hits Home – War on Terror', *The Daily Telegraph*, 12 March 2002

Richard T. Cooper, 'The Untold War', *The Los Angeles Times*, 24 March 2002

Phillip Coorey, 'Amid Freezing Days in Harsh Land, Our Men Long For a Beer – War Against Terror', *The Sunday Telegraph*, 12 May 2002

'Courage, Guts and Heroics – It's Just Part of Staying Alive', AAP, 28 November 2002

John Daniszewski, 'US and Afghans Savor Victory in Valley: Coalition Has Destroyed a Stronghold Used by al Qaeda and the Taliban', *The Los Angeles Times*, 15 March 2002

John Daniszewski, 'Anaconda Winds Down as Troops Scout al Qaeda, Taliban Stragglers', *The Los Angeles Times*, 18 March 2002

John Daniszewski & Geoffrey Mohan, 'Afghans Set Off to Root Out al Qaeda, Taliban Holdouts', *The Los Angeles Times*, 12 March 2002

John Daniszewski & Geoffrey Mohan, 'Assault Set Back al Qaeda', *The Los Angeles Times*, 15 March 2002

Roy Eccleston, 'A Helicopter Disaster amid the Fog of War, *The Australian*, 6 March 2002

Roy Eccleston, 'US War Architect Puts Faith in Latham on Iraq Pullout', *The Weekend Australian*, 7 August 2004

Roy Eccleston & Duncan McFarlane, 'SAS Broke al Qaeda Trap
– the War on Terror, Six Months On and It's Only Getting
Hotter', *The Weekend Australian*, 9 March 2002

Michael Elliott, 'Deadly Mission: Inside the Battle of Shah-i-Kot,
Where the Enemy Had Nothing to Lose and US Soldiers
Had to Fight for Their Lives', *Time Asia* magazine,
11 March 2002

Dave Enders & Phil Tegtmeier, '10th Mountain Division:
Soldiers Use Big Four Battle Drills to Maintain Combat
Edge', *NCO Journal*, January 2003

Ben Fenton, 'Bush Sheds Tears Over Deaths of US Soldier',
www.telegraph.co.uk

Mark Forbes, 'Nation Says Thank You to SAS Heroes', *The
Age*, 28 November 2002

Kathy Gannon, 'Troops Poised to Finish Off al Qaeda in War on
Terror', Associated Press, published in *The Daily Telegraph*, 8
March 2002

Kathy Gannon, 'Hundreds of Fighters Mass at Front Line for
Final Push on al Qaeda', Associated Press, 11 March 2002

Kathy Gannon, 'Troops Claim Success in Afghan Hills',
Associated Press, 13 March 2002

Jim Garamone, 'Coalition, Afghan Forces Attack al
Qaeda–Taliban Enclave', American Forces Information
Service, 3 March 2002

Jim Garamone, 'Troops Taking Fight to al Qaeda in Eastern
Afghanistan', American Forces Information Service, 4 March
2002

Jim Garamone, 'Allies Aggressive in Fight Against al Qaeda,
Taliban', American Forces Information Service, 5 March
2002

Steve Gee, 'US Bronze Star for SAS Hero', *The Daily Telegraph*,
24 July 2002

Adam Geibel, 'Operation Anaconda, Shahi Kot Valley,
Afghanistan, 2–10 March 2002', *Military Review*, May–June
2002, English edition

Barton Gellman & Dafna Linzer, 'Afghanistan, Iraq: Two Wars Collide', *The Washington Post*, 22 October 2004

Gerry J. Gilmore, 'US Troops Describe All-day Shahi Kot Battle', American Forces Information Service, 7 March 2002

Gerry J. Gilmore, 'Anaconda Battle Plan Sound, Franks Says', American Forces Information Service, 10 March 2002

John Gittelsohn, 'Soldier Recounts Fateful Operation Anaconda Battle', Knight Ridder/Tribune News Service, 3 April 2002

Bradley Graham, '7 Americans Died in Rescue Effort that Revealed Mistakes and Determination', *The Washington Post*, 24 May 2002

Rebecca Grant, 'The Echoes of Anaconda', *Air Force* magazine, April 2005

Darren Gray, 'SAS Seizes Rockets, Ammunition in Raid', *The Age*, 22 November 2002

Elaine Grossman, 'Was Operation Anaconda Ill-fated from the Start?', *Inside the Pentagon*, 29 July 2004, citing Major Mark Davis's master's thesis

Elaine Grossman, 'Anaconda: Object Lesson in Poor Planning or Triumph of Improvisation?', InsideDefense.com, Inside Washington Publishers, 12 August 2004

Pat Grossmith, 'NH Soldiers See July 4th in New Light', *New Hampshire Union Leader*, 5 July 2002

Paul Haven, 'Australia's Crack Troops Move in for Caves Battle', Associated Press, Reuters, published in *The Sydney Morning Herald*, 12 March 2002

Mark Hayward, 'Wounded Soldier Returns Home: Kyle McGovern was Early Victim in Operation Anaconda', *New Hampshire Union Leader*, 22 March 2002

'High International Praise for Troops – War on Terror', *The Daily Telegraph*, 29 March 2002

Grant Holloway, 'Aus Forces Heavily Involved in Anaconda', CNN.com, March

Ron Jensen, 'What Good am I if I Lose My Head?' *Stars and Stripes*, 14 June 2005

Damon Johnston, 'US Chiefs Watched Soldier Die on TV –
War on Terror: Australians in Battle', *The Daily Telegraph*,
7 March 2002

Terry Joyce, 'Area Couple Takes Pride in Son's Heroism',
Charleston.net, 5 January 2003

John Kerin, 'Heroes of Afghanistan Emerge from the Shadows',
The Australian, 28 November 2002

'Kidnapped Man Describes Cave Complex', *The Washington
Post*, 10 March 2002

Jason Lake, 'Kadena NCO Awarded Distinguished Flying Cross
for Afghanistan Operation', Pacific Air Forces News Services,
13 May 2003

Peter Londey, 'War Without Boundaries', *Wartime* magazine,
Issue 22, Australian War Memorial, Canberra

Bronwen Maddox, 'Anaconda Fails to Give Kabul Peace of
Mind', *The Times*, London, 13 March 2002

Victorino Matus, 'Sucking the Oxygen Out of a Cave during
Operation Anaconda, the United States Rolled Out a New
Weapon – the Thermobaric Bomb. It's Worse than a Daisy
Cutter, and It May Have Saddam's Name on It', *The Weekly
Standard*, 12 March 2002

Rory McCarthy, 'US Pays Afghan Warriors $384 a Month', *The
Guardian* & Reuters, published in *The Sydney Morning
Herald*, 6 March 2002

Robert H. McElroy & Patrecia Sleyden Hollis, 'Afghanistan,
Fire Support for Operation Anaconda', *Field Artillery*
magazine, September–October, 2002

Ian McPhedran, 'SAS in Hand-to-hand Mountain Combat –
War on Terror – Australians in Battle', *The Daily Telegraph*,
6 March 2002

Ian McPhedran, '36 US Troops Pinned Down: Australia's SAS is
the Only Hope – War on Terror – Australians in Battle', *The
Daily Telegraph*, 9 March 2002

Ian McPhedran, 'Calling Down Death is a Very Exact Science –
War on Terror – Australians in Battle', *The Daily Telegraph*,
9 March 2002

Ian McPhedran, 'Australia's Finest Tell of 18-hour War Siege', *The Mercury* (Hobart), 17 June 2002

Ian McPhedran, 'Salute to their Valour', *The Advertiser* (Adelaide), 28 November 2002

Ian McPhedran, 'Story of SAS Heroes who Dared and Won – War on Terror', *The Daily Telegraph*, 28 November 2002

Doug Mellgren, 'Australian Forces Arrive at Desert Base: US Troops More Aggressive in Reconnaissance Patrols', Associated Press, AP Worldstream, 2 December 2001

Greg Miller, 'Suspected Friendly Case Disclosed – Afghanistan: The First US Soldier Killed in Operation Anaconda may have been Strafed by Gunship, Pentagon Says', *The Los Angeles Times*, 30 March 2002

Sean D. Naylor, 'The Lessons of Anaconda', *The New York Times*, 2 March 2003

Sean D. Naylor, 'In Shah-e-Kot, Apaches Save the Day – and their Reputation', *Army Times*, 25 March 2002

Aaron Patrick, 'Military Ramps Up Australia's War Role', *The Australian Financial Review*, 9 March 2002

Patrick Quin, 'Al Qaeda Looking for Safe Haven', Associated Press, published in *The Australian Financial Review*, 27 May 2002

Carold Robidoux, 'Vets Carry on with Loyalty and Respect', *New Hampshire Union Leader*, 11 November 2002

Emelie Rutherford, 'Wounded New Hampshire Soldier Reunites with Family, Recalls al-Qaida Shootout', Boston University, Washington Journalism Centre, 16 March 2002

'SAS Helped Kill 300 Enemy in Afghan Fight', AAP, published in *The Sydney Morning Herald*, 11 May 2002

'SAS Put on the Squeeze', *Army: The Soldiers' Newspaper*, 28 March 2002

Craig Skehan, 'High Praise for Diggers who Helped Save Stricken Americans', *The Sydney Morning Herald*, 9 March 2002

Craig Skehan, 'Special Forces Kill 10 Enemy Fighters', *The Sydney Morning Herald*, 16 March 2002

'Soldiers Wounded in Operation Anaconda Receive Purple Hearts', CNN Saturday Morning News, CNN.com/transcripts, 16 March 2002

Susanne M. Schafer, 'US Troops Survive Ring of Fire From al Qaida', Associated Press, published in *The Daily Camera*, Boulder, Colorado, 8 March 2002

Rone Tempest, 'Purple Hearts for 6 Wounded in Afghan War', *The Los Angeles Times*, 9 March 2002

Mark Thompson, '11 Lives – The Soldier – Sudden Warrior: Randel Perez Didn't Join the Army to be a Hero. But in Early March, He Suddenly Became One', *Time* magazine, 1 September 2002

Ann Scott Tyson, 'Anaconda, a War Story', *The Christian Science Monitor*, 1 August 2002

'US Chief Upbeat after Rout in Afghanistan, Gardez', *The Sun Herald*, 17 March 2002

'US Claimed it Killed 500, So Where Are the Bodies?', compiled from *Times* wire services, *St Petersburg Times*, 17 March 2002

'US Uses Bunker-Busting "Thermobaric" Bomb for First Time', Agence France Presse, 3 March 2002

'US Warplanes Dodge Missiles: No injuries, Marines Say – Al-Qaida Prisoners Quizzed: Bin Laden Whereabouts Unknown', Guardian Unlimited, 18 December 2001

Jamie Walker, 'Diggers in the Thick of Anaconda Battle – September 11 – Six Months On', *The Weekend Australian*, 9 March 2002

MarianneWilkinson, 'Revealed: How Howard Brushed Aside the *Tampa*'s Medical Alert', *The Sydney Morning Herald*, 10 October 2002

Brian Williams, 'Is It Time for Guerrilla War in Afghanistan?', www.dawn.com/2002/03/15/int14.htm, 15 March 2002

Kevin Williams, 'Shaw Airman Makes History', *The Shaw Spirit*, 27 May 2005

Andi Wolos & Bob Necci, 'Afghan Leaflets Offer Reward for Killing Troops', www.aiipowmia.com, 7 April 2002

David Wood, 'Wounded GIs Recount 18-hour Ordeal Under al-Qaida Mortar Barrage', Newhouse News Service, 2002

David Zucchino, 'Operation Anaconda Leaves Bitterness in Its Wake', *The Los Angeles Times*, 14 April 2002

www.chinook-helicopter.com/index.html

www.defenselink.mil/sites/

www.defense.gov/transcripts/

www.globalsecurity.org

www.pm.gov.au/

www.whitehouse.gov/news/

AUSTRALIAN AND UNITED STATES GOVERNMENT PRESS RELEASES, TRANSCRIPTS AND REPORTS

Australian Department of Defence Annual Report 2001–2002

'Background Briefing on the Report on the Battle of Takur Ghar', official transcript released by the United States Department of Defense, 24 May 2002

Kelly Cahalan, 'Seventeen Receive High Honours for Heroism', US Air Force Press Releases, 14 November 2002

'Executive Summary of the Battle of Takur Ghar', United States Department of Defense, 24 May 2002, www.defenselink.mil/news/May2002/d20020524takurghar.pdf

Rebecca Grant, 'Operation Anaconda, An Air Power Perspective', Headquarters, United States Air Force, 7 February 2005

Robert Hill, 'Australian Special Forces Soldiers Honoured for Afghanistan Operation' press release from the Minister for Defence, Leader of the Government in the Senate, 27 November 2002

John Howard, Prime Minister of Australia, transcript of press conference at Australian Embassy, Washington, 11 September 2001

John Howard, Prime Minister of Australia, transcript of press
conference; subject: deployment of Australian troops in fight
against terrorism, 17 October 2001

John Howard, Prime Minister of Australia, transcript of press
conference prior to deployment of SAS Troops, Sheraton
Hotel, Perth, 22 October 2001

John Howard, transcript of the Prime Minister, the Hon. John
Howard, MP, address to welcome SAS troops back to
Australia, Campbell Barracks, Perth, 2 April 2002

'Interview With US Army Soldiers who Participated in
Operation Anaconda', official transcript from the US
Department of Defense, 7 March 2002

Secretary Rumsfeld and General Myers, Department of Defense
news briefing, 4 March 2002

'Special Forces Task Group Commander Honoured', media
release by Australian Department of Defence, 23 July 2002

*The 9/11 Commission Report. Final Report of the National
Commission on Terrorist Attacks Upon the United States*

US CentCom press briefing; 'Briefing Participants – General
Tommy Franks, Commander, Centcom', 4 March 2002,
Marriott-Waterside Hotel, Tampa, Florida

Frank Wiercinski, text of rallying cry 1 March 2002, at Bagram
Air Base, as published on *The Los Angeles Times* website
www.latimes.com/news/nationworld/nation/la-
rallyingtroops.story, accessed January 2003

ACKNOWLEDGEMENTS

This book would not have been written had it not been for my brother, Gavin 'General' Lee, a former signaller who served for sixteen years with the Australian Army and who, as a young corporal at 104 Signal Squadron in Sydney, worked with a younger digger by the name of Martin 'Jock' Wallace. Fifteen years later, Gavin believed that the story of his mate's bravery should be told, as it honours all members of the Royal Australian Corps of Signals, present, past and future. Signallers play an integral role in any combat situation involving the Australian Army, yet their heroics are often overlooked, particularly those of the soldiers in 152 Signal Squadron of the SAS Regiment. Thanks for the idea, Gav.

Do or Die is the story of one man's battle against al Qaeda and Taliban fighters in the mountains of Afghanistan on 2 March 2002. While much has been written about the War on Terror and Operation Anaconda, this is the first authoritative book from an Australian perspective about the Australians' role in a key battle against al Qaeda. I want to thank Martin Wallace for the privilege of letting me tell his inspiring story of courage, tenacity and adaptability. As a soldier, Martin Wallace is one of the best; as a gentleman, one of the very finest.

On the home front, I want to sincerely thank Margaret Wallace for revealing the boy who became the man, and another former SAS trooper, Travis Standen, Martin's best mate, who paints a picture of true Aussie loyalty.

The SAS Regiment is proudly secretive and protective of its operational, security and tactical matters and, as such, the Army's highest command did not want this story told. Fortunately, I had a great advocate in former defence minister Robert Hill, who saw the value of the story and supported my determination to write it. It's rare that a taxpayer thanks a politician, but gratitude to you, Robert Hill.

Thanks, also, to the head of Special Operations Command, Major General Mike Hindmarsh, who ultimately approved *Do or Die* and gave SAS troopers a rare clearance to discuss an operation in which they were critically involved.

Profound thanks go to retired SAS trooper Johnny for telling me how it was in his part of the valley on 2 March, as well as to SAS officer Lieutenant Colonel Rowan Tink, who commanded the Australians in Anaconda and gave generously of his time and knowledge to talk me through battle strategy and tactics.

To the Special Operations Command team of Brigadier Timothy J. McOwan, Captain Jason Logue, Captain Gabby Parker and Corporal Sean Burton, many thanks for all your assistance and photographs.

It is worth noting that all the soldiers in the Shahi Kot Valley fought their own battle and each has a story to tell. To a man, they shy away from being called heroes, but as now General Franklin 'Buster' Hagenbeck said during our interview at the Pentagon, there were many heroes in Hell's Halfpipe that day. Fortunately, some were interviewed for this book.

Special thanks, of course, go to Major General Hagenbeck for sharing his unique insight as commander of Operation Anaconda, and to Lieutenant Colonel Bryan Hilferty, the man who briefed the media each day at Bagram Air Base that March, and who later shepherded me through the Pentagon.

I am especially indebted to Frank Grippe, now a division

command sergeant major at the 101st Airborne Division (Air Assault), otherwise known as the Screaming Eagles, at Fort Campbell, Kentucky. His experiences on – and knowledge of – D-Day was invaluable. Immeasurable gratitude to Sergeant First Class Michael Peterson (retired) for his generous assistance, insight, photographs and good humour; and to Sergeant First Class Robert S. Healy and Private First Class Jason Ashline, for sharing their memories.

For further details about the actions of Sergeant Peterson's 120mm mortar platoon, I relied on sworn witness statements from US soldiers Captain James Scott Taylor, Sergeant Darren M. Amick, Specialist Eric T. Howell, Private First Class David Brown and Sergeant Thomas Oldham.

In reconstructing the opening eighteen hours of Operation Anaconda, and in researching and writing about the historical and political background of Afghanistan, I relied on personal accounts and recollections from several participants, and drew on the resources listed in the bibliography. As a former foreign correspondent, I am extremely grateful for the work of all journalists who reported from the front line history in the making. Their detailed daily reports helped build a picture of what it was like for the troops on D-Day. If there are errors, they are inadvertent but they are mine.

For those interested in reading about the entire operation, I recommend Sean Naylor's excellent book *Not A Good Day to Die*. Other fine references include Robin Moore's *The Hunt For bin Laden*, Linda Robinson's *Masters of Chaos*, Steve Coll's *Ghost Wars* and Gary C. Schroen's *First In*. For books on the SAS, see the bibliography.

Thanks to Catherine Fitzpatrick from then Senator Hill's office, and a sincere thankyou to photographers Frank Violi and John Berry, as well as the US Department of Defense and the US Army for permission to recreate official maps and use photographs.

A bouquet to my agent and dear friend Selwa Anthony; you make it easy and worthwhile. Thanks to the terrific team at

HarperCollins: Shona Martyn, Alison Urquhart and Mary Rennie. I tip my hat to lawyer Gregory Burn, an Army Reservist who stepped into action when needed, and to the editor of *The Sunday Telegraph*, Jeni O'Dowd, for supporting this project and giving me vital time to write it.

On a personal level, a massive and heartfelt thanks to my great mates and extended family who offered food, drink, laughs, encouragement and accommodation when needed: you know who you are, but David Burgess, Lynne Cossar, Jack Curry and Chris Soller (Washington DC), Miranda Devine, Debbie Hammon, Sharon Krum (NY, NY) and Linda Smith all deserve a special mention.

Eternal thanks as ever to my father, Kevin (Dixie) Lee, retired from the Royal Australian Navy; a man who showed exquisite taste in 1959 when he married a great woman, Valda May, who is forever missed but lives on so strongly in all our hearts and memories. And finally, but ever so importantly, I can't thank enough my husband, J.P. Clemence. You're my map-man and my ballast. With you beside me, life just keeps getting better.

Sincere thanks also to Stuart Robertson at John Blake for his terrific ideas, suggestions and great title.

'Thrilling, fast-paced account of Australian soldiers in a real war against a real terrorist enemy.'

- General Peter Cosgrove, AC, MC, former Chief of the Australian Defence Force (Retired)

'Sandra's well written story of Jock Wallace's experience in Hell's Half Pipe is awesome and about as accurate of an account of that battle as you could get. I couldn't put the book down and finished it in a day. I witnessed Jock's bravery several times that day; I have nothing but admiration for him and all the men of the Australian SAS. America has awesome friends and these guys are the tip of the spear. The leaders in 1-87 Infantry were the best I have ever served with and the soldiers were as good as they get. All you have to do as a leader is be willing to take the first step toward the sound of gun fire; Jock did that! Mistakes were made and corrected the next time out; 12 hours after we were extracted from the Pipe the men of the 120mm Mortar Platoon went back out to the valley in full strength. This time was pay back; no repeat of 2 March.'

- Master Sergeant Michael Peterson (Retired) 1-87 Infantry Mortars, US Army's 10th Mountain Division

'A very gripping and readable account of a historically very important battle.'
- *Australian & NZ Defender* magazine

'Lee has captured the feel and true life account of Jock Wallace's part in Operation Anaconda, which has now become part of Australian military history.'
- *Australian Peacekeeper* magazine